Who was the headless corpse? And why was his
head hidden on a tree on Robert Seaton's estate?
Nigel Strangeways is faced with one of the most
puzzling mysteries of his career.

"Nicholas Blake, one of our more literate mystery
writers, tells a suspenseful and tense story."
—*New Bedford Standard-Times*

"Tops in good English."—*The Kirkus Service*

"Mr. Blake is an extremely accomplished novelist,
with the rare ability to understand people whose
psyches are a mess and, at the same time, to
write about them without ever losing his own
balance or lightness of touch."
—*The New Yorker*

HEAD
of a
TRAVELER

HEAD
of a
TRAVELER

BY NICHOLAS BLAKE

PERENNIAL LIBRARY
Harper & Row, Publishers
New York, Hagerstown,
San Francisco, London

CONTENTS

HEAD
of a
TRAVELER

CHAPTER ONE

FROM NIGEL STRANGEWAYS' JOURNAL

7th June, 1948—Paul took me over to the Seatons for the day. "Bob Seaton'll be in your line," he said firmly: "writes poetry, you know." I did know. I informed Paul that Robert Seaton was one of the most distinguished English poets of our time. "Delighted to hear it," he replied, unruffled: "he's got a fine herd of Guernseys. Charming house, too. But you wait till you see his dairy." I said that, for me, the high spot of the pilgrimage would be the poet Seaton, not a herd of cows, however well appointed. I asked what he was like. "Who? Old Bob?"—Paul was filling up one of those forms that farmers have to fill up, and couldn't give me his undivided attention—"Oh, he's a good sort. Quiet little chap, you know."

The pilgrimage was only to the next village, in fact. Paul's farm is just outside Hinton Lacey. The Seatons' house, Plash Meadow, is in Ferry Lacey, two miles away. Ferry Lacey: one of those messy Oxfordshire villages—picturesque rural slums mixed up with brash little red-brick bungalows and villas.

The first sight of Plash Meadow, at the far end of the village, took my breath away. A perfect Queen Anne house. Long, low; mellowed, old-rose brick; irregular but successful placing of the windows. A fifty-yard stretch of lawn, smooth and lustrous as green glass, between the house and a low wall which separated it from the road. Everywhere, on this wall, on the house, in the beds to its left, on the wall of the farm buildings behind, there were roses. Drifts and swirls and swags of them. A cataleptic trance of white and yellow roses. One was surprised not to see them romping all over the two Wellingtonias which spire up from the lawn, at either end of the house. "There's a bower of roses by Bendemeer's stream." Only it's the Thames, flowing past, hidden by trees, a few hundred yards beyond the house, which stands on a bluff above it.

"It's the end!" I exclaimed.

"Yes," said Paul. "The road doesn't go any further. There's a footbridge down there, though, where the ferry used to be, and you can cross the river and walk over the fields to Redcote."

He had stopped the car for a minute outside the gate. I could hear a distant roaring, like the noise when you hold a shell to your ear, but deeper; a dying fall that never died; an immortal sigh. Was it from an infinite distance? or a delusion in my head, born of this place and its trance of roses?

Paul must have seen me listening. "It's the weir," he said, "half a mile upstream."

Well, it might have been worse. He might have said it was the mechanical milkers at work, I supposed.

"You don't milk cows at twelve-thirty in the afternoon," Paul replied, and drove in through the gate. We got out.

It was like getting out into a dream. Walking past the front of the house, glancing in at the drawing-room windows, one might have expected to see a group of brocaded figures arrested in courtiers' attitudes around a Sleeping Beauty, the stems of roses twining through their ceremonious fingers.

The impression was sustained when the door opened. A

2

dwarf stood there—a hideous creature in a green baize apron, grinning all over his face. Paul really might have warned me.

"Hello, Finny, how's tricks?" he said to this apparition, which replied with a series of adenoidal grunts and snuffles, then waddled in front of us to a door on the left of the hall.

We were in the drawing room. The spell persisted. A perfectly shaped room, windows on two sides, green paneled, Adam fireplace, rosewood and walnut pieces, curtains and carpet the faded magenta of Christmas roses, bowls of roses all over the place, a luscious Renoir above the mantelpiece—

"I see you're admiring my Renoir," says a deep voice from behind me.

I turn round. Paul introduces me to our hostess. Mrs. Seaton is very much *en grande tenue*: she receives me graciously, with the easy but practiced air of a duchess receiving a bouquet. A large, dark, commanding woman; big bones; rather beaky nose; sallow complexion; eyes smallish beneath heavy brows: plenty of social manner, but no charm. In the late forties, I'd say. She'll be a regular old battle-ax in twenty years' time.

I murmur polite and genuine admiration of the house. Her eyes light up, she positively looks ten years younger for a moment.

"I *am* rather proud of it. Of course, we've lived here for centuries—long before this house was built, I mean."

"You carry your centuries very well, Janet," says Paul. Mrs. Seaton flushes, unbecomingly, but not displeased: she is one who enjoys being mildly teased by a personable male.

"Don't be absurd, Paul. I was just going to tell Mr. Strangeways that my family, the Laceys, gave their name to these two villages. Our ancestor, Francis de Lacey, received the Manor from William the Conqueror."

"And then you married your house and lived happily ever after," said Paul. This, to me, entirely cryptic remark did

3

not go down so well with Janet Seaton. She turned away from him.

"The Poet will join us for lunch: he always Works in the morning," she said to me in a different, throbbing kind of voice, heavily capitalizing the key words. It could have been just funny; or it could have been cozy, in a period way: but for some reason I found the remark really blood chilling. So much so that I rudely pushed the conversation back to the previous move.

"So the house belongs to you?" I asked.

"It belongs to us both. Robert's father bought it from my father, and then Robert inherited it. Old Mr. Seaton renamed it Plash Meadow; but everyone here still calls it Laceys. Are you interested in Battersea enamel, Mr. Strangeways? There are some good pieces in this cabinet over here."

I said I was. Though the Seaton-Lacey transactions interested me far more. Mrs. Seaton unlocked the cabinet and took out an exquisite powder box. She held it a moment or two in her large, heavy-knuckled hands, then put it in mine. As I examined it, I felt her eyes upon me, like a physical pressure or a wave of heat from a furnace. I looked up. Caught a most peculiar expression on her face. Can I describe it now?—The fatuous self-satisfaction of a young mother looking at her first-born lying in a friend's arms, plus a certain controlled panic (will he drop my baby?) plus something else, something indefinable, urgently appealing, almost pathetic. When I handed the Battersea piece back to her, she sighed, almost gasped, as if she'd been holding her breath.

"Aha, the ruling passion again! Showing off your bric-a-brac!" came a pleasant, quiet voice from the doorway. A young man was standing there, arm in arm with a ravishing, yellow-headed girl, smiling at us.

"Now, Mr. Strangeways, here are my two finest exhibits.

Lionel and Vanessa. It's her half-term holiday. Come and be shown off, children," said Mrs. Seaton.

General handshaking. Close up, Lionel Seaton looks older —older than his age, too. Paul tells me later he was in the war, one of the Arnhem survivors, and has quite a collection of medals. But where on earth do they get their looks from? I am wondering. Surely not from Janet Seaton.

"We've been on the river," the girl says to me. "Lionel is absolutely mad. We tried to shoot a moor hen, *with* an air pistol, *from* his rubber dinghy. Of course, what happened was that the moor hen's intact and we're dying of frozen bottoms."

"Vanessa!" exclaims Mrs. Seaton. "You must forgive these children their shocking manners, Mr. Strangeways. They're very badly brought up."

She said it lightly; but a scowl appeared on Vanessa's face, making her look quite plain and colorless for a moment, as if the sun had gone in.

"We didn't have the benefit of Janet's bringing-up. She's our stepmother, you know."

It was an awkward little moment. But Lionel Seaton smoothed it over with an agreeably ponderous explanation of how the occupants of the rubber dinghy having to sit on the floor of the dinghy, and the floor of the dinghy being below the waterline, and the water being cold, inevitably the bottoms of the occupants of the dinghy, etc. etc. He added something about his good fortune in not having been one of those R.A.F. types, who had to spend considerable periods of the war paddling around the ocean in rubber dinghies.

He's a good boy. Has the self-contained, somewhat poker-faced air one often finds in the children of parents with genius or "strong" character.

Vanessa looks fourteen. Is actually younger? All-out hero-worship of her brother, who finds her inextinguishably funny, is protective, affectionate to her, and sheds about

5

ten years of his age in her company. The dear child is quite unaware she is healing her brother's war wounds.

Presently Mrs. Seaton held up a finger. The throbbing note, the note of a gong discreetly tapped by a perfect butler, entered her voice again.

"I think I hear the Poet coming downstairs. Yes, here he is."

And then—oh dear, it was like one of those Great Occasions, the street lined with bunting, the band ready to play, the guard of honor presenting arms, the crowds all agog, when round the corner comes, not Royalty, but a stray dog, or maybe an errand boy on a bicycle, and scuttles away down the ceremonial avenue.

Robert Seaton trotted into the room, smiling vaguely at no one in particular, a nondescript little man wearing a crumpled blue suit, which looked as if he'd slept in it.

He seemed about to shake hands with his own son and daughter; but Janet Seaton diverted him toward myself. As we shook hands, the dazed expression went out of his eyes, and his quality began to appear. A quality—I think I can put my finger on it now—of almost supernatural *attentiveness*. I had nervously begun to sketch out my fantasy, inspired by his roses, on the Sleeping-Beauty theme. He listened to me, or so I felt, not with his ears only, but with his nerves, his whole slight body, and with an inward ear (his eyes looking downward as if he strove to catch the echoes of my voice in his own soul). When I had finished, he glanced up, straight into my eyes for a moment: an impaling glance.

"The Sleeping Beauty. Yes," he said musingly. "And the thicket of thorns. Yes. But have you thought"—he seemed to be burrowing out of sight, like a mole, toward some deep meaning of his own—"have you thought what really kept her there? Not the thorns, but the roses. She was the prisoner of her own beauty, of her parents' determination that she

6

should be invulnerable and never allowed to meet her fate. The Queen took away all the spinning wheels, you remember. Yes, it was all the Queen's fault. I don't believe in that Wicked Fairy. The poor girl had nothing to do but moon about and admire her own reflection in the roses. So presently she went to sleep out of sheer boredom. I don't believe the part about pricking her finger on a spindle. And what's more," he added confidentially, "I don't believe in that Prince. He'd never have got through the thorns. It'd take the Beast to do that. 'Some rough beast.'"

"You *have* got your fairy tales mixed up, Robert," said his wife, who was now standing beside us. "Let's go in to lunch, shall we?"

The dining room. Dark, glowing, rich; not somber. A sheen on every surface—table, sideboard: two centuries of elbow grease and love. Empire chairs, candlesticks. Above the mantelpiece a portrait of the Lacey who built this house, after the Elizabethan manor, itself replacing an earlier construction, had been destroyed by fire. White roses nodding outside the window. Delicious food. The dwarf, Finny Black, serves at table: deft and quick, but it's disconcerting to have a servant peering *up* at you as he hands the vegetables. While he's out of the room for a minute, Mrs. Seaton says to me,

"Finny's a great character. An authentic Fool."

"Shakespearean, you mean?" Luckily I have caught the capital letter.

"Yes. He says the wisest things, doesn't he, Robert? Visitors always make him shy at first, though."

"He has persisted in his folly, then?" I venture. Mrs. S. looks blank at me, but her husband comes to the rescue.

"Mr. Strangeways is quoting from Blake—'If the fool would persist in his folly he would become wise.'"

"I think that's absolute rot," says Vanessa. "He'd just become a bigger fool. Which is what Finny has done."

7

"Oh, Vanessa, you know how that horrible chemical lemonade of yours takes the polish off the table! Wipe it up quickly!" Mrs. S. speaks in a voice of controlled exasperation. Vanessa polishes away with her napkin where she has spilled a little lemonade on the table, murmuring, "Out, damned spot!" She looks mutinous.

I ask Robert Seaton what he's working on just now. Before he can reply, his wife interposes: "Robert is writing his Masterpiece"—her voice is throbbing again—"an Epic Poem on the Great War—the 1914 war, I mean. Something in the nature of *The Dynasts.*"

Expression of blank misery on Robert's face for a moment. Writers hate having their current work talked about, of course. Good ones, at any rate. I murmur polite interest: say we've waited a long time for a new book of his (it must be nearly ten years, in fact). I tell him how his early work, his *Lyrical Interludes* in particular, was the first thing that gave me a feeling for poetry, when I read it at school. Paul, who has been concentrating on his food, looks up and says unexpectedly:

"Yes, but the best thing you've ever done is your *Elegy for a Dead Wife.*" He proceeds, after a sly glance in my direction, which says, plainly as words could speak, 'Oh yes, Nigel, even we ex-R.A.F. types can read,' to make a number of extremely sensible and sensitive remarks about this poem. Robert Seaton glows visibly. His rather ordinary, plain, worried little face becomes suffused, as it were from within, by a beautiful tenderness. Extraordinary transfiguration.

"It's a very painful poem," says Janet Seaton; then compresses her lips; then adds, as if the words forced their way through her lips willy-nilly, "For me, at any rate."

An exceedingly embarrassing silence. The "dead wife" of the *Elegy*, Lionel's and Vanessa's mother, still has power to haunt, then. I am suddenly consumed by curiosity to know all about her. Lionel breaks the silence:

8

"I say, d'you remember that Irish poet who came to stay, just before the war? You know, Dad—Peadar Mayo. 'Will I tell ya what's wrong with yer poouums, Seaton? They're not bad poouums, mind ya. But ya don't do what I do in me pooutry—ya don't tear yer heart out and lay it, raw and bleedin', on the page before ya. All this bejooled reticence of yours—ta hell with it, I say.'"

Robert Seaton chuckled. "Ah yes, he was a wild man. And then he went on to recite my *Elegy* to me, with tears pouring down his cheeks."

After lunch, he took me round the garden, etc. At back of house, which is L-shaped, the kitchen and servants' quarters occupying the horizontal stroke of the L, there's a large grassed court, with a whacking great chestnut tree in the middle. Beyond the courtyard a row of farm buildings —loose boxes, cow stalls, cart shed, the dairy, all under a long, lichened tile roof which has weathered to a Donegal-tweed pattern. On the left of the courtyard, facing the servants' quarters across the width of it, but detached from the house, a magnificent tithe barn. Seaton told me he'd turned it into a cottage and rented it to some friends called Torrance—a painter and his daughter: they were coming in to tea later.

We walked across the court, round the end of the farm buildings, into a walled orchard. In the near corner of it, a dozen yards or so wired off for poultry. The poet stood gazing intently at his hens for a minute: I waited respectfully: at last he said, with a curious little sideways glance at me, half quizzical, half abstracted,

"Hens always do look so much at a loose end, don't they?" His fine, deep voice brought it out so seriously, I couldn't help smiling. Well, no doubt it was just Keats over again with his sparrow picking about in the gravel. I asked if he looked after them and the cows himself. He said he used to, but he'd lost interest in them: he had a cowman and a

9

gardener again now: he milked the cows sometimes still—found it "soothing."

Over the orchard, through a finely wrought iron gate in the brick wall, into the meadow beyond. The famous Guernseys were grazing there, looking like Noah's Ark cows. Away on our left, a thick wood; on our right, below the pastures, the Thames. All wonderfully peaceful and well laid out for the eye.

"I thought of writing an English Georgic when I came back here. But I'm no farmer really, and Nature rather bores me *qua* Nature."

"When you came back?"

"Yes. After my father and elder brother died, I came in for the place. And the money. Very handy. Poets don't enjoy short commons any more than anyone else. Only it was too late. That's where we bathe, just down there. I'll show you."

I forebore from asking any of the questions which this last speech of his stirred up in my mind. He hadn't really been speaking to me at all. We sauntered down to the river; saw the place where the bank shelved gradually down into a natural bathing pool; climbed up the bluff a bit further on, Seaton pointing out the vestiges of the terraced garden of the Elizabethan manor house, which had stood at the top of the bluff. Then we were in the great courtyard again. Boughs of the chestnut were being violently agitated. An idiot face mopped and mowed at us from between the candelabra of blossom.

"Finny's always climbing that tree," said Robert Seaton. "Climbs like a monkey. Extraordinarily powerful forearms: I daresay you noticed it when he was waiting at table."

The appropriate comment failing me, I asked to see the dairy. It stands at the end of the row of farm buildings nearest the old tithe barn. Obviously no expense spared. Separator, pasteurizer, refrigerator, cheese molds, butter dryer and the rest of it, all very bright and hygienic.

Windows high up, floor and walls tiled, with good drainage so that the place can be sluiced down by hose. Robert Seaton points out all the advantages, in a burst of animation; then relapses into his companionable but abstracted mood. Can't keep his mind away from the epic of the Great War for long, I suppose: though I must say it's an odd subject for Robert Seaton.

We putter about a little longer. He shows me a well-equipped workshop and some unfinished articles of furniture he'd been making. I notice the dust is thick on them. Here too I get the impression of an only child of rich parents, given every toy that money can buy, and bored with the whole lot of them. I see a remarkably fine piece of wood carving lying on a bench, ask him if it's his work.

"No, Mara Torrance did that. She's got a gift, hasn't she?" Peering closer at the object, I get a shock: in the midst of the leaves and fruits carved out on the wood, intertwined with and fluently continuing their pattern, a nakedly Priapic scene hit my eye. And—what shook me most—the bearded face of the Satyr in it, tiny though it was, somehow conveyed an uncanny resemblance to no less a person than the poet, Robert Seaton. Involuntarily I glanced up at him. He met my eye firmly. The look of profound sadness, which always seems lurking just behind his features, ready to spring out and possess them, reappeared. He said,

"It's by way of being autotherapy, you know." I didn't know, of course. But there is a certain delicate dignity about Seaton, I find, which discourages even my inordinate curiosity from probing into his affairs.

Presently he leaves me to my own devices. I decide to look at the flower garden before rejoining the rest of the party. Walk past the barn, along a grass path lined with Irish yews and standard roses alternately, toward a summer-house at its far end. One of those revolving ones: its back has been turned to the path. I hear voices from inside. Been repressing my inquisitiveness too long: can't help listening. Lionel Seaton's voice, and one I do not recognize; a female voice, cool, husky and—no other word for it—gloating. As follows:

Unknown Female: "So you'd do anything for me, would you, darling Lionel? Anything? I wonder do you really mean that?"

Lionel Seaton: "You know what I want to do."

U.F.: "Oh yes. I'm to be—reclaimed. As if I were a marsh, or something. But suppose I don't want to be reclaimed?"

L.S.: "Quite happy as you are, eh?"

U.F.: "I have my moments. What more can anyone expect?"

L.S.: "A great deal, my dear girl. And you know it. Love: marriage: children. A normal ordinary life."

U.F.: "Oh, how dull you make it sound!"

L.S.: "I've had enough drama the last five years. Give me the bowler hat, the eight-thirty and the slippers by the fire."

U.F.: "You can have them. But *I'm* not interested. You and your dreary domesticity! No, I'm going to make a splash before I'm dead. I'll—"

L.S.: "A splash! Out of a bottle. That's all you—. No you don't, my girl! I'm rather good at unarmed combat, so you can just sheathe those long red nails of yours again."

U.F.: "No, you're not so dull now . . . Well, go on. Start reclaiming me . . . Come on, my little Arnhem hero, don't be frightened."

I judge it time to retire. Well, well. The lady is a holy terror, as my dear Superintendent Blount would say. But I fancy she has met her match.

At tea, an hour later, I meet her. She walks across the lawn to where we are sitting in the shade of one of the enormous trees; a big, lumpish, rather dirty-looking man with her. I am introduced to Rennell Torrance and his daughter, Mara. Recognize the voice in the summerhouse as

12

soon as she speaks. Dark, lank hair (why do all females connected with Art look as if they'd poured a bucket of varnish over their heads and forgotten to use a comb?): thick, magnolia-white skin: restless fingers: chain smoker? a bit of a dipso?

She holds me with a long, long stare from her slightly protuberant eyes. I can feel them on my face after I've turned my own away. During tea, she and Lionel pointedly refrain from mutual glances. Mrs. Seaton, I notice, keeps a weather eye lifting on them. Faintly uneasy atmosphere all round. Rennell Torrance holds the floor with a long diatribe against the "fashionable" English painters of the day—Matthew Smith, Sutherland, Hichens, Christopher Wood, Frances Hodgkin, all come under the hammer, regardless of age and sex. We've got to throw off the French influence and go back to Samuel Palmer. A disgruntled man, this Torrance, and presumably a failure himself as a painter. But he has a certain *panache* in his talk. After he'd blown off for ten minutes or so, he noticed my presence and asked what I was interested in.

"Crime," I said.

The man's eyes flickered toward his daughter, then back to me. His face had taken on a different expression—wary? stupid?

"What? You mean you read detective novels?"

"No, he lives them," said Paul. "He's hand in glove with Scotland Yard. So watch your step, all of you."

Vanessa Seaton clapped her hands gaily. "I say, that's wizard! When Torrance bumps off his rival painters, Mr. Strangeways will track him down."

"They're dead, most of 'em, already. And stinking," said Torrance.

Mara, staring hard at me again, asked me if I specialized in any particular branch of crime. Mrs. Seaton said, very quickly, she was sure I didn't want to talk shop.

13

"But I'm interested," said Mara, in a whining, little-girl sort of voice.

"Well, I've helped in a number of murder investigations."

The extraordinary tension, which seemed to have come into the air at Mara Torrance's last remarks, relaxed a little. Robert Seaton, very wide awake now, almost quivering with interest, like a terrier at a rathole, said:

"It must be fascinating. The detonating point, I mean. The point at which a given man or woman bursts into flame. I suppose it varies enormously."

"I'd like to see Lionel burst into flame," said Vanessa, giggling. "He'd burn with a beautiful orange glow."

"A pure white radiance," murmured Miss Torrance, with a rather disagreeable emphasis on "pure."

Lionel threw a cushion at his sister. "But most murders are premeditated, not sudden outbreaks of passion, aren't they?"

"This is a very morbid conversation, children," said Mrs. Seaton. Her husband did not take the hint.

"That's not what I mean, Lionel," he pursued. "Every murder is an act of violence, of passion, however long it's been premeditated. No, I'm talking about the flash point in every human being. Look—you may wish to get rid of someone, some intolerable situation: you lay your plans in fantasy; you're not serious about it, or you think you aren't: you imagine your weapon, your opportunity, your alibi, and so on: but all the time you're laying a train in reality. And then a moment comes when you find the train has been lit, the spark is creeping up it, you can't stop the explosion, now. You're doomed to act what you have dreamed."

"Oo-er," exclaimed Vanessa. "You are creepy, Daddy!"

I said something to the effect that the flash point would depend on whether the murder you planned in imagination was consistent with your own personality. If you planned a murder from the wrong motive, i.e. a motive unconnected

14

with the strongest element of your personality, with your ruling passion, the train would never be lit.

"But nobody would contemplate a murder unless what you call his ruling passion was involved," said Paul, very sensibly. "This begins to get interesting," Mara Torrance drawled. "Tell us what motive you think each of us would have, strong enough to push us over the edge."

I said I didn't know any of them well enough. The young woman made an eeny-meeny-miny-mo movement with her cigarette. It pointed at Mrs. Seaton.

"Come on, Janet. Mr. Strangeways doesn't know us well enough. So we'll tell him. You start."

"My dear Mara, I don't like these truth games. They always end in tears."

"Well, I'll speak for you, then. It's easy. Janet's ruling passion is Plash Meadow and all that therein is. She'd kill anyone to protect it. You next, Paul."

"I'm the purely altruistic type. I'd murder for the good of humanity. I'd like to get the leading politicians of the Great Powers into a room, and point a tommy gun at them, and tell them that, if they didn't come to an agreement within three hours to abolish the atom bomb, they'd have had it."

"Good enough. What about you, Father?"

Rennell Torrance mopped his lard-colored face. "I'm an Artist. I should only be interested in murder as an *acte gratuit*. I'd—"

"Hmph. Or if someone came between you and your creature comforts," interrupted his daughter, with a sort of humoring contempt. "You'd kill out of panic. Or perhaps for gain, if it seemed fairly safe, and there was really enough to be gained. Now Robert *would* kill for his art, wouldn't you, Robert?"

"You're probably right, my dear," said the Poet mildly. "Only I could never bring myself to facing my victim. It'd have to be one of those long-range murders—you know, the cyanide pill inserted in the bottle of aspirin tablets."

Vanessa, who had been brooding in a cloud of tawny hair, remarked meditatively, "I would like to poison Miss Glubb, our chemistry mistress. Some very slow poison. I would like to see her writhing at my feet—"

"Vanessa!—"

"—and just as she was about to expire, I'd give her an antidote. Or the stomach pump. How exactly does a stomach pump work, Mr. Strangeways?"

"You could use one on your own tum to advantage," said Lionel, prodding his sister's stomach. "It's really revolting, the way you swell up after every meal."

"Oh, do shut up, Lionel, you're horrible! And I'm *not* greedy."

"So we're left with Lionel," said Mara. "What would the *chevalier sans peur et sans reproche* do murder for?"

"Well, I might wring your neck one day, when you're in a specially exasperating mood."

"Ah yes. Crime of passion. That's got you taped," she replied with a shamelessly long, deep look at him.

There was a silence on the lawn. Wood pigeons cooed up above. I could hear the ground bass of the weir.

"Nobody has asked me what I'd do murder for," said Mara Torrance.

Nobody offered to, even now.

"Revenge," she said.

"Oh, goody," said Vanessa. "Like me and Miss Glubb."

Finny Black came trotting up to remove the tea things.

"And what about our Finny?" drawled Mara.

Mrs. Seaton turned upon her formidably. "Mara, I absolutely forbid you—you know Finny's not—"

"All right, all right. Finny's a piece of Plash Meadow, and mustn't be disturbed. I know. Aren't you, Finny?"

The dwarf clucked and beamed at Mara Torrance. When

he'd returned into the house, Robert Seaton turned to me and said,

"It's quite an interesting point. Finny will copy any action he has seen. That's how my wife trained him."

"You mean," said I, "if he actually saw a murder committed, he might go and commit an identical one on another victim."

Robert Seaton nodded. His wife got a firm grip on the conversation and turned it in another direction. It was very amiable, carefree, placid, from now on. An hour later Paul and I left. They stood on the drive, waving good-by: the good poet, embowered in his roses, embosomed in his charming family group. How proper, and how rare, that a true creator should have so beautiful, so calm a setting to work in. As we turned out of the drive into the road, the roses seemed to close in upon him with a gentle, genial familiarity, and enfold him. Such graciousness. Such peace. . . .

CHAPTER TWO

A TRUNK WITHOUT A LABEL

Two months after his visit to the Seatons' home, Nigel
Strangeways received a telegram:

STRANGEWAYS: *Welbeck Club, London, W.1.*
BODY IN THAMES 1½ MILES UPSTREAM FROM HINTON
LACEY STOP ARE YOU INTERESTED QUESTION MARK

PAUL

To which Nigel replied:

WILLINGHAM: *Robb Farm, Hinton Lacey, Oxfordshire.*
NO WHY SHOULD I BE FISH IT OUT IF IT WORRIES YOU VERY
BUSY

NIGEL

Two days later, while he was working at his monograph
on the subject of graphology in relation to the manuscripts
of certain twentieth-century poets, a second telegram arrived:

STRANGEWAYS: *Welbeck Club, London, W 1*
POLICE BESIEGING PLASH MEADOW STOP JANET SEATON
IN GREAT FORM O/C THE DEFENSE STOP HAS ALREADY
CLONKED INSPECTOR STOP ARE YOU INTERESTED NOW YOU
OLD VULTURE QUESTION MARK

PAUL

Nigel did not reply. Paul Willingham never wrote letters and refused to have a telephone in his house, on the score that he had done quite enough talking over the intercom during the war: so there was nothing for it but to go down and ask him to explain his rigmarole. But Nigel first rang up his old friend, Superintendent Blount, at New Scotland Yard: he had no intention of interrupting his work merely on the strength of a flippant telegram from Paul. At the same time, it could not be ignored that a body found in the Thames one and a half miles *up*stream from Hinton Lacey was a body found in the Thames half a mile *down*stream from Ferry Lacey; and presumably the police would not visit Plash Meadow just to admire the roses.

"Blount? Strangeways here. Sorry to bother you, but do you know anything about a body found in the Thames two or three days ago—in Oxfordshire, near a place called Ferry Lacey?"

"E'eh, why, good Lord, the assistant commissioner's just been talking to me about it this forenoon. Now isn't that a vairy strange coincidence? The Oxfordshire chaps have asked for our help."

"What is it? Suicide? Murder?"

"Och, it's murder all right. Don't you ever read the newspapers?"

"Only the *News of the World*. And it's not Sunday yet. Who's the victim?"

"That's what we've got to find out," said Superintendent Blount, with a grim chuckle. "But how d'you know about it if you haven't read the papers?"

"Well, I've met the Seatons, who live—"

"The devil you have! Are you free this evening? I'd like to have a chat with you after I've seen Inspector Gates— he's the local chap in charge of the investigation."

"The one Mrs. Seaton clonked?"

"Eh, what's that? Oh yes, the lady appears to be some-

19

thing of a Tartar. Now, would you be free about 10 P.M.? . . ."

Nigel decided not to look up the last few days' news-papers, but to wait till Blount gave him the story, ungarbled. Shortly after ten that night, the two of them were sitting in Nigel's room with a bottle of whisky between them.

"A vairy sweet dram," said Blount, smacking his lips. "Where d'you get the stuff? Are you in the black market? Well, good luck to you. Now, about this body of yours . . ."

The facts, as related by Blount, were as follows: On the previous Sunday, at 9:20 in the evening, a young couple on holiday had pushed their punt into a reed bed by the south bank of the Thames, intending to moor there for the night. Thrusting his pole down into the mud, the young man felt an obstruction. He fished with the boat hook, and pulled up the body of a man which had been caught in the reeds underwater. The girl disembarked and went for help to the nearest farm, while the man remained by the body. In due course the police arrived, and the body was taken to a mor-tuary. Post-mortem examination revealed no signs of as-phyxia: therefore ("apart from other evidence," said Blount grimly) death had not been caused by drowning. Rigor mortis had passed off: the palms of the hands and soles of the feet presented a bleached appearance, and there was brownish discoloration of the surface veins of the body, but not yet the green hue in the abdominal region which comes as the second stage of colliquative putrefaction. These signs gave the time of death within approximate limits of from 36 hours to five days before the discovery of the corpse.

Since dead bodies do not come to the surface and float in less than eight or ten days from the time of death, the victim must have been put into the river at or near the spot where he was found. Because of the weir not far upstream, there was a strongish current, which might conceivably have rolled the body some little distance along the river bed: the police might conduct experiments with a dummy to test this. But, to sum it up, everything pointed to the body having been put into the river not later than the night of Friday-Saturday, or earlier than the previous Tuesday, at some point between Ferry Lacey and the reed bed where it was found, if it was not actually placed in the reeds. No attempt had been made to weigh the body down, which was unusual in cases of this sort. Search of the river banks for traces of the corpse's disposal had been rendered almost hopeless by the trampling and debris of the members of a London angling club, who had been fishing this reach all Sunday. But the local police had found no suspicious marks on the section of bank nearest the reed bed. The possibility that the corpse had been conveyed to this point by boat, and dumped into the water, was likely enough; inquiries were being made on these lines too.

The superintendent reeled off these particulars, then stopped short and applied himself to his whisky with a somewhat leery look at Nigel.

"So how was he murdered?" Nigel asked.

"There were no marks of violence—e'eh—on the body."

"Poison?"

"No trace of poison in the organs," replied Blount, evidently enjoying Nigel's mystified expression.

"He wasn't drowned. He wasn't poisoned. He wasn't shot, stabbed, or beaten to death. What sort of a corpse is this?"

"He was wearing a mackintosh—no other clothes at all. Faint traces of bloodstains were found on it, in spite of the immersion," continued Blount with stolid complacence.

"But how the devil?—"

"Mostly on the *outside* of the mackintosh. The deceased was judged to be about five feet, eight inches in height."

"What d'you mean, 'judged to be'? Haven't the Oxfordshire police got a tape measure?"

Blount's climax, for which he'd certainly worked hard enough, now arrived. He said,

21

"Well, e'eh, ye'll no' judge precisely of a man's height when his head is missing."

The superintendent sat back and savored Nigel's amazement.

"Just so," he went on, after a pause. "The head had been hacked off the neck, verra clumsily; amateurish work—"

"T'ck, t'ck, t'ck."

"—and they can't find it anywhere, what's more. Inspector Gates has had the river dragged for a mile either way, and—"

"But if the body was brought by boat, the chap might have been murdered and his head disposed of hundreds of miles away."

"Aye, just so. But there was a tear in the mackintosh, and the wee piece of stuff torn from it was found on a barbed-wire hedge on the edge of Foxhole Wood, about a mile from the footbridge at Ferry Lacey."

"Well, what's your trouble, then? The chap must have been a local. Who's missing in the neighborhood?"

"Nobody's missing," replied Blount. "And what's more, my boy, we've had men working through the list of missing males for the whole of Great Britain, and the body does not answer satisfactorily to any of the descriptions given."

"Then why was his head cut off?"

"Exactly, Strangeways! You've put your finger right on the spot," exclaimed Blount, with as near an approach to excitement as Nigel had ever seen in him. "You cut off a man's head, or batter his features, to prevent your victim being recognized. You remove his clothes so that tailor's labels and laundry marks shall not be identified—the mackintosh was a cheap one, by the way, from the Universal Tailors—could have been bought at any of several hundred branches—we're trying to trace it, but—" the superintendent shrugged. "Now why should the murderer go to all this trouble, if the victim was an absolute unknown anyway? Of course, it's early days yet. But this body seems to have turned up simply

22

out of the blue. It just doesn't correspond with any of the descriptions of missing persons. I tell you, it's no' canny. Well now, what do *you* make of it?"

"Perhaps he did. Turn up out of the blue, I mean," said Nigel meditatively. "From a far country. Was he wearing leather boots?"

"Leather boots? I've just told you that, except for a mackintosh—"

"Yes, of course," murmured Nigel. "But—" he began to quote:

O suitably-attired-in-leather-boots
Head of a traveler, wherefore, seeking whom,
Whence, by what way, how purposed art thou come
To this well-nightingaled vicinity?

"What is all this tommyrot?"

"First lines of Housman's parody of a Greek tragedy. Very apt. Asks all the questions we've got to answer. Ferry Lacey's a quiet, peaceful place; a dead end. You wouldn't go there on your way to anywhere else. Small population—five hundred perhaps. If a stranger turned up there, he'd stand out like a black sheep on a snowfield. The whole village would be talking about him."

"We've had no reports of any stranger being seen in the village last week."

"Which implies that he didn't *want* to be seen. Arrived at night, perhaps. And why was he walking through that wood where he got caught up by the barbed wire? Perhaps because he had a rendezvous there: perhaps because he wished to avoid the roads. Both explanations involve secrecy. You know, Blount, there's one class of missing persons your lists won't altogether cover. Deserters from H.M. Forces. Add in returned prisoners, displaced persons, all the flotsam and jetsam of war."

"Is that all?" said Blount dryly.

"A little tactful gossiping in the neighborhood should discover whether there are any families with dubious relatives—any skeletons in cupboards or black sheep or prodigal sons. How old was this corpse of yours?"

"Fifty-five to sixty, the doctors reckon."

"Not a deserter, then. But—"

"Rather ill-nourished. But tough and sinewy for his age; had done hard manual work recently:-also been living some time in the East—pigmentation of the skin." Blount went on, poker faced.

Nigel threw up his hands. "As you know all about him, why come to me?"

"Just to admire the trained theoretic mind exercising itself on inductive thought. Aye, 'head of a *traveler*,' verra good, Strangeways, verra good," said Blount, slapping his own bald head enthusiastically. "But let's have some more induction."

"Well, then, clothing of corpse. Mackintosh left on because label of British outfitters would give nothing away. Rest of clothes removed because they bore signs, in their cut or material or on the labels, what foreign parts our traveler had come from, and might lead to the discovering of his identity."

"Just so. We're making inquiries at the ports and the shipping and airway offices of course, but it'll be a terrible long tedious affair. Anything else?"

"I find this mackintosh business rather odd, don't you?" said Nigel slowly. "Why bother to put it on again after removing the rest of his clothes? Was it *his* blood on the mackintosh?"

"Same blood group, anyway."

"But mostly on the outside. You'd think that, if he'd been battered to death, or had his throat cut, a lot of blood would have trickled down *inside* the mac."

"Uh-huh."

"Which suggests it may not have been his mac at all. It

may have belonged to the murderer, who put it on to keep the victim's blood off his own clothes."

"Aye, that's possible. But it still doesn't account for his putting the mac on the body afterward. Much safer for him to burn it, or hide it, together with the victim's clothes. Not that it's ever safe to try to hide or burn articles of clothing. Remember the Lakey case in New Zealand?"

Nigel had opened a drawer of his bureau. He took out a large-scale ordnance map and opened it on the table before them.

"Here's Ferry Lacey. Let's see, now. There are three railway stations within about five miles of the village. Redcote and Chillingham Junction on the main G.W.R. line, Hinton Lacey on a small branch line. But Redcote's the wrong side of the river—the opposite side from this wood you say he came through. That leaves Chillingham and Hinton Lacey. But a chap wishing to avoid notice would never get out at a small branch-line station. So my bet is Chillingham Junction. Quite a busy place. Station on outskirts of town. He could take this road, walk four miles, then strike off the road, into Foxhole Wood, and it's a short cut to Ferry Lacey. He must have known this part of the country pretty well, to know about the short cut."

"Just so," said Blount. "But the only evidence we have, so far, that he came through the wood is that wee bit of mackintosh on the barbed wire. And you've just suggested it may not have been his mackintosh at all."

"Oh hell! Tripping me up on my own words! You solve it, then. It's all yours, this muddy mystery."

"I'll look after the routine investigation. But, e'eh, you wouldn't be thinking of taking a holiday in Oxfordshire yourself, would you?"

"Certainly not. I'm busy."

"Because you have friends there, and you'd pick up a lot more gossip than flatfoots like Gates and myself."

"Oh, talking of Gates," said Nigel, "what's this about him getting into a free fight with Mrs. Seaton?"

Blount looked shocked. "Oh, well now, that's a fearful exaggeration. Gates was merely inquiring, in the way of his duty, whether any members of the household had seen a stranger about during the last week. And it seems they have a wee dwarf creature as a servant—"

"Yes. Finny Black."

"—and Mrs. Seaton refused to allow Gates to question him; said he was dumb, or half-witted, or something. Gates persisted. And she slapped his face. Gates is new to the district, mind you: and maybe he was a thought tactless. But—"

"Huh. The Gestapo hanging together."

"—but it's a serious thing, assaulting a police officer in the execution of his duty. Oh dear me no, won't do at all. Then the lady threatened to bring the chief constable and the lord lieutenant and the whole boiling down on puir wee Gates' head. It seems she has a great deal of influence in the county. So Gates thought he'd better say no more about it."

Blount drained the last of his whisky and reached for his battered felt hat. "Will I be seeing you in the country?"

"Well, I could stay with Paul Willingham: and I'd like to get some samples of Robert Seaton's manuscripts for a monograph I'm writing. So perhaps—"

"That's the boy! I knew you'd not keep your long nose out of the business—"

The door closed on Blount's stocky figure before Nigel could find the apt reply. . . .

"I thought you'd not keep your long nose out of—"

"The next person who refers to my nose, in whatever terms, will be felled to the ground," said Nigel. It was the evening after his conversation with Blount: he and Paul were sitting in the bar of the Lacey Arms at Hinton Lacey. "And do try to use your loaf. I shan't hear anything if the locals find I'm connected with the police," Nigel continued in a low voice.

"I shall say you're a man from the B.B.C. It always impresses my neighbors. God knows why. I shall say you're the producer of one of those corny programs—you know—Here's Wishing You A Jolly Good Bung-Ho—you know the sort of twaddle. And you've come here to put them all on the air. They'll eat it. Evening, Fred! . . . Tom! This is a friend of mine, Mr. Strangeways. He comes from the B.B.C. and he's going to—"

"I don't come from the B.B.C. And I'm *not* going to buy you a drink, Paul. If you gentlemen would care—"

"Thanking *you*, sir," said Tom and Fred in rapid unison.

"The B.B.C.," began Tom presently. "That's a remarkable organization, look at it what way you will. Mind you, I don't hold with that 'ere Light Program. All bloody yup, to my way of thinking. But these symphonies—classical music, like —I'm partial to them myself. Sir Boult, now, there's a fine conductor for you." Tom wiped off the ends of his ragged mustache. "You're not by any chance associated with the Light Program, sir, I hope, for I'd not wish to give offense."

"No. No connection at all," said Nigel, darting a poisoned glance at Paul. "In fact, I've nothing to do with the—"

"Perhaps the gentleman is on the engineering side," suggested Fred. " 'Tis all a mystery to I—these high frequencies and kilowatts and meggiecycles and such. But I suppose they'm an open book to you, sir. Come to think of it, my missus says to me, just as I was stepping out to come along to the Arms, 'Fred,' she says, 'this effing wireless of yourn have pegged out again, and I was set to listen to that nice Dickens serial while you was at the boozer,' she says. So to make a long story short, when Mr. Willingham mentions as how you're a gentleman from the B.B.C., sir, I says to myself—"

"But"—began Nigel.

"—I says to myself, why Fred, I says, perhaps the gentleman could spare the time to step along to my humble abode, tomorrow morning, say, and have a look at my old wireless. Put it to rights in two shakes of a cat's arse, you would, I'll take my oath. Not that I wants to put you to no trouble, sir."

"But—"

"You just think it over, sir. Please yourself. Your very good health."

When the two old farm laborers had edged back to the bar, Nigel turned on Paul.

"I'll murder you if you involve me with any more of the local highbrows. How the devil d'you suppose I—"

"Keep weaving, old boy. You did fine. It's all in the build-up. Now we'll try Jack Whitford. Jack!"

A stalwart, tousle-headed man—he had just come in with a lurcher, which had instantly curled itself up under one of the benches—strolled over. Paul introduced them.

Nigel said: "In case Mr. Willingham tells you I'm from the B.B.C., it's a lie."

"Ah. Terrible bloody liar Mr. Willingham is," said Jack, beaming amiably. "Seen you talking to those two old fools. You going to put them on the air, mister? Couple of quaint old country bumpkins nattering about how they used to mow the fifty-acre by hand in their young days? It turns me up some of the stuff the B.-bloody-C. puts out about us country folk."

Nigel gave it up. "I'm not interested in that sort of thing," he said. "But this murder of yours—that'd make a good feature program. The effect of a murder upon the neighborhood, I mean."

He was aware that silence had descended upon the barroom of the Lacey Arms. Jack Whitford was gazing at him enigmatically out of those pale blue eyes, which had the sailor's steady, distant focus.

28

" 'Tidn't no murder of ours," he said. " 'Tis they Ferry Lacey chaps. Proper wild lot of bastards they are at Ferry Lacey. We're law-abiding folk at Hinton."

Paul Willingham laughed. "Especially at night."

"What the eye don't see, the heart don't grieve for," said Jack.

Nigel said, after a pause, "I know a chap, down in Devonshire where I used to live—he was a Somerset chap, actually —he used to take a long pole into the woods and fasten some sort of firework made of sulphur to one end, and light it, and poke it up among the branches. And the fumes stupefied the roosting pheasants. They just fell off their perches into his hands, like ripe apples."

Jack Whitford slapped his thigh. "That's a good 'un! Never heard of that before. Stupefied the s.o.b's! Well, I'll be damned!"

The ice was broken. Presently Nigel asked the poacher if Foxhole Wood was preserved. Jack Whitford gave him a wary glance.

"Mr. Strangeways is all right," put in Paul.

"Ah. It is. And wired up. Now. But you can get in, and out, if you knows yer way," Jack replied, with his quick, ferocious smile.

Nigel pumped him again, cautiously. The wood, it seemed, had once been part of the Lacey property. James Seaton, father of the poet, had sold it to a London syndicate. The syndicate had installed a gamekeeper, and in general made things difficult for local enterprise. They had even, after a bit, wired up the gate of an immemorial right-of-way through the wood.

"How long ago was that?" asked Nigel.

"Matter of eight or nine years. Old Mr. Lacey now—the squire as used to be—he'd never have allowed them London bastards to get away with that."

"I wonder Mr. Seaton doesn't do something about it," said Paul.

"Oh, reckon he's all for a quiet life. We know who wears the trousers over to Laceys these days."

A contemplative silence fell. Presently Jack Whitford raised his face from his beer mug.

"I could have told that lug of an inspector something."

"He was on at you too, was he?" said Paul.

"Ah. That's a nosy-parker. I sent him about his business. Not even a local man. 'You stick your nose in where it belongs,' I says to him, straight."

Jack took another swig of beer.

"Can't be too careful with that sort. 'Had I seen any strangers about, any night last week?' 'And me tucked up in bed with my missus?' I says; 'don't be daft, I don't go out looking for trouble, like some. How should I be seeing strangers?'"

"I suppose he was after the man who murdered the chap found in the river," said Nigel innocently.

"You never knows what the coppers are after. Don't bloody know, themselves, half the time." Jack paused. "Funny you should mention Foxhole Wood. I saw a chap there last week—last Thursday night, it'd be." He lowered his voice confidentially. "Thought it was Mr. Seaton at first. Wouldn't have been the first time I'd seen him at night. Passed as near to me as you are, he has, many a time: composing his poems, I reckon. Ah, he'm another of us night birds."

"Perhaps it *was* Mr. Seaton you saw."

"Well, he had a look of him, first glance. But he passes by, very quick, where I'm standing behind a tree. And Mr. Seaton always walks slow, see? And then this s.o.b. turns off the ride, down the old right of way. And I hear him presently climbing over the gate—the one I told you about, with barbed wire all over it. So I knew it couldn't be Mr. Seaton. He'd never use that gate."

"Did you notice how this chap was dressed?"

"Had a mac on. Couldn't see nothing else. He flitted past me like a shadow. Reckon he needed it, too."

"How d'you mean?"

"Hell of a thundershower we had, that night."

"You know," said Paul, "this body they found in the river —it had a mackintosh on."

Jack Whitford gave him a bland, crafty look. "Plenty of mackintoshes about in these parts, Mr. Willingham."

"What time was it when you saw this stranger in the wood?"

"Not long before midnight."

"Funny if it turned out to be the bloke who got murdered," said Paul. "Well, drink up, Jack, and we'll make a four-hand." . . .

When the game was over, and Paul and Nigel were preparing to leave, Jack Whitford leaned over to Nigel.

"You'll not put down anything I said just now in one of your radio programs, will you, mister?"—a sharp, foxy grin. "I've got a reputation to lose, see?"

Nigel reassured him. "It's a queer thing, though," he added, "a stranger walking through a wood in the middle of the night. You'd think he'd stick to the roads."

"You've said it. And I'll tell you something more. You've not been in Foxhole Wood yourself?"

"No."

"Well, just you try walking through it at night. Proper bleeding rabbit warren of paths it is, half of 'em overgrown too. You'd lose your way, I'll lay you a dollar."

"And this chap was walking fast ahead, as if—"

"Ah, as if he knew it blindfold."

"And yet he took the path that had been wired up?"

"Ah. Bit of a riddle, ain't it? Well, cheer-oh, I'll be seeing you."

As the two friends strolled up the village street, Paul said, "Interesting evening? I think I handled it pretty well for you."

"You damn' near wrecked the whole thing with that farcical B.B.C. stuff. I could have wrung your neck."

"Pish. Establishing an identity for you. Most important in a place like this."

"I like that poacher of yours. He's no fool."

"It *was* the murdered man he saw, I suppose?"

"Or the murderer. But what's really interesting is the riddle he set me. And I think I've guessed the answer."

CHAPTER THREE

DEAD END

Aᶠᵗᵉʳ breakfast the next morning, Nigel set out to walk to Ferry Lacey by a detour through Foxhole Wood. On his way he telephoned to Robert Seaton from the public call box in Hinton Lacey and received a warm invitation to lunch. He then took the road toward Chillingham. A couple of miles along this, he came to the outskirts of Foxhole Wood, on the right of the road. If the unknown traveler, whom Jack Whitford had seen in the wood just before midnight the previous Thursday, had walked from Chillingham Junction to this point, it would have taken him the best part of an hour, for the Junction was four miles away. Both the route and the time he had chosen suggested a wish for secrecy. Therefore it was unlikely that he would hang about at the station after getting out of his train. Therefore his train had probably arrived there somewhere about 11 P.M. Nigel made a mental note to find out from the stationmaster what trains stopped at the Junction around this time, and where they came from.

It was possible, of course, that the unknown had not traveled by rail at all: he might have taken a bus, or hitch-hiked, or even hired a car. Or again, he might have come to Chillingham by train and got a lift from there to Foxhole Wood. But these were doubtful possibilities, for each of them

33

would involve a greater risk of the recognition he seemed to have feared: sooner or later, if there were to be a hue and cry after him, someone would come forward who remembered giving a lift to a man of his description. But a crowded train, particularly a long-distance express, would be a pretty safe method of travel: and expresses from both Bristol and the South Wales ports passed through Chillingham on their way to London.

Nigel took out his large-scale map, set his stop watch going, and turned into the wood, just where a notice warned Trespassers, in exceptionally stringent terms, that they would be Prosecuted. The bridle path along which he walked was fairly well defined: his map told him that it was a right-of-way—no doubt the one the London syndicate had closed. But, as Jack Whitford had said, the wood was a warren of paths. At night, unless one knew the path well, it would be almost impossible not to stray down one of the tracks, hardly less narrow than the right-of-way itself, which led off from it.

The morning was bright, and fresh for August. The leaves made a lace of light and shadow. Presently Nigel came to a broad ride, furrowed by the wheels of tractor and trailer which had been at work on thinning out the wood. This ride, according to his map, bisected the wood on a diagonal, and the right-of-way ran down it for several hundred yards to the right, then branched off to the left again, its opening half-overgrown with brushwood. It was here that Jack Whitford had seen the stranger making for the edge of the wood. At night, no one unfamiliar with the wood could have found so readily the point where the right-of-way branched off from the main ride.

Nigel followed it for a quarter of a mile. Then the trees thinned away and he was confronted with a high, narrow gate, positively swathed in rusting barbed wire. There were footprints and crushed undergrowth all around, traces of the police search. Nigel struck off the path, emerged from the wood further to the right, and stood blinking in the sunshine, which showed him a vestigial path running across a meadow toward Ferry Lacey, and the glittering ringlets of the Thames. The path led him into the Seatons' pastureland, where it forked, one branch going right handed to the village itself, the other toward the iron gate in the walled orchard of Plash Meadow. Nigel noticed that this gate was locked, and the key not there, but the wards and hinges were oiled. He glanced at his stop watch: it had taken him twenty-one minutes to walk from the far side of Foxhole Wood to this point; say one and a half hours, by night, from Chillingham Junction to Ferry Lacey—not more, perhaps ten to fifteen minutes less if the traveler had walked fast the whole way.

Nigel now turned back from the gate and strolled down to the river. He scrutinized for a few moments the short shingly incline which dropped away below the bank into deep water —the bathing pool Robert Seaton had shown him during his previous visit. One could easily launch a boat from here, he said to himself. Or a corpse. Only the corpse was found half a mile downstream. And Paul had told him that there were no boathouses on the stretch of river immediately below the Ferry Lacey footbridge.

"Not my job, anyway," he muttered.

It was at this moment that, looking up, he saw, just round the corner of a clump of reeds to his left, a head resting upon the silver Thames, as it might be John the Baptist's on the platter—dank, drowned, black hair falling about the dead-white face, whose eyes were fixed upon his. For a second or two he gaped at it, stupefied and unrecognizing. Then the mouth of the head opened. A cool voice said,

"Why don't you come in? You look hot. Been chasing someone?"

It was Mara Torrance. Nigel's heart resumed its norma
beat.

"No. You come out. And do stop staring at me like Johr
the Baptist. You gave me quite a turn," he added irritably.

The young woman emerged, dripping. She unloosed the
shoulder straps of her scarlet bathing dress and lay down
on the bank beside him.

"I thought you'd be turning up soon," she said. "*And* witl
heads on your brain. I presume they haven't found it yet, o
you wouldn't have been so startled by mine."

"The police? As far as I know, they haven't."

"Did I really look like a corpse—from the neck upward,
mean? It's not very flattering of you," Miss Torrance pursued

"You don't now."

"What *do* I look like then, Nigel Strangeways?" He
eyes, shaded with one hand from the sun, stared insolentl
into his.

"Oh, you look very nice. And you also look like a girl wh
has a good deal of sleep to make up," said Nigel, lookin
down at the magnolia-white face, the skin puffy about th
eyes.

"I don't sleep well without a man in my bed. And that'
not so easily arranged in these parts."

Nigel laughed unaffectedly. "Good gracious! Are you try
ing to shock me? With simple physiological facts?" The girl'
right hand, which had turned palm upward on the grass an
slid toward him, clenched itself. "You ought to get marriec
then."

"So Lionel tells me. But it's no good. . . . I'm not . . .
can't . . ." Her voice faltered. She tried again. "He's too muc
under his stepmother's thumb for me. Could you fancy Jane
as a mother-in-law?"

"Lionel?" said Nigel, surprised. "I should have though
if anyone was under her thumb, it's Robert Seaton."

36

"Oh, Robert can afford to be under her thumb: or to seem to be."

Nigel glanced at the girl sharply. It was the first perceptive unegotistic remark she had made.

"You admire him very much?" he asked.

"Robert? I—I venerate him. He's the only really good man I've ever met. He was wonderful to me, when I was—when something foul happened. A long time ago. But that's not important. He's a great poet."

"Yes . . . Well, to revert to your insomnia for a moment. What about last week? Did you sleep badly every night? Friday night, for instance?"

Nigel was aware of a quick tension, and relaxing of it, in the girl beside him.

"Oh, Friday? No, we all slept like logs that night, I should imagine."

"Why was that?"

"Because we'd had such a hellish time the night before."

"Oh?" said Nigel, gazing noncommittally down his nose.

"Yes. There was a cracking thunderstorm. Not long after midnight. It went on and on. Went away and came back again. I hate thunder and adore lightning. I watched the storm out of my bedroom window."

"Which way does it face?"

"Over the courtyard."

"You didn't see any mysterious strangers gliding along— with or without heads—I take it?"

"No. The police have asked me all this, anyway. It's a frightful bore."

"And the rest of the family had a bad night too?"

"Well, Robert and Janet did, certainly. I saw them crossing the courtyard, soon after half-past twelve—the first drops of the thundershower were just beginning to fall. And Vanessa apparently saw them there again, half an hour later, when the second thunderstorm was in progress."

37

"What on earth were they doing?"

"I asked Janet the next morning. She said she'd got worried about Kitty—that's the mare—being frightened by the storm, and maybe kicking her loose box to bits. So she went out with Robert to see."

"And the second time? When Vanessa saw them?"

"Oh, Janet said she must have been dreaming. Vanessa stuck to it that she had seen them, in a flash of sheet lightning, just under the big chestnut tree."

"What? Sheltering under it?"

"No, hurrying past it, away from the house. I expect Vanessa *was* dreaming. But Janet needn't have been so brusque with her. As a matter of fact, she was very queer and edgy all Friday, took to her bed before dinner."

"Janet?"

"Uh-huh."

"And what about the others? Lionel, for instance?"

"Oh, Lionel claims to have slept through the whole thing. Says the war taught him to sleep through any bombardment." Mara added, rather pettishly, "He has to have his eight hours of sleep every night. Very regular habits, our Lionel."

"And your father? Did the storm keep him awake?"

The young woman paused before answering. "I shouldn't think so. He—well, he was a bit plastered that evening. Why are you asking me all this, anyway?"

"Thursday night may turn out to be rather important."

"But it was Friday night you began asking me about."

"A slip of the tongue," replied Nigel blandly.

"'Slip of the tongue!' You liar! You've just been leading me on. It's contemptible!" She was sitting bolt upright now, positively glaring at him.

"Now you mustn't get worked up. The police will soon be asking you all a lot of questions about Thursday night. You've just had a dress rehearsal with me. That's all there is to it. And you've told me nothing that could possibly incriminate anyone, as far as I can see. After all, there's no evidence that the murdered man came to Plash Meadow. Yet."

"I think you're rather a frightening man, Nigel Strangeways," she said, looking at him doubtfully.

"And I think you're not nearly as wicked a woman as you try to make out."

She seized his hand, drove her nails viciously into it and threw it away from her.

"Don't be paternal to me!" she exclaimed furiously. "Don't you dare to be—" She ran away from him, into the river, and swam strongly out on her back. It occurred to Nigel that a strong swimmer could have towed the corpse some way downstream, then let it go. He stood up.

"Won't you walk along to the house with me?" he called.

"No, I'll have to creep in by the back way. Janet doesn't like me showing off my figure in full view of the front windows. She's a great one for the proprieties. Why don't you come along to our barn after lunch? See you then."

Nigel waved and set off along the bank. He went through a gate into the lane that led up to the village from the footbridge, climbed its steep slope for a hundred yards or so, then he was in front of Plash Meadow.

The house looked different. It seemed less enchanted, more awake than when he had last seen it. The roses—that was it: most of them had withered, and there was a tarnished look on the few that were left. It was a beautiful house, oh yes; but only a house now, not a brilliant, enervating dream any more. What on earth am I doing here? Nigel mused. What sort of a trap am I walking into? And why should the idea of a trap come into my head at all? A great poet, his well-born and distinguished wife, his son, his daughter—what could be more reassuring? Just because a headless body is found half a mile away from their house, I come here with a mind already half-poisoned, looking for the sinister detail in every hole and corner, in every artless word. A girl plunges into a river, and I have to think of a corpse being towed out from the bank.

Nigel pulled himself up, realizing that the house was beginning to cast its spell on him again, roses or no roses, and more swiftly this time. No, there *are* certain queer anomalies, he said to himself. As, for instance, why should Janet Seaton, that race-proud woman and stickler for the proprieties, allow a raffish couple like the Torrances to live in her barn? And how did Mara Torrance, who so venerates Robert Seaton, come to do that wood carving in which he so discreditably figured? And why had Robert called it "autotherapy"? And when was it—

"Hello! You look awfully worried. Have you come about our murder?"

Vanessa Seaton's head, in its tawny cloud of hair, had risen up from the other side of the low garden wall, a foot away from his own face. Nigel gave a dramatic start.

"Heavens! You frightened me out of my wits. Where did you spring from?"

"I've been tracking you. Our Lieutenant—" she blushed rosily "—in the Guides, you know—Lieutenant taught me tracking last term. She's wizard at it. The great thing is to sink into the landscape, freeze quite still if anyone looks in your direction. Then you're practically invisible."

"Hmm," said Nigel, eyeing Vanessa's plump contours in a marked manner. "And did you trail the police too, when they were here?"

"You bet I did. There were hordes of them. Well, three at least. All over the garden and orchard. Peering at the ground." Her voice sank to a hoarse and bloodcurdling whisper. "Do you know what they were looking for? *Freshly turned earth!* That's what Lionel says. A new policeman came this morning. His name is Superintendent Blount. He's just down the road now, talking to Hubert."

"Hubert?"

"Our gardener."

"I must have a word with him. Like to come?"

Vanessa drew back, took a run at the wall, vaulted it and fell in a heap on the other side. "I don't seem to have got the knack of landing yet. Lieutenant can do it absolutely pro style. But she's our gym mistress too, of course."

She walked up the lane beside him, chattering hard. They passed a row of cottages on their right. Beyond this row there was a path, meeting the lane at right angles. Vanessa led the way down it. At the far end Nigel saw a stile and the path continued over the meadows beyond: he recognized it as the other fork of the right-of-way. If the unknown had not taken the left-hand one, leading to the orchard gate of Plash Meadow, he must presumably have come down this way into the village.

"That's Hubert's cottage," said Vanessa, pointing through a gate in the hedge to their left.

"Will you go in, and if the superintendent is still there, tell him Mr. Strangeways would like a word with him."

"I say, d'you *know* the superintendent? Could you get his autograph for me? I simply didn't dare ask him for it."

"I expect so."

When Blount emerged from the cottage, towed by Vanessa, Nigel said,

"Good morning, Superintendent. I've told Miss Seaton you'll give her your autograph."

"Oh well, now, oh well now," said Blount, patting his bald head.

"So run back to the house and get your album, Vanessa."

The girl galloped off. Nigel quickly told Blount the information he had received from Jack Whitford, adjuring him not to make any trouble with the poacher for having

41

withheld it from Inspector Gates: there might be more information to come from that quarter.

"Aye. It gives us a line. I'm much obliged to you, Strangeways. We'll take it up at the Chillingham end, too. The Thursday night. In Foxhole Wood, shortly before midnight, this chap was seen, eh?"

"And it takes about quarter of an hour's brisk walking from the wired gate to Ferry Lacey. You know about the right-of-way, I presume, and how it forks."

"Uh-huh. Any more gossip?"

"Plenty. It'll keep for a bit. Can you come along to Paul Willingham's farm, at Hinton Lacey—say nine o'clock this evening? We'll have a chat."

"Very well. By the bye, your deserter theory won't do. Gates got in touch with the Service authorities. As far as we can tell, no lads from this village are on their list of deserters."

"Oh, that's cold rice now. What you've got to find is somebody who knew this part of the country very well, but left it for good nine or ten years ago."

Blount raised his eyebrows interrogatively. A tremor of the earth's surface announced the return, at full speed, of Miss Vanessa Seaton.

"I'll explain this evening," said Nigel hurriedly. "Now, out with your pen and sign, please."

As they walked back to Plash Meadow, Vanessa told Nigel that her stepmother would like to see him privately before lunch. She took him to a small sitting room, where they found Mrs. Seaton doing her accounts. She rose and received him graciously.

"Do sit down, won't you? All right, Vanessa, run along now. . . . Mr. Strangeways, I wanted a word with you. Vanessa tells me this Superintendent Blount is a friend of yours. Perhaps you could advise me. You see, he has asked if I—if we have any objection to the police searching this house. Naturally, I asked him if he had a search warrant. He hadn't of course. And I must say it seems to me quite preposterous—I mean, it was bad enough having that fool of an Inspector Gates badgering us all. And I gave the police a free hand to search the grounds and outbuildings, several days ago. But the house! Well, really!"

"Blount cannot very well proceed without a warrant. But it's everyone's duty to assist the police to the best of—"

"I consider it my Prime Duty, Mr. Strangeways, to protect my Husband from worry and interference," said Janet Seaton grandly. "His Work must always come first with me. I think it quite monstrous that, because some unfortunate person gets killed—nowhere near my house, incidentally—Robert should be pestered. And just when his new Poem has reached a point that demands the greatest concentration."

"Yes. I see that. But I'm sure the search could be managed so that your husband wasn't disturbed."

"It's not only that. It's the indignity of it all—a pack of policemen ransacking one's home! I have some very valuable things here, as you know. Irreplaceable things. If they were damaged—"

"I don't think there's any likelihood of that. Scotland Yard men are extremely skilled and careful."

"But I *can't* see the necessity for it."

"It's just to make sure that this man who was murdered didn't come here. He might have been a burglar and tried to break in, for instance. Or a fugitive from justice."

"But, good gracious me, if he'd broken in, if he'd left clues here, *we* should have found them."

"On Friday morning, you mean?"

"Yes. If that was the morning after—after it happened. I didn't know the police had fixed it so definitely."

Nigel seemed to detect a certain unwonted flurry in Mrs. Seaton's rhythm at this point—a check, a recovery, a rush in her words, like the gait of a hurdler who has just touched the top bar with his foot, but recovered himself well enough to make up the lost ground. She went on,

"I'll think over what you say. Well, we mustn't keep the Poet waiting any longer. He's expecting you."

It's either pure innocence or a phenomenal effort of will power, thought Nigel as they went upstairs, that she should refrain from sounding me further about the Thursday night.

Robert Seaton was sitting at a small table in the far corner of his study. The window overlooked the courtyard, the out-buildings, and the rolling pastoral country beyond: but the table was set so that his back was turned to the window when writing. There were bookshelves lining three of the walls. On one of them stood a bronze bust of the Poet, by Epstein. The room was light, fresh and tidy looking: but somewhat austere, compared with the elaborate richness and artistry of the downstair rooms; no pictures, no valuable bric-a-brac.

"I've got 'em all for you," said Robert Seaton cheerfully. "You must thank my wife for that. No idea they hadn't been thrown away. But she'd kept 'em all under lock and key."

He pointed to a pile of five or six small notebooks on the table.

"Robert is too modest," said Mrs. Seaton. "I knew they would be of interest to posterity."

"Posterity? Poof! That's a very big word. I'm sure Strangeways doesn't want to be called posterity."

"You know what I mean, Robert." Mrs. Seaton sounded rather piqued. Nigel seemed to sense a change in Robert Seaton. He was brisker, more alive than in June, as though something had been released in him. The air after a thunderstorm, thought Nigel: damn it, I've got thunder on the brain!

"Now here," the poet was saying. "What's this? Oh yes, *Lyrical Interludes*." He had taken up the top notebook from the pile. "Mmm. I had nothing to say in those days, but I said it rather well. You'll find it quite easy to follow. I've always done my first drafts in pencil—afraid they're almost illegible—" Looking over his shoulder, Nigel saw the page scored all over with corrections and alternatives. Robert Seaton turned over. "Then the subsequent drafts of each poem are in ink. You'll see how they worked out. Quite simple. Well, here you are, then."

He laid the pile of notebooks in Nigel's hands.

"Oh, Robert, do you think you'd better?—I mean, I'm sure Mr. Strangeways will be very careful of them. But—"

"Nonsense, my dear! If he's to work on them, he must take them along."

"I was just thinking, wouldn't it be simpler if he stayed with us at Plash Meadow while—we should be delighted to have you, Mr. Strangeways, if Paul could spare you for a few days."

"Excellent idea," said Robert Seaton, rubbing his hands briskly. "Why not? Of course you will, my dear fellow." An impish gleam came into his eyes. "You'll be able to divide your time between your work and your hobby. You've heard about our local crime, I suppose?"

"I have indeed."

"Splendid! Capital! That's fixed, then. When can you come? Tomorrow? The sooner, the better. Take some of the garrison duty off Janet's shoulders."

"Robert! Really! I'm sure Mr. Strangeways doesn't—"

"My wife has the most exaggerated ideas about the sacro-sanctity of my work. I really believe she'd allow the police into this room only over her dead body."

"Mrs. Seaton was telling me you've reached a critical point in your new long poem."

"Long poem? Oh yes. To be sure. I—"

"Robert doesn't like talking about a poem he's actually at work on," Janet put in firmly.

"No. I quite understand," said Nigel.

"Well, I'm moving ahead, anyway. Janet gave me this pen

45

a few weeks ago. Called a Biro. Ever seen one? It must have brought me luck. Scribble, scribble, scribble. But I suppose even it will dry up one day."

"You can get it refilled at Axters. Shall we go down to lunch?"

At lunch, Nigel brought the conversation round to the great thunderstorm of last week. He was aware at once of tactful efforts by Mrs. Seaton to change the subject; but Vanessa, with an air of unassuaged grievance, persisted that she had *not* been dreaming.

"I saw you both crossing the court," she said to her parents. "*Honestly* I did. And it was after the thundershower, because the grass was gleaming wet. I looked at my watch and it said five to one. I couldn't have dreamed about looking at my watch. It'd have changed into a turnip or ice cream or something, if I'd been dreaming."

"Vanessa, we've been into all this." Mrs. Seaton turned to Nigel. "We all had a very disturbed night. I went out soon after the first thunderstorm began, to see if Kitty—that's the mare—was frightened: she's very timid. Vanessa must have seen us then, and got it mixed up with a dream."

"But I tell you it *wasn't* then! I—"

"You mustn't contradict your mother," said Robert Seaton gently. "Anyway, what does it matter?"

"My veracity is being impugnated," Vanessa exclaimed, with a virgin-and-martyr air which made Lionel Seaton chuckle.

"Impugned, Fatty. Impugned," he said. "Either impugned or impregnated. You can't have it both ways."

"I shall say 'impugnated' if I wish," returned his sister, with great dignity. "It's a perfectly good word. And don't call me 'Fatty'! You should have more respect for womanhood."

The rest of lunch conducted itself quite amiably, with a great deal of family jokes and jargon bandied about. Finny Black, chuckling and gurgling at the sallies of laughter from the two young people, waited upon them deftly. Nigel thought to himself that the Seaton menage was taking its local crime very much in its stride.

As it turned out, however, he was not quite right about this. After lunch, when Lionel and Vanessa had gone off together, Mrs. Seaton took up the subject of Vanessa's "dream" again.

"We thought it best to tell her she'd imagined it all. But the fact is, she did see Robert and myself that night. I'd better explain—" she glanced at her husband "—since Mr. Strangeways has hinted that the Thursday night may be important."

She went on to say that Finny Black was apt to be over-excited by thunderstorms. It had happened several times before: he'd been found wandering about the house or grounds in a rather demented state ("like a child—an over-sensitive child"). They had gone to his bedroom, to make sure he was all right. The room was empty. So they went out of doors, and looked about the grounds for him, calling his name softly so as not to alarm him further.

"And did you in fact find him?" Nigel interposed.

"Not then. He turned up about an hour later, drenched to the skin," said Robert.

Mrs. Seaton, lowering her voice confidentially, said, "You see, Vanessa is highstrung. And she's never quite taken to Finny. That's why we took the line we did. It would have been most unwise to let her know that Finny may sometimes be wandering about the place, in the dark."

Nigel thought privately that it was still more unwise not to have warned Vanessa about the possibility of a demented and gibbering dwarf bumping into her room one night. However, it was not his concern. He meditated for a moment asking them why they kept Finny Black on, if Vanessa didn't like him. But what he finally said was,

"Yes, I see. That explains it. Tell me, Mrs. Seaton, you and

your people have been associated so long with this village, I
expect you know the history of every family in it: tell me,
do you remember anyone leaving the village, perhaps under
a cloud, nine or ten years ago? A man of forty-five to fifty?
One who had lived here all his life till then, or at any rate
was thoroughly familiar with the surrounding countryside."

As he amplified his question, Nigel was quite horrified by
its effect upon his host and hostess. Janet Seaton's sallow
face darkened with a painful flush, and her big-knuckled
hands clenched on the arms of her chair. Robert Seaton took
his pipe out of his mouth, positively gaping at Nigel.

There was a stricken, dead silence when he stopped. Then
both of them began to speak together, and both broke off.

"Really, it's too extraordinary," said the Poet, at a second
attempt. "Isn't it, Janet? I mean, your whole description fits
perfectly, Strangeways. But—"

"Fits whom?"

"My elder brother, Oswald."

"Robert, I don't think Mr. Strangeways is—"

"But it *does*," said the Poet, brushing aside his wife's protest with an impatient gesture. "It was ten years ago. And he
was—let me see—fifty, no forty-nine then. And he certainly
knew this countryside like the back of his hand."

"But he didn't leave under a cloud, I'm sure," said Nigel.
"Did he go abroad? Where is he now?"

"Oh no," said Robert Seaton. "He didn't go abroad. He
disappeared one day. And—well, the next day I heard that
he'd drowned himself, poor chap."

CHAPTER FOUR

THE DARK BACKWARD

BEFORE they parted, it was arranged that Nigel should install himself at Plash Meadow on Monday. That would give him one more full day with Paul. As he strolled across the courtyard to the old tithe barn, he was thinking how satisfactorily things had panned out: he would be able to devote next week to a study of Robert Seaton's manuscripts, undistracted by misgivings about the Ferry Lacey crime; for, after what the poet had just told him, and particularly the *way* he had told it, Nigel could not seriously imagine that he had accepted the hospitality of a murderer. It was a pity, of course, that Oswald Seaton had drowned himself ten years before. Theoretically, he would have fitted into the picture very neatly—family black sheep returning, embarrassment all round, blackmail perhaps, off with his head. He could imagine Janet Seaton going to almost any lengths to preserve her status quo. But that idea didn't have to be reckoned with now, thank goodness.

Nigel walked round the barn, idly noting that one door opened onto the courtyard, while there were French windows at the end facing the drive which led out into the lane, and on the far side lay a neat little enclosed garden—rose bushes, a lawn, a few apple trees. Turning back again, after a glance at this garden plot, he found Mara Torrance opening the French windows. She let him in to the studio. This was a big, high, cool apartment, occupying half the length of the building, its whitewashed walls carrying right up to the arched and timbered roof. The rest of the barn had been divided into two stories: kitchen-dining room and offices below; above, three small bedrooms and a bathroom. Access to this upper floor, which had originally been the barn loft, was by a steep stair ladder from the studio: the loft had a balustrade, and from below presented the appearance of a musician's gallery.

At Nigel's request, Mara had taken him round the place, pointing out its features in a bored, *dégagé* manner. Nigel had glanced out of her bedroom window, from which she had seen the Seatons crossing the courtyard on the night of the storm: he had noted that this bedroom was furthest from the staircase, Rennell Torrance's nearest to it, and a cell-like spare room in between.

Now they were back in the studio. While Mara went to prepare coffee, Nigel mooched around, scrutinizing the pictures hung low on the walls, the canvases stacked against them. Rennell Torrance was clearly a prolific painter. Evidence of genius was less noticeable, however. The subjects of his canvases were romantic; the treatment ambitious, slovenly, grandiose. He sets himself up to be a "visionary" painter, thought Nigel: but his visions are synthetic—pitiable attempts to inflate a respectable, small talent into the proportions of greatness. There was a monotony about the pictures; their general impression on the eye was that of a series of unfinished studies for a masterpiece not yet begun.

Nigel turned away to a side table littered with dirty glasses, painting materials, old magazines. One of these lay open at a photograph of the Seatons and Torrances grouped against the front of Plash Meadow. It had the usual society-paper's vapid caption.

Artistic Entente (read Nigel). *The distinguished poet, Robert Seaton, poses* en famille *outside his beautiful old house at Ferry Lacey. Mrs. Seaton was one of the Laceys, from time immemorial lords of the manor in this part of the world. With them are the painter, Rennell Torrance, and his attractive daughter. The Torrances live in an old tithe barn adjoining Plash Meadow, converted for them by Mr. and Mrs. Seaton into a ravishing* atelier *(see picture below).*

The magazine was dated July of the previous year. Nigel put it down and approached another table which stood before an artist's throne. On this table stood a round object concealed by a cloth. Nigel took off the cloth. What he saw made him draw in his breath sharply. It was a head. Molded in clay. A head, unmistakably, of Robert Seaton. The object made every single canvas in the studio look third rate: It had an extraordinary power and vitality. But the shocking thing was that the face of the poet had been given an abominable untruth. Every feature was perfectly recognizable, almost photographically correct; yet the whole effect was one of evil—a sultry, gloating kind of evil. It was the face of a devil, basking in his own damnation.

"Crikey," murmured Nigel, putting back the cloth.

"How dare you do that!" came the furious voice of Mara Torrance from the doorway. She slammed down the coffee tray on a table, and thrust herself between Nigel and the clay head, almost as if protecting it. "How dare you go prying at my work!"

"So *you* did it?"

"I hate people looking at my things when they're unfinished. Sorry to break out like that," she said, more equably.

"Unfinished? I see."

"What d'you mean?"

"Well, I was going to ask if that's the way you really see Robert Seaton."

"Oh. Oh no." A bewildered look came into her face. Her voice went small and faltering. "I don't know how it got like that," she said. "I—it frightens me. I'd better start again."

"It's very good, though. Very good indeed. Terrifyingly good."

"What's very good?" said her father, coming into the room. Nigel indicated the head.

"Oh, that. Yes, Mara has inherited some of my gift. It'll be one in the eye for Janet, anyway." Rennell Torrance sniggered fatly, plumped himself down in a chair and poured out a cup of coffee. "Well, she asked for it."

"Asked for it?"

"Yuh. A few days ago—when was it, Mara?—last Saturday—Janet was in here. We got talking modern art. Hopeless old bourgeoise, Janet is. Mara got a bit heated. About the abstract chaps. That's Mara's usual line, you know—three curves and a twiddle, label it 'Object,' and bob's your uncle. Anyway, Janet said Mara couldn't do a portrait bust, a realistic job so's you could recognize the sitter, not if she tried for a hundred years. Janet said people only do that abstract stuff because they're incapable of straight naturalism. Pretty crude of old Janet, I must say, though I wouldn't altogether disagree with her. Anyway, this chump here, my daughter proceeds to fall for it, hook, line and sinker. 'Oh, can't I just?' she says in effect. So she roped in Robert and got him to sit for her."

"And you think it *is* a good likeness?" said Nigel after a moment's pause.

"Oh, it was coming along pretty well. Haven't looked at it for a day or two."

He hauled himself out of his basket chair, slouched over to the table and took the cloth off the head. Nigel saw his back go rigid. A queer sound came from the man's throat.

52

He almost overturned the head by the violence with which he flung the cloth over it again. As he stumbled back to his chair, his pasty face was green.

"Sorry," he said. "My heart goes wrong on me now and then. Mara, get me a drop of brandy, there's a good girl."

"I'll get you some water. You had quite enough brandy after lunch."

When the girl had left the room, Nigel said, "It's not really Robert Seaton, is it?"

"What the devil d'you mean? Who else should it be?" The painter spoke with remarkable vehemence for a man who had just had a heart attack. "Robert sat for it. Ask Janet. She made him sit for it."

"What I meant was that it's not Robert Seaton's normal expression," replied Nigel, mildly and quite truthfully. . . .

Soon after nine o'clock that evening, Superintendent Blount drove up to Paul Willingham's farm. His first words to Nigel were,

"So you're going to stay at Plash Meadow next week, I hear. That's vairy convenient."

"Glad you approve. But let me tell you this, Blount: I'm much more interested in Robert Seaton's poetry than his homicidal tendencies, if any. I shall do my best to defeat the ends of justice, should it prove necessary. We haven't so many good poets in the country that we can afford to hang one."

The superintendent looked extremely shocked at this unethical statement. Then his face took on the gratified expression of the Scot who has tracked down a joke single-handed.

"I doubt you're pulling my leg, Strangeways. Of course, we have no grounds for suspicion against Mr. Seaton, as yet. But the household in general—that's another matter."

Blount proceeded to enlarge on this. After the information

53

Nigel had given him this morning, he had narrowed his inquiries in Ferry Lacey to the period round about midnight of Thursday last week. He had discovered that a woman, living in the cottage nearest to the Seatons' gardener's cottage, had been expecting a baby that night. Her husband had gone to the call box shortly after 11 P.M. and telephoned to the doctor. The doctor was out at another confinement, but the message would be given to him on his return. The husband—it was his wife's first child—had been anxious. From midnight till nearly one in the morning, when the doctor had finally arrived, he had stayed out of the house, either in the porch or the road, awaiting the doctor's arrival. He was quite certain that, during this period, no one had come down the path which led from the right-of-way across the fields, past his cottage, into the road. This evidence, if it could be relied on, must imply that the unknown man had taken the left-hand fork of the right-of-way, leading to Plash Meadow.

"And another significant fact," Blount went on. "This chap tells me he saw Mr. Seaton walking down the road, toward Plash Meadow, a while before the doctor arrived. He couldn't be exact about the time: thought it might have been about quarter to one."

"Did you ask Seaton about this?"

"Yes. He said he'd been out for a walk. He often walks at night, it seems—nothing unusual about it. And he'd taken shelter for a wee while when the first thunderstorm came on."

"I see," said Nigel slowly. "Of course, when you're anxiously waiting for a doctor to arrive, time goes very slowly."

"What's in your mind?" Blount glanced at him keenly.

"There seems to be something wrong with the timetable. Seaton ought to have got home before 12:30. However, I expect this worried young husband misjudged the time. Or else Mara Torrance got it wrong."

Nigel told Blount the substance of his conversation with Miss Torrance.

"Oho. We must look into that," said Blount formidably. "Well now. Trains. There's an express from Bristol, gets in at Chillingham Junction at 10:58. And another, from the South Wales ports, which gets in at 10:19. They were both running up to time that night. The Bristol one sounds the more likely, on the face of it. The ticket collector can't help. But Gates has made inquiries at and near by the station: no evidence of anyone hanging around there between 10:19 and eleven o'clock. No reason why he should hang about, as far as we know. On the other hand, Gates hasn't found any witness yet who saw our man walking away from the Junction on the road to Ferry Lacey. But it's early days yet for that. Gates'll be making inquiries all along the road, as far as Foxhole Wood."

"I take it you've not found the man's head yet, or his clothes?"

Blount shrugged his shoulders. The county police had examined the grounds of Plash Meadow, and every allotment and cottage garden in the village, soon after the discovery of the corpse. But you couldn't go digging up the whole countryside in search of one head: and none of the village people had reported sounds of digging that night. Blount had asked the Seatons' gardener, only this morning, if he'd noticed any signs of freshly dug earth in their garden on the Friday, any implements out of place in the tool shed. He had not. "Though, mind you," Blount added, "these country people are vairy close. I'd no' put it past them to lie themselves black in the face to protect the Seatons—the Laceys, perhaps I should say. It's a vairy feudal type of community still."

This very afternoon, shortly after Nigel had left, two of Blount's men had begun a thorough search of Plash Meadow. Mrs. Seaton had made no objection, when the superintendent asked her permission, though she had insisted on following them round the downstairs rooms to make sure they didn't damage her priceless possessions. Nothing at all had been found. In the meantime, Blount had interviewed every member of the household. They told him nothing that Nigel hadn't heard already about the Thursday night.

"Of course, I could get no sense out of that unco wee dwarf," said Blount. "He juist yammered at me. And I've yet to interview Miss Torrance. She'd gone out when I arrived."

Inspector Gates had found no traces of blood anywhere in the farm buildings during his original search. This afternoon, Blount had questioned the dairyman. But the result was again negative.

"Why the dairyman?" asked Nigel.

"Well, you see, the dairy is tiled. It could easily be hosed down."

"At night? But that'd be a frightful risk, surely? Somebody might hear."

"Not if it was done—e'eh—while a thundershower was in process. But the dairyman could not definitely say that the place had been sluiced down since he hosed it himself the evening before."

"I still think you're concentrating far too much on Plash Meadow."

Blount looked wounded. "Indeed I'm not. I've an open mind. But the murdered man was last seen walking in that direction. And the house stands a little away from the rest of the village. You'd think, if he'd gone anywhere else, to one of the cottages, say, and been killed there, and his head and clothes somehow disposed of—well, all the odds are that one of the neighbors would have heard something, noticed something wrong and started gossiping, isn't that so? We've got to make a start somewhere."

"Any of the Plash Meadow household taken a trip recently?"

"Mr. Lionel Seaton went up to London last Saturday: staying the week end with friends. We're following that up, of course. None of the others left the neighborhood. Och, but they've had all the time on earth to get rid of the clothes."

"But the head wouldn't be so easy to get rid of?"

"An old house like Plash Meadow will have two-three secret panels and suchlike, I dare say. But I can't go tearing the place apart till I've some more evidence."

"Till you know whose head you're looking for, eh?" asks Nigel.

"Just so." Blount gave him a meditative look. "Tell me, Strangeways, do you know anything about Mr. Seaton's brother?"

"Oswald Seaton? I know he's dead, if that helps you at all."

"Och aye. He's legally dead, all right."

"How d'you mean, 'legally' dead?"

"He committed suicide. Ten years ago. Drowned himself. In the Bristol Channel."

"Well?"

"But, you see, the body was never found."

Nigel sat back and threw up his hands. "Really, Blount, this is too much! D'you mean he left his head on the beach and—"

"I mean he, the *corpus*, the man Oswald Seaton, was not found. He left a pile of clothes and a suicide note in the boat he jumped out of. Finis. Body never recovered. But the tides are tricky thereabouts. He died intestate. Robert Seaton, being his next-of-kin, applied for letters of administration. In due course, after all possible inquiries had been made, the court gave leave to presume death, and so Robert came in for the property. The suicide note was perfectly genuine— business worries and so on—people had noticed Oswald Seaton acting strangely, some days before—worried, drawn

57

looking and all that. But nothing criminal: he hadn't been embezzling; nothing to suggest a *fake* suicide: otherwise, of course, leave to presume death wouldn't have been near so readily given."

"Who told you all this? His brother?"

"Robert Seaton corroborated it just now. But I knew it before. We look up the records of anyone even remotely associated with a case, as you well know."

"Well, then, if it was a perfectly straightforward suicide—"

"Yes, there it is." Blount sighed. "But he'd have fitted the requirements. A man who knew this countryside well enough to take the short cut through Foxhole Wood, but hadn't been here for ten years—since that gate was wired up—otherwise he'd not have tried to get out of the wood that way. And it is a funny thing, too," Blount added musingly, "you and your 'head of a traveler'—he'd been one. Head traveler for his father's firm. Manufacturers of electrical equipment."

"What about the original police report on the suicide? No distinguishing marks on the body? Can't Robert Seaton help?"

Blount shook his head. "It'd be something if we could definitely eliminate the possibility that the murdered man was Oswald Seaton. But, as it so happens, what with the state of the corpse here, and the period of years that has passed, Robert Seaton couldn't be expected to identify it. The original report is rather negative on distinguishing marks —no bones broken, no birthmarks. Age, height, size of feet and hands—they correspond pretty well: but that part of the description would fit hundreds of men. No, Strangeways, I should simply be wasting my time trying to link up this murder here with a ten-year-old suicide—"

"Disappearance, you mean."

"If you like to be pedantic. But the police and the probate court were satisfied. That ought to be good enough for us."

"I think," said Nigel after a pause, "I shall have to do some digging on my own, then."

"Digging? Where?"

"Digging up the past."

Nigel's first excavations took place the next morning, the site being Paul Willingham. The gist of their leisurely conversation, as Paul unloaded his memory in the little stock-scented kitchen garden of the farm, tabulated itself for Nigel under the headings of F. for fact and H. for hearsay, something like this:

(F.) Old Mr. Lacey, father of Janet, lost heavily in slump of 1930. Compelled to sell Plash Meadow: Sold it to James Seaton, father of Oswald and Robert, successful manufacturer of electrical equipment, self-made man, factory in Redcote, other side of river. Old Mr. Lacey died soon after. Janet and her mother took cottage in Ferry Lacey. (H.) Janet set cap at Oswald: nothing doing.

(F.) Oswald and Robert—boyhood in Redcote when it was a small, unspoiled market town—familiar with countryside, fished in Thames at Ferry Lacey, etc.

(F.) Oswald went into father's business: worked way up: head traveler: was virtually running business from 1932 to 1936, when the father, already invalidish though indomitable, died.

(F.) James Seaton: a hard, strait-laced man—petty bourgeois, nonconformist conscience. Left whole property to Oswald. Robert cut off with shilling many years before, because (a) he had married, very young, against his father's wishes, a beautiful but lowborn Redcote girl, (b) he had refused to go into the family business, announced determination to support self by writing. (H.) Robert had very bad time in early years; great poverty; first wife died of (?) malnutrition, (?) lack of medical care.

(F.) After father's death, Robert, a widower now, paid long visit to Plash Meadow. (H.) Janet set cap at *him*,

59

Oswald not having come up to scratch. (F.) They becam
engaged in 1938, shortly after Oswald's suicide. Robert sol
factory when leave to presume Oswald's death had gon
through. In spite of death duties, very well off on proceeds
(H.) General gossip in countryside that Janet married hin
to get Plash Meadow back for the Laceys.

(F.) Torrances first turned up in district about 1937. Cara
van holiday in August. Rennell Torrance had already di
vorced wife, obtained custody of only child, Mara, the
about fourteen. They returned, caravanning, the next sum
mer. Nothing further known of them till they came to live i
the old tithe barn in 1945. No known connection, befor
then, between Torrances and Seatons.

(F.) Finny Black: brought back to Plash Meadow b
Robert and Janet Seaton after their honeymoon. No accoun
given of his provenance. The pair honeymooned in Dorse
(H.) Village gossip that Finny is Robert's bastard son.

"So there you are," said Paul, leaning back in his dec
chair and gently fishing a stray bee out of his beer mug
"That's the best I can do for you. What d'you make of it
What's your theory?"

"I haven't one."

"Well I have then. I suggest to you that the man we kno
as Robert Seaton is not Robert Seaton at all."

"Indeed? Who is he?"

"Brother Oswald. Oswald had the reputation of being
bad hat. Addiction to popsies—the younger the better. H
gets into bad trouble over one, fakes a suicide, pays Robe
a large bribe to clear out of the country, shaves off hi
beard—"

"Oh, he had a beard, did he?"

"—yes, and returns to Plash Meadow impersonatin
Robert. He was only a couple of years older, after all, an
quite like Robert to look at."

"So alike that Lionel and Vanessa were taken in?"

"Well, they hadn't seen their father much the last few years, after his wife died. He sent them to live with relations, you know. Janet, of course, realizes the truth and thus blackmails Oswald into marrying her. Then, ten years later, Robert returns from abroad. Oswald is threatened with exposure and slays him. How about that for a solution? Bang-on, wouldn't you say?"

"It's a mass of large holes, with nothing even to tie them together. On what do you base this farcical theory?"

"On the fact that the alleged Robert Seaton has written no poetry for the last ten years," said Paul, leaning earnestly forward.

"But—"

"You've only got his word for it, and Janet's, that he's been composing an epic of the First World War. Very shaky, old boy. Don't you believe it. All those tiddly little notebooks you brought back yesterday—nothing new in them, is there? You ask him for the manuscript of something he's written since 1938. Bet you a pint you don't get it."

"And where do the Torrances come in?"

"The Torrances? Well, let me see now; I hadn't got them in the picture yet. I know!—Torrance, waking from a drunken stupor on the dunes, sees Oswald lay a heap of clothes and a suicidal note at the brink of the Bristol Channel, then slink off inland again. He investigates, discovers the hanky-panky, and blackmails Oswald up to the eyeballs. So 'Robert,' the *ci-devant* Oswald, has to provide Torrance with a cozy home for life."

Nigel gazed gravely at his friend.

"I think you had better stick to agriculture," he said.

Paul grinned. "You reject my reconstruction *in toto*? Can't say I'm surprised. I only thought it up a minute ago."

"Nevertheless," said Nigel, "you've laid your clumsy great fingers on two quite crucial points. I wonder—. D'you know anyone round here who knew the Seatons well in the old days?"

Paul thought for a bit. "There's old Keeley. Edits the *Redcote Gazette*. He's a local man: might be able to help. I could give you an introduction to him. In fact, I could drive you over tomorrow morning. I promised him some eggs, and I've got to see a man about a calf—that takes care of the petrol aspect. Then I can drop you off at Plash Meadow on the way back."

At 11:30 the next morning, Nigel was sitting in the editor's room. Paul had made an appointment for him by telephone, and brought him in to the *Redcote Gazette* office, a dingy building near the station.

Mr. Keeley, a gray-haired, fatherly-looking man in shirt sleeves, took the basket of eggs from Nigel and plumped it down in the litter on his desk.

"Thank Mr. Willingham very much, will you? The wife'll be glad of these. Funny how we've got back to the old system of barter these days."

"And what does Paul get in exchange?" Nigel ventured.

"Ah, that'd be telling," said Mr. Keeley comfortably. "Sit down, do. Here, let me clear a chair for you." The editor seemed to have all time at his disposal. He loaded a pipe in a leisurely manner; rang for cups of tea: only when these were brought did he sit back in the editorial chair, and with the guarded, slightly uneasy look of the journalist who finds himself for once at the giving end of an interview, ask Nigel what he could do for him.

Nigel had decided to put his cards on the table. He spoke of his association with Superintendent Blount, and his acquaintance with Robert Seaton. He said he wanted to fill in the picture of the Seatons' past, of which he only knew the bare outlines at present. He hinted that, on the barter principle, he would do his best in return for Mr. Keeley's reminiscences, to see that the *Redcote Gazette* got an exclusive story of the Ferry Lacey affair as soon as it could be released.

"What's this Ferry Lacey murder to do with Bob Seaton?"

"Ah, that'd be telling."

"I don't know that the *Gazette* is so interested in exclusive stories, Mr. Strangeways. We're not Fleet Street. And we have a high opinion of Mr. Seaton in these parts."

"You can't have a higher opinion of him than I have. Police investigations are a hellish experience for anyone who gets involved, and I want to take the brunt of this one off him as much as possible."

"Aye, he's had enough trouble in his life, has Bob. I'm not keen to make any more for him."

"Believe me, Mr. Keeley," said Nigel earnestly, "I'd not be here if I thought there was any danger of that. It's simply that this investigation has become concentrated on Plash Meadow, let's hope only temporarily. I admire Seaton tremendously. I'd like to help him, and his family of course. But I can't until I know more of the background."

The editor gave Nigel a long, considering look. Then he lumbered to the door, half-opened it, called out, "Mr. Arthur, I'm not to be disturbed for half an hour," and sat down again.

"You knew Seaton as a boy?" Nigel asked.

"Aye, we grew up together here—him and me and Oswald. Went to school together and got up to all sorts of mischief."

"Old Mr. Seaton, their father, was a bit of a terror, so I gather."

"He lived according to his lights, Mr. Strangeways. He put Redcote on the map, give him that. Started with a little shop and worked up to this factory. Regular, old-fashioned success story. Oh, he was a genius in his way. But Redcote's not been the same since. It's a betwixt-and-between sort of place now—half industrial, half rural—can't make up its mind what it is. Not that James Seaton cared what happened to Redcote. He was out to make his pile; and he made it; and then he tried to become a country gentleman."

"But, as a person, a father?"

Mr. Keeley very deliberately moved a pot of paste to one side of his desk, took up a pencil and began doodling. The Oxfordshire accent became more noticeable in his voice.

"I don't mind telling you, my blood boils even now when I think of the way he treated those two. Beatings, browbeatings, sermons, emotional outbursts. He was Chapel, you know. A real hell-fire Puritan. And damned tricky in business, like those canting Chapel hypocrites are apt to be. That's off the record—must remember my local advertisers! I suppose, in a way, it helped to make Bob a poet. He had to escape, and writing was *his* escape. But it's a wonder he wasn't warped for life, like his brother."

"Poets have a pretty hard center."

"Aye, he was always tough in his way, was Bob—what's the word?—resilient. Old James Seaton had to respect him for it. He found it was dangerous—well, useless—to try and drive Bob too far."

"How d'you mean?"

"Well, when Bob was just down from Oxford—he'd got a scholarship and his father had been all over him for a bit—he fell in love with Daisy Summers. She worked in the factory. A sweet, pretty girl, good as gold—aye, she was the belle of Redcote. But it wouldn't do for James Seaton. His son marrying a factory hand, a workman's daughter, oh dear me no! There was a fearful row. Bob married her, of course: he stood up to his father all right. But that, on top of his refusing to go into the firm—well, it finished him for James. Proper old-fashioned send-off he got. 'Never you darken my doors again.' And he didn't. He went to France in 1917. When he was demobbed, he and Daisy had a terrible bad time. I used to see quite a lot of them: I was in Fleet Street then. Bob scraped along on odd jobs—a bit of journalism here, a bit of lecturing there—anything so long as he could have plenty of spare time to write his poetry. It's a bitter business, that hand-to-mouth kind of life. And with a wife and child—. Still, they were happy, oh magnificently happy, taking it all in all. Till the second child came. Daisy got very ill. Bob pocketed his pride and wrote to his father asking for money. First time he'd done it. But he was older now, and you don't fuss about your pride so much when you're older. Well, James Seaton had forgotten nothing and forgiven nothing. He wrote back to say Bob could come into the business, if he'd give up his writing. Would you believe it? Bob was pretty well known as a poet by then, too. But old James thought of poetry and the theater, and all that sort of thing, as the Devil's work. I believe Bob might have done it, given it up, for Daisy's sake, only she wouldn't hear of such a thing. She was a stanch lass. No, perhaps he wouldn't have, after all. Anyway, she died. He hadn't the money to send her abroad, which the doctors said would save her. So she died. I don't like to think what his feelings were. It was his poetry, when you get down to the bottom of it—his poetry which had killed her. And only a year or two afterward, James himself died. Too late. Poor old Bob, he's had a hard life. You hear people talk about the elevating effects of poverty—the Artist-in-the-Garret stuff. By God, Bob could tell them. I reckon he'd do anything rather than go through all that again."

There was a silence. Then Nigel asked, "Weren't you surprised that he married again?"

"No. He was lonely: he wanted a mother for Vanessa: he'd found marriage a happy state of affairs. But I *was* surprised he married Janet Lacey. Or that she married him. She's a high-and-mighty one, for all that her family had come down in the world."

"Perhaps she took pity on him?"

"He on her, just as likely. He's always been apt to do unexpected, quixotic things. He's a queer mixture. That dwarf he has—d'you know, Bob told me he'd found him being stoned by a gang of louts in a village near where he and Janet were honeymooning, so he up and brought him home to Ferry Lacey, just like that. Don't know how he got round his missus."

"She seems very fond of the dwarf now."

"No children of her own. But old Bob gets what he wants, in his quiet way. God knows how he does it."

"Perhaps because he doesn't want much."

"Concentrates, you mean? Very likely. He'd need it all, to put anything over on his present missus. Talk about a will of iron! Why, she runs Ferry Lacey and Hinton Lacey, and she'd run Redcote too if she got half a chance. She's fifty years behind the times; but she believes so strongly in herself as Lady of the Manor and the Last of the Laceys, and in whatever she's doing, that she carries everything before her. I wouldn't care to get in her way. My predecessor here printed an editorial criticizing something highhanded she'd done in local affairs—this was before she married—and dammit if she didn't turn up at the office next day with a hunting crop! Only one thing she wanted and never got."

"What was that?"

"Oswald Seaton. Not that she wanted *him*. It was Plash Meadow, the Laceys' old property—that's what she was after. Yes, she'd even marry a fellow like him to get back the Laceys' inheritance: shows the strength of a ruling passion, doesn't it? But she'd met her match for once."

"What was Oswald like?"

Mr. Keeley raised his eyes. "If I tell you that her worst enemy wouldn't have wished Oswald onto Janet Lacey, it'll give you some idea. *De mortuis* and all that, but he was a thorough-paced rotter. Efficient enough in the business. But his father's upbringing ruined him as a human being. He was sly, specious, wriggle out of anything. And *cruel*! I don't

now that it *was* all his father's fault, even. I remember—
Oswald was only about seven then—going into their house
and hearing Oswald's voice: he was saying, 'I'm going to
put your feet into the fire first, and you'll scream. Then I'll
put your legs in, and you'll scream louder and louder, but
I shan't have mercy. All your blood will boil and bubble.
It's hell's fire, and I'm going to burn you up in it bit by bit.'
I went into the room. He was just putting his sister's doll
through the bars of the grate. I've believed in original sin
ever since that day, Mr. Strangeways."

"So his death was no loss?"

The editor, his tongue pushed against the side of his
mouth, executed a particularly elaborate doodle on the blot-
ing pad before replying.

"That suicide. Yes. He was not universally lamented. I
couldn't have been happier myself. I've a couple of
daughters, and between you and me and this pencil, nobody's daughters were safe with Oswald Seaton about. Well,
I *could* have been happier still. If they'd found the body."

"But surely—"

"Oh, I know there was no doubt about it really. But, as I
told you, Oswald could wriggle out of anything."

"Wriggle out of his own death, even?"

"He'd have a damned good shot at it."

"Why did he commit suicide?"

"Business worries. That's what they said. He left a letter,
you know. All tidied up."

"But you don't quite believe it?"

"When a rat's cornered," said Mr. Keeley with a sober
emphasis, "it fights. I won't say the Seaton business wasn't
having a difficult time just then: there was severe foreign
competition, for one thing. But—oh well—" he rumpled his
white hair "—I've rambled on long enough. Is there anything
else?"

"I suppose your paper carried a long report of Oswald

Seaton's death. I'd like to see the file copies, if it's not troubling you too much."

"Yes, we did. Janet Lacey threw her weight about a lot—tried to have it hushed up. I'm afraid she doesn't like the *Redcote Gazette* one little bit. So I don't see as much of Bob Seaton as I'd wish. But then, he's a famous man now. Aye, it's a long time since we split our infinitives side by side in grammar school. And I'm still splitting 'em."

Nigel thanked the editor warmly for his help. After a quarter of an hour's reading in the *Gazette* library, where he studied the suicide of Oswald Seaton in the paper's back numbers and in a sheaf of clippings from other journals, Nigel left the building. He and Paul Willingham had lunch together at the Golden Lion. As they were getting into Paul's car, Nigel, who had been very distrait during lunch, said,

"Could you stop at a toy shop on the way out?"

"Any toy shop?"

"Yes."

Paul Willingham gave him a sharp look; then, checking whatever facetious comment Nigel's request had brought to the tip of his tongue, let in the clutch.

CHAPTER FIVE

HEAD IN CLAY

NIGEL STRANGEWAYS was reclining in a deck chair on the lawn. The little pile of Robert Seaton's notebooks lay on a table at his side: but, whether it was the house standing there before him, like a beautiful woman, demanding all his attention, or whether it was the hazy, stilly closeness in the air, through which the weir hummed and roared more insistently, he could not turn his mind to the poet's manuscripts. Everything this afternoon seemed as if charged with fatality. What was the weir distantly, insistently trying to say? A petal detached itself from one of the tarnished roses on the house front and went dithering down to earth, and when it landed, Nigel positively relaxed, as though he had expected the earth to be shaken by its fall. A dove suddenly cooing in a treetop high overhead startled him like a siren.

Nigel mentally shook himself, took up one of the notebooks. But it lay open on his lap, unregarded. The beautiful house would allow no rival. So you're jealous, he found himself idiotically murmuring; are you trying to vamp me, or to get rid of me? I can deal with flesh-and-blood charmers. But a brick-and-mortar one, older than the subsoil on which she sits, older in experience, ripe and bursting with the juice of human hopes, human graces and tragedies—ah, take your glassy eyes off me!

Deliberately and rudely, Nigel got up, turned the back of his chair to the house. He had seen it last June, lapped in its rose-sleep. He had seen it last week, looking flushed, a little frowsty, but more vital, more of this world, as if it had just wakened up. And this afternoon, Plash Meadow was changed again for him. It had come nearer. It was appealing now, he fancifully put it, not through its beauty any more, but out of its frailty: the fine features, the disdainful look had melted into an expression of pretty helplessness. Or was it something worse? Was it apprehension? Panic? Guilt?

Nigel spoke aloud, half-turning his head:

"Oh, do shut up! You're driving me crackers."

"But I haven't said a word yet."

Nigel started convulsively and looked round. It was only Lionel Seaton, who had approached noiselessly over the lawn.

"Sorry," said Nigel, "I was talking to your house."

"Sorry to interrupt the conversation," remarked the young man politely. "I sympathize with you, though."

"Eh? What? Oh, it drives you crackers too, does it?"

"Sometimes." Lionel Seaton sat down cross-legged on the grass in front of him, his eyes fixed on Nigel's face. "It's about time I got away."

"A job, you mean?"

"Yes. Of course I was only demobbed last year. Janet'd have liked me to go up to Oxford. But—" the clipped, army voice broke off.

"But you want to be out on your own?" Nigel suggested.

"Yep. If I knew what to do. Unfortunately I went straight into the army from school. I'm not equipped for anything, except killing people. Might emigrate. Australia seems keen on getting British to go out."

"That's a long way away."

"It couldn't be too far away from Europe for my liking."

70

"I suppose," said Nigel tentatively, after a pause, "your father does cast rather a big shadow."

Lionel Seaton gave him a sharp, rather hostile look. "There's nothing wrong with—"

"I meant it must be difficult to be the son of a genius."

"Oh, I see. Yes. In that sense they both cast rather a big shadow."

"Your stepmother too?"

"Yep. They don't need me here. Neither of them."

"Well then, there's nothing to keep you."

"You think not? There's the police, for one thing."

"They won't be here forever. What else?"

Lionel Seaton was silent for a few moments, gazing meditatively at Nigel, who felt that the name of Mara Torrance was not far from his lips.

"Vanessa," said Lionel at last. "I'd like to see her through."

"See her through what?"

"Well, Janet does her best," the young man returned rather obliquely. "But they don't get on exactly like a house on fire, as you've noticed. And my father—well, he's got his work; and then, it was Vanessa's birth which really caused our mother's death; so he naturally—. But I'd like to see her safely married. She's the sort of girl who might fall for some fearful type, you know—some winsome, neurotic egotist. She's madly vulnerable."

"She'll have to make her own mistakes."

"Well, at any rate I can see her through this present dust-up," said Lionel slowly, his keen face averted.

"It shouldn't affect her, surely?"

"Oh come now," Lionel replied impatiently. "Not affect her, with the police pretty well drawing a cordon round Plash Meadow? We've had 'em in and out for a week. They seem to have got it into their heads, God knows why, that this chap was bumped off hereabouts."

He paused, as if inviting comment or denial. When none was forthcoming, he looked straightly at Nigel.

"I hope we can trust you."

"Trust me?"

"You know very well what I mean," the young man formidably replied. "No fifth-column work."

"I'm neutral. At present. I admire your father very much."

"He's taken to you, too. So there's all the more reason why——"

"All of you seem in a conspiracy to protect him," interrupted Nigel. "But, from what I've seen of your father, he can look after himself quite adequately."

"Oh, do you think so?" Lionel Seaton had the air of one giving impartial thought to an unexpected point of view. "Well, you may be right. But it's not at all the tradition in our family."

"Ah, that's his negative capability. He's a poet. He's so receptive to the person or thing he's involved with at the moment that each person sees in your father an image of himself."

"I don't follow you."

"Well, take Paul Willingham. His first words to me about your father were, 'He's a good sort. Quiet little chap. Got a fine herd of Guernseys.' Mr. Keeley called him tough, resilient. His family thinks of him as a rare, delicate vessel which has got to be protected."

"You mean he plays up to everyone's different ideas of him?"

"Unconsciously, yes. But it's more than that. He *becomes* the person he's with, almost."

The young man considered this. "And what does he become, with you?"

"Why, an amateur criminologist, of course. He got terrifically excited the other day when I was giving a description of the kind of man this chap who was murdered must

72

be. Turned into a regular sleuth-on-the-trail for a moment. He was absolutely impersonal—said it might have been a description of his brother Oswald."

"He did, did he?" said Lionel, with what Nigel could have sworn was an admiring intonation. "Hello, there's Finny with the tea things. My father's a hero to *him*, anyway. Does that mean, according to your theory, that Finny's really a hero himself."

Nigel laughed. "Oh, you mustn't ride my hobbyhorse too hard."

"As a matter of fact, he is. He rescued my father once from the bull we used to have. Stood right in its path, and beat it off with a stick. Jolly good show by the little imp. But he's strong as a lion."

"Strong and silent. Is he completely dumb, in fact?"

"To the best of our knowledge. Why?"

"When I was here in June, your stepmother talked about him as a Fool who said such wise things. Don't you remember?"

"Oh, that's just Janet's nonsense. Haven't you ever heard a doting woman use exactly the same words about her dog?"

"I see."

They fell silent as Finny Black approached. He laid the tea table under the cedar tree beside them, without his usual nods and becks and wreathed smiles. The dwarf almost scowled at Nigel: there were beads of sweat on his little, hideous face, and his movements lacked their usual deftness.

"Looks as if there might be a thunderstorm before long," said Lionel, mopping his forehead. "Phew, it's close, isn't it?"

The front door of Plash Meadow opened. Robert and Janet Seaton emerged. As they approached across the lawn, a piercing momentary qualm transfixed Nigel Strangeways. He had observed that the poet was carrying his head under his arm.

"Not bad, is it?" said Robert Seaton, carefully placing the head on the table.

Mara Torrance had done something to it since Nigel saw it last. The evil had gone out of it; but so had the vitality. It was now a very respectable, dead likeness.

"I'll ring the hand bell if I want some more hot water," said Janet to Finny Black, who was staring at the head with a wild, intent, puzzled expression. He lolloped away, glancing back over his shoulder several times.

"You shouldn't have let Finny see it," said Lionel. "It might upset him. This afternoon, particularly."

"Oh, nonsense," said Robert robustly. "Why should it? How d'you like it, Strangeways?"

"Well, it's a good photograph."

Janet Seaton bent her prominent eyes upon him. "But the spirit is not there? I entirely agree with you. A piece of laborious, insipid realism, nothing more. It would do very well for the Royal Academy."

"Oh, you mustn't be hard on Mara," said Robert, laughing. "After all, you challenged her yourself to produce a good likeness. It's not her usual line at all."

"She shouldn't have undertaken it, then," replied Janet Seaton censoriously. "Are you interested in the plastic arts, Mr. Strangeways?"

"Moderately."

The remarkable woman went off into a lecture on non-representational sculpture, thickly larded with expressions like "cubic factors," "pure meaning," "plane, volume and tension," "dynamic correlation of masses," "hyperconscious equilibrium."

There was a respectful silence round the tea table when she had finished, broken at last by her husband's saying,

"Is that, er, what you're going to tell the Women's Institute on Saturday?"

"I shall simplify it for them, naturally," his wife replied, with a lack of humor which Nigel found quite devastating.

"Janet has been reading it all up in an article by Herbert Read, I suspect," said Robert Seaton. There was a certain mischievousness about the remark which did not seem quite in character.

Nigel indicated the pile of notebooks.

"I'd like to come and beard you in your den this evening, if I may," he said to Robert.

"Of course. About six? I've got to do a bit more work on a poem first."

"It's going well, is it?"

A faint, secretive smile, like that of a shy child receiving a bag of sweets, gave the poet's face a beatific expression.

"Yes, it's going well," he said, "it's all going very well, I think."

He rose, tucked his head under his arm again and walked briskly into the house.

At six o'clock Nigel entered Robert Seaton's study. The poet was sitting at his desk, the clay head in front of him. His face had a tranquil, drained look. They discussed certain points about one of the poems in the manuscript book on which Nigel had been working since tea. Then Robert Seaton rang the bell and asked Finny Black to bring up some sherry. Presently the dwarf returned with a decanter and glasses on a tray. He seemed unable to take his eyes off the clay head on Seaton's work table. His face twitched: it was white and puffy this evening, like a circus midget's.

"All right, Finny. You can go now," said the poet gently, and turned away to pour out the drinks.

Nigel, hands in pockets, had moved across to the work table and was bending over it.

Robert Seaton brought a glass of sherry to him.

"Here you are. Good lord, what the devil?— Did you do that?"

The sherry slopped over, as Seaton pointed at the clay

75

head, which appeared to have grown, in one instant, a bristling and satyrlike beard.

"Yes," said Nigel.

"You have a remarkable turn for inverted metaphor, young man," said the poet. "Bearding me in my den, indeed!"

"I just wanted to see what it looked like. I bought the beard in a toy shop in Redcote this afternoon."

"And what *does* it look like?" asked Robert Seaton, his head cocked to one side in the attitude of a blackbird listening for a worm on the lawn.

"It looks exactly like the face of the satyr in that bit of wood carving by Mara Torrance—the one you showed me when I was here last June."

"By Jove, so it does! You're quite right," said the poet with animation. "You'd better take it off now. I wouldn't like Vanessa to wander in and see it. She mustn't see her father as a satyr. And really," he added, "I'm not one."

There was a curiously unembarrassed silence. The two men sat down in armchairs.

"Of course," said Nigel at last, "it's your affair. I ought to apologize for—well, unseemly curiosity."

"If it was just my affair—but, the trouble is, it's Mara's, much more than mine. It's Mara's secret."

"She admires you tremendously. She told me you'd been wonderfully kind to her in the past."

Robert Seaton made a deprecating gesture. "I fancy you have guessed something of the truth. Enough, anyway, for you to realize how carefully we must all go, just now," he said slowly. "Excitement is so bad for her. Any stirring up of the past. Let it lie, my dear fellow, if you can. No pranks of this sort with her."

"Of course not. But, you know, a police investigation is bound to stir up the past."

The poet sighed. "Yes, I suppose so. It's a great nuisance."

"I'm afraid it must be interfering with your work a lot."

76

That faint, inward smile showed on Robert Seaton's face again.

"Well, no, I can't pretend it does. I really seem to be finding it quite stimulating. And then, of course, Janet makes an admirable watchdog. I think even your friend the superintendent has his work cut out to get past her. He was in again this morning, by the way."

"Oh?"

"Apparently someone in the village saw me returning from a nocturnal prowl that night. And it doesn't fit in with the time when Mara said she'd seen Janet and me crossing the courtyard to have a look at Kitty. I presume the chap got it wrong. Your superintendent seemed quite satisfied anyway. But I don't like the idea of Mara being badgered."

Nigel forbore to remark that his friend the superintendent had an outstanding gift for *appearing* satisfied with a piece of evidence. What he actually said was,

"If you don't mind my offering a bit of advice, I hope you won't, through your natural wish to keep Miss Torrance's affairs secret, give the police the impression that you're being evasive about happenings in the much less remote past."

"This murder, eh? The police are welcome to everything I know about *it*," replied Robert Seaton bravely.

"Good. Well, I'll go and have a wash before dinner."

A few minutes later, when Nigel was brushing his hair and singing to himself in his harsh baritone, the door of his room opened.

"I heard you singing," Vanessa said. "May I come in? I didn't know you were in here."

"Oh?"

"I mean, it isn't the usual guest room. That's the other side of the passage."

"Looking out over the courtyard?"

"Yes." Vanessa wandered inquisitively about the room,

picking up Nigel's brushes, sniffing his shaving soap. She seemed to be screwing herself up to an important statement. "Phew, it's jolly stuffy, isn't it? Hadn't you better open a window. It's very unhealthy, sleeping with your window shut. Lieutenant—you know, she runs the Guides, I've told you about her—she does exercises in front of an open window every morning, summer or winter: she says every girl ought to; she says it's the best preparation for Healthy Motherhood." Vanessa cast a languishing glance at him. "You haven't any china dogs you don't want, by any chance, have you?"

"Do you collect them?"

"Yes. Would you like to see my collection? I started it last January. Felicity—she's my best friend—collects Egyptian scabs."

"*What?* Oh, scarabs?"

"Mm. I think they're rather eerie myself. I mean, there might be a curse on them. Buck up! What a time men take tying their ties and that sort of rot!"

She seized his hand and dragged him out of the room, down the passage. There, taking a key from her little reticule, she unlocked a door.

"See? Aren't they a lot of preciouses?" she said, pointing at the mantelpiece and breathing heavily with possessive pride.

Nigel examined the array of china dogs. "I like this one best," he said.

"Sssh! So do I actually," said Vanessa in a breathy whisper. "But you shouldn't say it out loud. That's favoritism. You'll hurt the feelings of all the other poor doggies."

"It's a valuable collection. D'you always keep the room locked?"

"In the daytime. Only I often forget to. And if you've any valuables, take my advice and keep your room locked too."

"But surely nobody—"

78

"Well, not intentionally. But things do sometimes disappear." Vanessa gazed at him earnestly. "It's supposed to be a family secret, but I'll tell *you*. We have a kleptomaniac in the house. It's very sad."

"Do you know who it is?"

The girl shook her hair over her face and gave him a coy glance through it. "I mustn't tell you that. But I expect you can guess." . . .

After dinner they had music. Lionel Seaton played Chopin preludes and some Schumann with considerable virtuosity, his keen, young-old face turned to an unearthly and abstract beauty in the darkening room. Presently, candles being lit, Vanessa was persuaded to sing. Her voice, singing Scots folk songs, was pure and thin and wavering as the candle flames, which shook from time to time with a waft of air through the open windows. After two or three songs, she stopped, saying it made her sweat all down her back. The atmosphere tonight was indeed oppressive, thick as lukewarm, congealing soup. Nigel felt a tension in the air; but whether it came from the elements alone, he could not say. At any moment he expected to hear the first mutter of thunder from beneath the distant rim of the sky. Janet Seaton, her fingers gripped tight together, half reclined on a window seat gazing out. Nigel fancied it was a relief to her when, at eleven o'clock, he said he was sleepy and would go to bed.

Up in his own room he did not undress, however, but took from his pocketbook a sheet of paper headed with a large question mark, and studied it. The notes were somewhat cryptic, jotted down from time to time during the last few days:

"(i) Mara's wood carving; the original expression on the clay head. Satyr. Satyromania? Poof! Was it O. or R.?"

Nigel took out his pencil and drew a line through "R."

"(ii) Is Finny Black really dumb?"

Nigel added, "No proof yet."

"(iii) Which was right, Robert/Janet or the expectant father? This could be crucial, IF. . . . Essential fix exact time thundershower began. Where did R. take shelter? Were his clothes wet when he got back? Etc.

"(iv) Who keeps key of (a) orchard gate, (b) dairy? How many keys?

"(v) Was R.T. really 'plastered' that evening? Did L.S. really sleep right through storm?

"(vi) Did L.S. arrive at friends' house that week end with same amount of luggage he left Plash Meadow with? (Blount).

"(vii) J.S. 'a stickler for the proprieties.' Why the T.'s then?"

Nigel added, "Depends on answer to (i)."

"(viii) The society magazine with photograph of family. Might explain much, IF. . . ."

Nigel now wrote in another question:

"(ix) Does or does not J.S. approve of abstract art? If answer *yes*, why the clay head? If *no*, why her line this afternoon?"

Nigel studied this last question. He was still picking away at it in his mind when a growl of thunder invaded his thoughts. He put the paper away, went to the window. The last dregs of light were draining out of the sky. Nigel moved away, silently opened his door, looked up and down the passage, then slipped into the room opposite—the one, Vanessa had told him, where guests usually slept. It was empty. Nigel very gently opened the lower half of its window and sat down on the window seat. The storm was approaching from this side, from the north. Congested, indigo clouds, darker than the night, were piled up untidily one on another in precarious heaps which it seemed a single thrust of lightning would send toppling over. The night held its breath, then released it in a sudden, hot puff which stirred the foliage of the chestnut tree. From behind the cloud-massif, a sheet of lightning flared up and shook the sky, outlining the fantastic scarps and ridges and pinnacles of the thunder-clouds. As Nigel watched, the lightning flickered more energetically, till it was almost continuous, darting and vibrating all over the tortured heavens. Like wagon wheels down a stony defile the thunder rumbled nearer.

Nigel felt in his pocket, to make sure his electric torch was there. He believed that something was going to happen tonight, and he believed he knew what it was. His eye turned more frequently now to the door of the wing to his right where the servants' quarters were. He waited a long time, his head out of the window now, his gaze alternately dazzled by lightning and muffled by the darkness which followed each flash.

Presently he became aware of a door slowly opening; not the door of the servants' wing, but one directly below him. He was not the only watcher at Plash Meadow tonight. Whoever it was down there who had opened the door, did not attempt to move: he must be standing on the threshold, looking out toward the courtyard, waiting. Nearly five minutes passed. Nigel became obsessed by a fancy that the person down below was waiting for a seventh great flash, so that he might dart out unseen through the ensuing trough of darkness, like a boy on a beach calculating the precise moment between two waves when he can dash to the water's edge and retrieve some treasure cast up by the storm.

Then at last the door of the servants' wing did open. The next moment a livid, protracted glare of lightning revealed a figure running full tilt across the courtyard. It moved with a scuttling, crablike gait, if you could imagine a crab running as fast as a man; but once it bounded into the air in the manner of a dog hunting through bracken, and as it did so Nigel saw something bounce upon its back. The figure was Finny Black—no doubt about that. And the thing on his back, the globular thing hanging from his shoulders that, glimpsed momently in a second flash of lightning, might have been a gross black spider riding him—

Nigel saw the figure swallowed up by another wave of blackness. There was a scrabbling noise. And when lightning lit up the scene again, nothing moved out there but the foliage of a lower branch of the chestnut tree. Nigel ran down the passage and quickly descended the stairs. A peal of thunder crashed over the house. As he emerged from the door, Nigel noticed a figure flitting over the courtyard. It was much bigger than Finny Black: the other watcher, no doubt.

Making a detour by the old tithe barn, Nigel approached the tree silently from the opposite side. He could hear a voice, calling gently out of the darkness at the foot of the tree:

"Finny! Come down, Finny! It's only me."

It was the voice of Janet Seaton, and there seemed to be a great sadness in its soothing tones.

From far above there came a scuffling noise, immediately drowned by a head-splitting crack of thunder. In the silence that followed, Mrs. Seaton quietly called,

"Come down, Finny, at once. And bring it with you. Bring it down with you. It's not yours, Finny."

She might have been gentling a restive horse. The lower branches shook. The figure of Finny Black appeared, swinging down from bough to bough with a horrible alacrity. He landed lightly at Janet Seaton's feet, jumping from the lowest bough. A flash of lightning showed a string bag dangling from his shoulders, and in the bag, as Mrs. Seaton took it from Finny, the clay head of her husband.

Nigel walked forward.

"Don't you think," he said, "while he's about it, he'd better fetch down the other one?"

CHAPTER SIX

HEAD IN AIR

JANET SEATON whipped round, letting out a little scream. She shrank away from Nigel, till her back was against the giant bole of the chestnut tree.

"What are you doing here?" she exclaimed. "Go away! Finny! Help!"

The next moment, Nigel was fighting for his life. As if infected by her panic, or like a dog instinctively leaping to defend its mistress, Finny Black went for him. The dwarf jumped up upon Nigel, wound his legs round Nigel's waist, and groped for his throat. Taken completely by surprise, Nigel staggered a pace backward and, a little half-heartedly at first, tried to pry the dwarf off his chest. It was like fighting a child, so light was the body which had clamped itself to him—but a child, he soon realized, of uncanny strength. Finny's long arms were thick and sinewy as conger eels. His fingers sank into Nigel's throat. For a moment Nigel saw the dwarf's distorted, sweating face glaring into his like a mad baby's: then the face was hidden in his shoulder, where he could not get at it, and the fingers tightened.

Nigel threw himself forward on to the ground—it seemed the only hope—trying to stun the dwarf with his weight. Finny grunted as he hit the ground, and his arms fell away. He was lying quite still now, apparently stunned. Nigel began to get to his feet. "I hope to God I haven't broken his neck," he thought. But he was still only on his knees when the dwarf suddenly came to life again, rolled furiously to one side, and before Nigel could grab him had bounced up on to Nigel's back. Nigel was able to give one shout for help, then the fingers were gouging into his throat again. He staggered toward the tree, in a desperate attempt to knock Finny off against its trunk. But Finny clung to him like an adhesive bubble. Nigel was dimly aware of Janet Seaton hovering near by, giving little distracted cries and sobs, then ineffectually trying to tear the dwarf off his back. The pain in his throat became appalling. There was a continuous thunder in his ears, but whether it came from the sky or from inside his bursting head, he did not know. I must fall backward this time, he bemusedly thought. There were feet running—or was it the pounding of his heart? A voice called out sharply,

"Finny! Stop it at once! D'you hear? Stop it!"

Then Nigel, almost fainting, became aware that the steel fingers had gone from his throat, the midget weight from off his back. He sank down against the tree, harshly coughing and gasping.

"My dear chap, I'm terribly sorry. What on earth happened?" Robert Seaton was saying, out of the darkness.

Robert and Janet bent solicitously over him.

"I'll be all right in a minute," he croaked.

"I'll go and get some brandy," said Mrs. Seaton.

"And bring a towel or something, soaked in cold water," her husband called out as she went toward the house.

"I'm afraid it was my fault," Nigel whispered after a few moments, feeling his throat. "I alarmed your wife, and I suppose Finny thought she was in danger. Where is he?"

"He ran away. I really can't forgive myself for letting— It's this thunderstorm. Finny always gets overexcited. I suppose Janet must have been looking for him. But he won't always obey her when he gets like this."

"I'm glad he obeys you, anyway. Look, could you go and ring up the police straight away? We must have a man here."

"Is it really necessary?" Robert Seaton's voice sounded painful. "I mean, couldn't we—couldn't you give him another chance?"

"I shan't prosecute Finny, or anything like that. Of course not. But he's got to be found. Quickly."

"Very well. Will it be all right if I leave you? Oh, here's Janet."

It was Janet. And Lionel Seaton. And, a minute after, Rennell Torrance came up with his daughter.

"I'm just going in to telephone," said Robert Seaton.

"Who's here? What's been happening?" asked Torrance in a thick voice.

"Didn't someone shout?" said Lionel. "It woke me up."

"Here's your brandy, Mr. Strangeways. I'll put this towel round your neck. Don't try and move yet. There. I came out to look for Finny," Mrs. Seaton explained to the others, "and Mr. Strangeways must have heard us, and he came out too and rather startled me. I didn't realize who it was. Then Finny attacked him. I'm dreadfully—"

"Is that Finny over there?" said Nigel.

As they all looked away, peering into the darkness, Nigel poured his brandy on to the grass. He had no reason to suppose there was anything but brandy in the glass; but he could take no risks just now. He must stay by the tree till the police came.

"I always told you you ought to get rid of him," said Torrance grumpily. "It simply isn't safe. Well, if there's nothing I can do, I'm going back to bed. Jesus! What's this?"

The man's foot, as he turned to go, had kicked against the clay head, lying forgotten in the grass. A sheet of lightning made an exposure of the scene—Mrs. Seaton, fully clothed, the others in dressing gowns, all wearing the dead, pop-eyed expression of diners caught by a photographer's magnesium flash.

"Christ! It's the head!" exclaimed Rennell Torrance. "In a string bag. It's—"

"Don't panic, Father!" came Mara's cool, contemptuous voice. "It's my head of Robert. And please don't kick it around," she added, as Nigel's electric torch was switched on to reveal Rennell Torrance gingerly turning over the head with his foot.

"Panic? What d'you mean? Don't talk to me like that, you little bitch!" said her father shockingly.

"We all seem to have heads on the brain," said Lionel. "What's it doing out here, anyway? This place is turning into a madhouse."

"I think it's just going to rain." Janet Seaton was in control again. "We'd better all go to bed. Mr. Strangeways, d'you feel well enough to walk in?"

Nigel groaned, in what he hoped was a convincing manner, half-rose to his feet, and collapsed again.

"I'm sorry. I—"

"Lionel, you help him. And Rennell, please. We can't have him getting wet after the shock. Mara, run along to bed now."

"No," said Nigel. "We've got to find Finny first."

"That's all right," said Robert Seaton, who had just come out of the house. "The superintendent will be over here in a few minutes."

"The superintendent?" said Janet. "But—. I said, go to bed, Mara! And do button up that dressing gown. It's positively indecent!" Her voice seemed full of a suppressed rage.

"Here's Mr. Strangeways been half strangled, and Janet has eyes for nothing but my bosom," retorted the girl, with an edgy laugh.

"I do really think you'd better come in, Mr. Strangeways," said Janet. "You see, I put a little sedative in your brandy.

You ought to have a good sleep. The police will look after things now."

"I must just have a word with Blount before I pop off, though."

And Nigel did, in private, a few minutes later. The superintendent had driven over, with his detective sergeant, from the Hinton Lacey pub where he was staying.

"Look, Blount, I'm supposed to have swallowed a sleeping draught, so I'd better go to sleep. Anyway, I've just been strangled, and that takes it out of one. Did Bob Seaton tell you what happened?"

Blount nodded.

"Well, I want you to do two things. I'll explain tomorrow, when I wake up. Put Sergeant Bower under that chestnut tree and tell him not to stir an inch from it, not if it's struck by lightning. And to let no one else near. I may be wrong, but—. The second thing is, if Finny Black is found, don't let him come back into the house."

"Will he be dangerous still?"

"He might be. But he might also be *in danger* here."

The admirable Blount, perceiving by the frayed thread of a voice in which Nigel spoke that he was almost exhausted, asked no more questions but promised to do what Nigel had suggested.

"One other thing. Bob Seaton is the only person who has any control over Finny in his present condition," whispered Nigel. "If you *do* start Inspector Gates on a man hunt, I'd recommend sending Seaton with them."

"Oh, Seaton's gone out after him already. With his son."

Nigel shrugged his shoulders. It would have to look after itself. He allowed Blount to support him upstairs and help him undress. Hardly had the bedroom door closed again when Nigel was sound asleep. . . .

The next morning Nigel was wakened by the sound of his door opening. Vanessa's mop of tawny hair slid into view.

"Janet wants to know what you'd like for breakfast. I say, have you got mumps?"

Nigel's hand moved involuntarily to his throat, which was tender enough indeed, and felt the towel still swathed round it.

"Oh, this? No." His voice began as a painful croak. "I was a bit too sharp, and I cut myself."

"Cut your throat?" Vanessa's eyes opened wide. Nigel perceived she had an exceedingly literal mind. He said,

"I was speaking metaphorically."

"Oh, I see," replied Vanessa, with the informed air of a member of a household where metaphor was quite the legitimate thing. "There are two kinds of cereal, eggs, coffee or tea."

"I'd like coffee and a boiled egg."

"O.K." Vanessa teetered round the door, looking mysterious. "I shall bring it up myself. The household is thoroughly disorganized. Guess what has happened?"

"The cook was struck by lightning last night."

"No. Finny has disappeared. *And* there's a man under our big chestnut tree. I took him out some tea and toast."

"Good—I mean, I'm sorry to hear about Finny."

"I'm not. Of course, it's very inconvenient, with servants so difficult to get nowadays. But Finny *is* rather gruesome. And besides—can you keep a secret?" asked Vanessa, who obviously could not. "Well, he *stole* sometimes."

"That's what you were hinting at last night? The kleptomaniac?"

"Mm. He can't help it, Daddy says. And of course we generally find the things again. He has caches, like a magpie."

"What, in the house?"

"In the garden or the orchard generally. But further away sometimes. We found the last one in Foxhole Wood. Lionel followed him there. He'd taken three of my china dogs, and Li saw him hide them in a bush. The funny thing, talking of magpies, is that just beside the bush there was one of those gamekeeper's gallows things, with dead magpies and rooks and jays and squirrels hung from it. I think it's very crool, don't you? Oh Lor'! There's Janet calling. Coffee and a boiled egg, you said, didn't you?"

When Vanessa returned with the breakfast tray, she announced,

"Superintendent Blount, of New Scotland Yard, is here to see you."

"Ask him to come up. What are you doing this morning, Vanessa?"

"I shall go for a long ride on Kitty after I've helped with the housework. I find I can think best on horseback."

"What are you going to think about?"

"Oh, I can't tell that till I start thinking, can I? But Lieutenant says that Beautiful Thoughts are essential to a Rich and Fully Satisfying Life. So I'm practicing hard this hols. Good-by."

Nigel was gingerly swallowing his egg when Blount came in.

"How are you feeling this morning, Strangeways?"

"Fine, thanks. Tell me, Blount, do you ever have beautiful thoughts?"

"E'eh, well now—"

"I was afraid not. Perhaps if you'd joined the mounted police, it might have been different."

The superintendent stared at him with some anxiety. "Are you sure you feel quite the thing? No pains in the head?"

"Quite sure. Any sign of Finny Black yet?"

"No. Gates has it in hand. He'll not be long at large, not a wee dwarf like him. Too conspicuous. Now, tell me—?"

"What's your form at tree climbing, Blount?"

"I was pretty handy at it as a bairn," replied the superintendent, with the overbright air of one humoring a lunatic.

"Because someone has got to swarm up that chestnut tree.

89

I suppose nobody's tried to entice your sergeant away from it?"

"No. Everything's been very quiet. Bower can climb the tree. He's a younger man, and it'll be a change from standing under it. What's in your mind, Strangeways?"

Nigel took another cautious swallow of coffee. Then, ticking the points off on his fingers, he said,

"First: Finny Black is apt to go haywire in thunderstorms; there was a thunderstorm the night of the murder, another one last night. Second: when I was staying here in June, Robert Seaton said that Finny would copy any act he had seen done. Third: Finny is a kleptomaniac; he had a cache in Foxhole Wood, near one of those gamekeeper's gallows with vermin swinging from it. Fourth: last night Finny pinches a clay head of Robert Seaton, executed by Miss Torrance, puts it in a string bag—notice the string bag particularly—and swarms up the chestnut tree with it."

"A string bag," remarked Blount, his eyes sparkling now with sagacity, "because that would be the simplest way of suspending a clay head from a branch, like he'd seen the vermin suspended from the gamekeeper's gallows?"

"You're really very good indeed, Blount," said Nigel warmly.

"And—e'eh—you're suggesting that there might be—e'eh —other acts the wee dwarf would imitate, when the thunder had turned his brain?"

"Exactly. He might copy something he'd seen done under similar conditions, or repeat some action of his own."

"It seems to me the sooner Bower gets up that tree, the better."

"Wait till Vanessa Seaton has left the house. She's going out for a ride soon. We don't want her about the place. It might interfere with her Beautiful Thoughts curriculum."

"And what about the others?"

"It might be helpful if they were present, including the

Torrances. Can you think up some pretext for getting them all out there? Of course, it may be an entirely false alarm. It's quite a long shot after all. But there've been other pointers. Tell you about them when Bower has done his stuff."

The village church clock had just struck eleven when they assembled round the chestnut tree. As he strolled out of the house with Robert Seaton, Nigel noticed Janet in earnest colloquy with the superintendent: she glanced up at the tree, and whatever she was saying, it evidently took Blount considerably aback.

"I hope he's not going to keep us long," said Robert Seaton. "I want to get back to my work."

But Blount did not hurry the proceedings. He took Sergeant Bower aside for a whispered conversation. Then he asked for a ladder, and there was a further delay while Lionel Seaton found the gardener and the gardener fetched the ladder. If Blount's object was to strain the nerves of the little party at the foot of the giant tree, he was not unsuccessful. They stood about, fidgeting, finding little or nothing to say to one another—why should they, after living so close together all these years? Or they might have been strangers, met for the first time, with the ice still to break. To Nigel, standing apart, it was as if he observed the members of a house party gathered for a photograph, kicking their heels, making self-conscious jokes and desultory conversation, half excited, half resentful while the host fusses with his camera, each of them preoccupied with his own ego, with an intention not to be caught out by the camera, to put his best face forward.

In the fresh, robust light of this August morning, the air cleared by the thunderstorm overnight, the courtyard grass sparkling with rain, the five of them stilled into their final poses as the gardener approached with his ladder. Janet Seaton, planted bulkily there, arms folded, frowning, now moved a little closer to her husband, as if to protect or to receive protection. The poet, who had been standing with his hands behind his back, an abstracted look in his eyes, took his wife's arm—a natural, homely gesture. The sun shone upon Lionel's golden head and Mara Torrance's dark one, close together: the girl's face was a grayish-white, the color of newspaper left out in the rain; the sunlight cruelly emphasized its haggard look. Lionel muttered something to her, and she glanced up at him with an expression of gratitude which made her seem younger, less raffish and defiant. A few yards away, Rennell Torrance fished in his pocket, pulled out pipe and pouch. His eyes, one might have thought, were studiously avoiding the rest of the group, the two policemen, the gardener, and the tree itself. His hand shook as he lit the pipe. He glanced at Nigel through the smoke, his heavy lower lip pouting; glanced, rather theatrically, at his wrist watch, shrugged his shoulders and shifted his feet.

Lionel Seaton stepped forward to help the gardener with the ladder. He was self-composed, alert, interested.

There was another pause, while Blount conferred again with his detective sergeant.

"Are we going to be kept here all the morning?" Rennell Torrance grumpily inquired of no one in particular.

"Will you all step back a little?" said Blount smoothly, heightening the illusion that a house party was about to be photographed.

Plash Meadow watched the scene with all its windows, holding itself calmly aloof, as a house well might which had seen two hundred years of good and evil.

At last Sergeant Bower advanced to the ladder, climbed steadily up and disappeared into the thick foliage. Mara Torrance was heard to inquire, in her most irritatingly casual voice, "Have we been summoned out here to watch a bobby climb a tree?"

"I shall explain presently," said Blount. "It's a little experiment of mine." His tone was paternal. His eyes sleepily scrutinized them all, standing where he had put them, outside the shade of the tree, the sun spotlighting their faces.

A hoarse shout came from halfway up the tree. Then a louder rustling, as the detective sergeant climbed faster to his now visible objective.

"Now don't worry, dear," said Robert Seaton to his wife. "He's quite safe. It's a very sound old tree."

"But he's going so high up."

They might have been discussing the exploit of an eight-year-old son.

"I've got it, sir!" called the sergeant from high overhead. There were grunting noises as he started to descend. Then suddenly a muffled "Damn!" and a louder "Look out, below!" Something was falling through the leaves, scraping and sliding down from branch to branch. Mara gave a little scream. Robert Seaton's arm tightened on his wife's. The next moment, like a swollen, giant chestnut, a roundish object dropped from the lowest foliage, bounced upon the grass, and rolled to the feet of Rennell Torrance.

"Clumsy ass!" growled the superintendent.

Torrance glared down on the object at his feet. His pipe fell out of his mouth. He began to tremble all over; his hands made little blind fending movements in front of him: then he ran a few paces away and was violently sick.

"Wh-what is it?" cried Mara.

The superintendent strode over to the object on the grass, picked it up by its hair and dangled it before them—the severed and decomposing head of a man.

"Does anyone recognize this?" he asked in the matter-of-fact tones of a clerk at a Lost Property Office.

There was another moment of stunned silence. Then Lionel Seaton coolly said,

"Well, it's not very well preserved, of course, but it has quite a look of you, Father."

"*No!* It hasn't, it hasn't, it hasn't, it hasn't!" Mara Tor-

93

rance's voice rose to a long, rasping scream. Mrs. Seaton advanced upon the girl, slapped her face very hard two or three times. Mara's screaming was cut off suddenly. Janet took the girl, sobbing now, awkwardly into her arms.

The poet went up close to Superintendent Blount. "It's incredible!" he murmured.

"What's incredible, sir?"

"That's my brother. My brother Oswald."

"But he's dead, Father," said Lionel. "I mean—"

"He's dead now, anyway."

The voice of Sergeant Bower broke in. "Very sorry, sir. The net slipped out of my hand. It got caught on a branch and the head rolled out of it before I could—"

"Never mind, Bower. It was damaged enough already." And Blount gazed meditatively at the face, hideous with putrescence, wormholed by the beaks of birds, a dirty rag of flesh—all that remained of the neck—hanging away from the underjaw on the left-hand side where there were still the clear signs of a long, incised wound running from the left ear to just below the point of the chin.

The superintendent turned to Robert Seaton again. "I wonder could I trouble you for some brown paper, and the loan of a hatbox, if you have such a thing."

CHAPTER SEVEN

JANET SEATON CONFESSES

"SO THERE's another possible reason for cutting off the head,"
said Nigel.

"To conceal the way he was killed? Mphm. Don't see how
it helps us, though."

"Narrows down the search for a weapon," Nigel suggested.

"Any sharp instrument could have done it. The wound
won't tell us much, I reckon, after all this time."

"Perhaps not. But, once the murderer had made a wound
like that, you'd expect him to cut through it, not below it,
when he was taking the head off. I suppose you've been into
the razor question?"

"Yes, Mr. Seaton and his son use safety razors. Finny Black
doesn't have to shave. Mr. Torrance has a cutthroat razor,"
said Blount.

"He has, has he?"

"Yes, but any sharp blade could have done it. A carving
knife."

"Surely not, Blount? All the indications are that Oswald
Seaton would be very much on his guard when he returned
here. He'd expect a whetted knife, rather than a fatted calf."

The two men were talking in Superintendent Blount's
bedroom at the Hinton Lacey pub. It was late on the same
day that the head had been found. Nigel continued,

"Oswald returned to Plash Meadow in a highly furtive way. We're agreed on that?"

"Uh-huh."

"Now, this fake suicide of his, ten years ago. The police had nothing against him. There was no question of a criminal charge, which he'd flee the country to escape?"

"No."

"But he did, presumably, leave England. And he certainly staged a very convincing suicide. But, by all accounts—the editor of the *Redcote Gazette* would certainly bear this out— Oswald was not the sort of chap who'd give up his money, his position and everything, except under extreme pressure. He was a rat. He'd wriggle out of anything, Mr. Keeley said. And if he was cornered, he'd fight."

"Verra like. But what's this to do with the weapon that killed him?"

"I'm working along to that. I suggest there's only one thing which could have made Oswald fake a suicide and leave the country—he'd committed a crime, some very grave crime, which had not come to the ears of the police. I suggest that more than one person knew about this crime. If it had been one person only, Oswald would have done his best to silence him. But even he would hardly dare to try to bump off four people."

"Why d'you say four?"

"Because I've reasons for thinking that there were four people who knew something very much to Oswald's discredit. But let's skip that for the present. I suggest pressure was brought to bear upon him by one or more of these people. Either you leave the country, or we expose you to the police."

"Blackmail, eh? But why didn't he just leave the country, then? Why the fake suicide? You mean the suicide was part of the bargain, part of the price he'd got to pay for silence?"

"Exactly."

"And who profited from Oswald's apparent death?" Blount pursued. "His brother."

"His brother. And Janet Seaton. And indirectly the Torrances."

"His brother chiefly. Well, then?"

"Well, something happens which suggests to Oswald that it may be relatively safe for him to come back to England. Or perhaps it's just that he's on his beam-ends and desperate."

"Wait a minute, now. That's vairy problematic and vague."

"Not entirely. I noticed in the Torrances' studio, a copy of a society paper with a picture of the Seatons and Torrances outside Plash Meadow and a caption saying the Torrances lived here. The paper was a year old. You know the way back numbers of English papers are found lying about abroad—in bars, or hotels, or waiting rooms. I think it possible that Oswald may have seen this particular magazine, and—"

"But why should a picture of this group at Plash Meadow give him the all-clear to come back to England? You're implying that, because the Seatons and the Torrances were living together now, the danger to Oswald—the danger of his secret being exposed—was gone. It doesn't make sense to me."

"Not gone, necessarily. But diminished enough for him to take the risk of returning. I can't explain this side of it further till I've had another talk with Mara Torrance. Call it a hypothesis. What follows? Oswald works his passage back to England. He lands at Bristol, say, and lies up there. It may be that he communicates with someone at Plash Meadow, to take soundings. He is not confident at all of the reception he will get. He turns up here, by night, in the most unobtrusive way possible. He's obviously going to be suspicious, on his guard still. That brings me back to the weapon. Can you imagine Oswald Seaton allowing anyone at Plash Meadow near him with a carving knife. You can't conceal a carving knife at all comfortably on your person. A razor, or a whetted clasp knife, you can."

"But it's exposure, not murder, he'd be apprehensive about?"

"I agree. But, when you're nervous, you're nervous of everything. Think of the setup. He arrives here at night. Someone meets him, either by appointment or by accident, we can't tell which. Now, unless Gates and his men are absolute fools, the murder was not done in the house. There'd have been a hell of a lot of blood."

"You can take it from me it wasn't. No stains anywhere. No clothing, carpets or rugs hidden or sent away to be cleaned."

"Then it was done outside the house. Where? In the garden or the orchard? Possible. But the murderer couldn't rely on all traces of blood being washed away by the thundershowers; and Gates would almost certainly have found some. The outbuildings? Worse still. But the dairy: that could have been sluiced down under cover of the noise of a thundershower. How could the murderer get Oswald into the dairy? By playing on his fears of exposure. Just hide in here, old man, for a few hours, till we've thought out the position and what we're going to do next. But I don't see Oswald trusting this person enough not to keep a wary eye on him. Or her. A carving knife negligently carried in the hand would disquiet him, I fancy."

"All right. I give up the carving knife. But your whole hypothesis breaks down on motive. If everyone at Plash Meadow knew Oswald's secret—"

"Not everyone, necessarily. Mr. and Mrs. Seaton, I suggest, and Rennell, and Mara Torrance."

"—Why should Oswald have to be murdered? He could be made to disappear again by a threat of exposure."

"If his secret was that he'd done someone here a grievous wrong, there'd be a revenge motive. Let us imagine that, of the Plash Meadow households, A. was prepared to forgive and forget, and had encouraged Oswald to return: but Oswald is intercepted by B., the one he'd originally wronged, who still nourishes an inveterate hatred of him."

"Och, these A.'s and B.'s!—it's all too much in the air. Where does Finny Black come in, anyway?"

Nigel drew meditatively on his cigarette. "Do *you* think Finny did it?"

"There's no evidence."

"The head in the tree?"

"Anyone could have put it there."

"Anyone active enough to climb the tree," said Nigel. "He wouldn't risk bringing out a ladder for the purpose."

"I'll tell you what I think about Finny Black." Blount leaned forward in his chair. "First, he had no motive we know of. Second, although he got queer in thunderstorms, there's no record that his queerness ran to violence. Third, if it did, it would be crazy violence—he'd not think about covering his traces; he'd not take his victim into the dairy, and Oswald wouldn't meekly follow him there either."

"Agreed. So—?"

"So, if it wasn't the murderer himself who disposed of the head—and why should he choose such a—e'eh—such a far-fetched place to put it?—then the only possible explanation is that Finny Black saw the murder done, or maybe just came upon the head while the murderer was away disposing of the body, and ran off with it up the tree."

"Having, by a strange coincidence, a net bag with him to put it in?"

"The murderer might have fetched that already, so that he could convey the head away without getting blood on his clothes," said Blount. "It'd be natural for him to get rid of the body first, because it was the more difficult to conceal. He'd not dare leave it lying about in the dairy: but he could hide the head there temporarily without much danger."

"I'm afraid you're right," said Nigel. "And, of course, if Finny *saw* the murder—"

"Aye, the poor crazed loon maybe did well to run away."

"Not that he'd be much use as a witness. He *is* dumb, isn't he?"

"Yes, I've been into that. But he's not a cretin. He could understand questions and he can write a bit." The superintendent sighed heavily. "This is a most unsatisfactory case, though. Here's a house, at the back end of nowhere. The old cook is hard of hearing; apparently she slept right through the thunderstorm that night. Finny Black is dumb. There's a village girl who comes in to clean every day; but she noticed nothing wrong the next morning. Gates and I have been right through the village: but, apart from the chap who saw Mr. Seaton returning from his walk, not a soul has one single piece of evidence to contribute. The press, as you know, has publicized our request for anyone to come forward who was on or near the river that night, in the vicinity of the footbridge. Results entirely negative."

"It looks as if you'll have to do all your own work for once, instead of getting the great British public to do it for you."

Blount brushed this aside with a curt gesture. "And the whole thing is cold, anyway. The body was not discovered till three days after the murder, and it wasn't till we found the head this morning, a week after *that*, that we could begin to pin the thing down to Plash Meadow."

"Too bad. What are your plans?"

The superintendent outlined them. The investigation would now become three pronged. With the aid of old photographs borrowed from Robert Seaton, and photographs of the severed head, it was hoped that a composite picture could be produced to give a fair likeness of Oswald Seaton. This picture would be reproduced in the press, carrying the usual appeal for anyone who had seen this man recently to come forward. Provided with copies of it, Inspector Gates would try to trace the traveler's journey down to Ferry Lacey. Copies would go to airports and seaports; shipping companies and air lines would be asked for co-operation in tracing the original: and the Bristol police would be requested to inquire at all lodginghouses and hotels, since the scanty evidence still seemed to point at Bristol as the most likely link between Oswald Seaton's sojourn abroad and his arrival at Ferry Lacey.

Secondly (and here the superintendent groaned) the whole business of Oswald Seaton's "suicide" would have to be reopened. Blount had already applied to his assistant commissioner for a detective inspector of the C.I.D., a pertinacious subordinate of his, named Slingsby, to be detailed for this work. "If Slingsby can't root it up, nobody can," he told Nigel. It was obviously essential to examine this "suicide" again now, although at the time both the police and the probate court had been satisfied: all the more so, if Nigel's hypothesis was correct that it had been staged under pressure from one or more of the parties who had benefited by it.

The third prong of the inquiry would, of course, be directed at Plash Meadow. Here, Blount was on much more difficult ground, at any rate until Finny Black was found. He had already interviewed every member of the two households. Mara Torrance, questioned again, had admitted she might have been wrong about the time when she'd seen Mr. and Mrs. Seaton cross the courtyard: she had not looked at her watch, it seemed, but had thought it was not long after she'd heard the church clock strike half-past twelve; but she agreed now that it might have been quarter-to-one which she'd heard striking.

As for the others, their stories appeared to be unassailable. It could be argued that it was rather odd for the Seatons not to have seen or heard anything suspicious that night. They had been out of the house twice, they said: once to have a

101

look at the mare, Kitty; then, about half an hour later, when they discovered that Finny Black was not in his bedroom, to look for him. Each time, they agreed, they had passed near the dairy: but they had not gone inside even during their search for Finny. Still, there was no inherent contradiction in their story. Oswald Seaton might well have wished to avoid them; he might even, conceivably, have been dead before they came out of the house the first time; alternatively, he might not have been killed till after they had returned from their search for Finny: this search, they said, had occupied them five to ten minutes—they'd broken it off when the second and heavier thundershower came down. The dairy was normally locked up by the dairyman, after the evening milking: this man believed he had locked it on the fatal night, but could not absolutely swear to this. The front door of Plash Meadow was also locked, but on that particular night Robert Seaton had not, to the best of his recollection, locked the door leading to the courtyard at the back, either on returning from his walk or when he and Janet had come in after looking for Finny.

"There's one thing I'd like to know," said Nigel at this point of the superintendent's résumé. "Why did Janet Seaton start worrying about her mare during the first thunderstorm, but not about Finny Black till the second one began?"

"It had occurred to me too," said Blount dryly. "But she explained it quite reasonably. She says that, when the first thunderstorm began, she went along to Finny's bedroom to see if he was all right. She found him asleep. That was soon after midnight. She decided to sit up then till her husband came back from his walk: she expected him back sooner, she says. When he did return, he told her he'd heard the mare kicking about uneasily in its loose box. So she went out with him to soothe the animal down. By this time, both of them felt wakeful, so they decided not to go to bed till the storm was over. They sat up in Mrs. Seaton's boudoir, reading.

After about half an hour, they decided they would go to bed. Just then the second thunderstorm broke, so Mrs. Seaton thought she'd just have another look at Finny first. This time, he wasn't in his room. So they went out and hunted for him. When they returned, unsuccessful, they did go to bed at last —they have separate rooms, as you know—and fell asleep quickly, both of them."

"They're a very protective family," remarked Nigel as he rose to go. Blount had offered to drive him back, but Nigel preferred to clear his head by a walk through the night air.

"The question is, whom are they protecting?" said Blount.

"Oh, everyone is protecting everyone else. Robert Seaton gets it all round: he's the most precious object in the whole collection. Lionel is madly protective toward Vanessa. Finny Black's aberrations call forth extreme solicitude on the part of Robert and Janet. Then there's Mara Torrance—Robert treats her as if she were his own daughter; Lionel is far from indifferent to her, in his quiet way; Janet tolerates her, which is saying a good deal: they've all woven a veil of silence round young Mara. No, Blount—the question is not *whom* are they protecting, but *from what*. We mustn't be misled into thinking that they're all in a conspiracy to cherish a murderer. They may be. But I fancy we shall have to get through several protective layers, which may have little relevance to this crime, before we come to *him*."

And I myself, thought Nigel, walking briskly back to Ferry Lacey, have enlisted in the bodyguard. His own status at Plash Meadow, after the discovery of the head, might have seemed highly questionable. He had, after all, been spying on Janet Seaton the previous night. And indeed it was part of the gathering mystery that a character so fierce and autocratic as Janet should have accepted his share in the night's work without protest or apparent rancor: apart, of course, from virtually setting Finny at his throat; but that might have been no more than the reflex action of a suddenly startled woman. At any rate, Nigel had restored himself to her good graces this afternoon by dealing with the swarm of reporters who had descended again upon Plash Meadow as promptly as if the fall of Oswald Seaton's head had been audible for fifty miles around the chestnut tree.

So here I am, reflected Nigel, at once a member of the bodyguard and a nigger in the woodpile. Though God knows what the nigger is supposed to be doing in the woodpile. Do I want to discover the murderer? From all one knows of Oswald Seaton, his taking-off was a consummation devoutly to be wished. What I really want is that Robert Seaton should be allowed to write his poetry. In fact, I'm already sucked into the general conspiracy to cherish and protect his genius. Well, why not?

An owl hooted rudely from a tree at the roadside.

"You disagree?" Nigel addressed the unseen skeptic. "You're telling me that Robert Seaton's genius is the one thing at Plash Meadow which can safely be left to look after itself? Maybe. But there's one little commodity genius cannot manufacture for itself, or do without. Time."

"Hoo! Hoo! . . . Hoo! Hoo!" exclaimed the owl.

"Ah, who indeed? Well, tomorrow I shall unwrap the first layer of the mystery. . . ."

At half after eleven the following morning, Nigel went into Janet Seaton's sitting room. The house was silent. Robert had been distrait at breakfast, and retired to his room immediately afterward, an intent look upon his face as though his powers were all concentrated on the delicate, invisible thread of poetry to be drawn, unbroken, out of the inner darkness where he had laid it down the day before. Lionel and Vanessa had gone off to the river. In the little garden-close beside the old tithe barn, Mara Torrance was sun bathing: her father, sprawled in a deck chair, read the newspapers.

"May I have a talk with you?" asked Nigel.

Mrs. Seaton looked up from her accounts. "Of course. I was rather hoping—I feel I owe you an apology. Have they heard anything about Finny yet?"

"I'm afraid not."

"I can't understand it. He's never stayed away so long before. Mr. Seaton and I are getting anxious about it. I didn't like to say anything at breakfast, in front of Vanessa."

Nigel was struck, not for the first time, by the incongruity between Mrs. Seaton's appearance and her address. It was as though a hard-bitten hunting woman spoke in the ceremonious periods of a Jane Austen dowager.

"I'm afraid I rather lost my head the night before last," she pursued.

Lost yours and found another's, thought Nigel. He said, "It's I who should apologize. I must have startled you badly, coming out of the darkness like that. I've a regrettable tendency toward melodrama, and have never quite succeeded in breaking myself of it."

Janet Seaton made an abrupt gesture with her heavy-knuckled hands, as if to push aside such a flippancy.

"You knew the—the other head was there, up in the tree?" she asked.

"It must have seemed as if I was spying on you. But I happened to see Finny start across the courtyard. I was looking out of the window—"

"Looking out? But your window's—"

"Not out of *my* window. When the storm began, I went into the room opposite—the room where you generally put guests, Vanessa told me—because the storm was approaching from that side of the house, and I wanted to watch it."

From beneath her heavy eyebrows, knitted in a frown, Janet Seaton gave him a somewhat formidable look.

"You haven't answered my question yet, Mr. Strangeways."

"Well, I did suspect the other head might be up there,

yes." Nigel paused, his pale blue eyes fixed inquiringly upon her. "So did you, I fancy?"

"I? Really, Mr. Strangeways!"

"In fact, you as good as told me so. Not intentionally, of course."

The painful flush came over Janet Seaton's face, darkening its sallow skin. She rose abruptly from her desk, went over to the window seat and plumped herself down on it, face averted.

"I think you had better explain yourself."

"Do you mind if I smoke? . . . It began with the clay head of your husband. I was told that you had provoked Mara Torrance into doing it."

"You were told? By whom?"

"I gathered it was so," Nigel went on patiently, scrutinizing the stiff, bulky figure outlined against the window. "I gathered that you had thrown doubts on Mara's ability to do a straightforward, realistic portrait head. You made a violent attack upon the abstract, nonrepresentational school. So her father told me, at any rate. Yet, at tea the other day, you showed considerable knowledge of this school, and sympathy for it. Naturally this suggested to me that your previous attack on it had not been quite ingenuous. Just a minute," said Nigel as Mrs. Seaton made an impatient movement, "let me go on. I'm simply explaining how I reasoned. If you had no *arrière-pensée*, if you just wanted Mara to do a head of your husband, it was surely a roundabout way to get it. Why not have asked her straight out? And then this clay head, obtained in a rather devious manner, is exhibited on the tea table, in full view of Finny Black, on a thundery afternoon when he is already showing the signs of mild dementia which such weather brings on him."

Janet Seaton's heavy head made a little, weaving movement from side to side, like that of a fly-tormented heifer.

Nigel felt a stir of pity for her: but his curiosity was stronger, and he went on,

"It occurred to me that the whole thing might be a contrivance on your part to get Finny to lead you to the head of the murdered man. You suspected, at any rate, that he might have hidden it. And, if he had done so on the night of the murder, he might repeat the action again with the—with a make-believe head."

"I think I know what you're going to ask me," came in a numb voice from the woman at the window. A crucial question was indeed on the tip of Nigel's tongue: but he decided not to put it yet. Instead, he asked,

"Wasn't that what you had in mind? And the reason why I was not put in the usual guest room?"

"You're very intelligent, Mr. Strangeways." Janet Seaton turned to him. She was unable to conceal a look of relief, of reprieve almost. Her fingers unlocked themselves on her lap. "You're quite a dangerous guest to have in the house, you know," she added with an attempt at archness.

"So there we were," Nigel pursued. "A thundery night. The decoy head in position, so to speak. Finny getting worked up. The dangerous guest tucked safely away on the other side of the house—and, by the way, I couldn't help noticing you were on edge that evening, and relieved when I went up to bed. Yes, I have to confess that I didn't go into the other room just to watch the storm. Presently you came out and stood at the door giving on to the courtyard. And then Finny, who'd presumably fetched the clay head from your husband's study and taken it to his bedroom, emerged from the servants' quarters. You were on the watch, and followed him out to the chestnut tree. And I followed you. A shocking abuse of hospitality, I fear."

Janet Seaton smiled at him uncertainly. "And I lost my head, and as good as got you strangled by poor Finny. A shocking abuse of my position as your hostess. May I have one of your cigarettes?"

"Oh, I'm so sorry." Nigel lit it for her, noticing how her hands still trembled. "Did you suspect Finny had done the murder? Or did you think he'd just come upon the severed head by accident, and hidden it?"

There was a marked pause before Janet Seaton spoke. "I'd no idea, one way or the other. There was no evidence then, you remember, that the—that it had been done here at all. Or who the victim was," she said slowly. "All I knew was that the head had disappeared. And that Finny is apt to take things, and to behave rather strangely during thunderstorms. Somehow the two things got linked together in my mind. So I made the experiment."

"I see. Did your husband know what you were up to?"

A momentary look of hauteur came into Mrs. Seaton's face, induced no doubt by Nigel's rather disrespectful mode of referring to her "experiment."

"He knew what was in my mind."

"And approved what you were doing?"

"But of course." Her rising intonation suggested that she was not accustomed to solicit Robert's approval for her conduct. The Lacey blood was very much in the ascendant again.

"What I can't understand," remarked Nigel mildly, "is why you went to such extraordinary lengths to protect Finny Black."

"To *protect* Finny?"

"Yes. The whole procedure, from the purveyance of the clay head onward, was so much under cover. If you'd merely thought Finny might have had some connection with the murder, with the missing head, why not have suggested that experiment to the police, or to me?"

"But I had no proof." Mrs. Seaton sounded a bit flustered. Then she recovered herself and said in her stateliest manner,

"It is surely quite natural to look after the interests of one's dependents. We Laceys have always prided ourselves on—"

"Oh come, Mrs. Seaton, that really won't do at all," exclaimed Nigel, who could be formidable too on occasion. "You are a woman of very considerable intellectual powers. You couldn't have failed to realize what construction the police would place upon your behavior."

"My behavior? I don't understand you," she said icily.

"Your keeping it all so dark. Let me tell you, then, what the police will say. They'll say that it was quite inconceivable for you to have done all this in the interests of a dependent —and a half-wit dwarf at that." Janet Seaton visibly flinched. "They'll say that your actions can only be interpreted in one way," Nigel went on, "and that your secrecy can only be accounted for in one way. You, or someone you love, killed Oswald Seaton. The head was removed to prevent identification of the victim. Finny Black stole the head and hid it, in the temporary absence of the murderer, perhaps while he was putting the body into the river. You, or the murderer, know that there's no safety until the head is disposed of. You suspect Finny may have got it. You dare not ask him openly to produce it for you, because that would give you away. So you work out an elaborate and secret method by which Finny may lead you to the head without himself or anyone else knowing what's afoot. Would anyone lay herself open to such obvious and appalling suspicions, the police will ask, on behalf of a—"

"Stop!" Janet Seaton almost shrieked it. Her fingers writhed and clenched in her lap as she fought for command of herself. Her face was turned away again. Presently she said,

"Have you ever wondered why Robert and I had no children of our own?"

Nigel shook his head uncomprehendingly. Janet Seaton's eyes glanced all round her exquisite room, as if seeking strength or comfort in its familiar beauties, or as if seeing them now for the first time, or the last—the highlights on the rosewood and walnut furniture, the hand-painted Bristol glass bowls on the mantelshelf, the little Constable glowing like a gem above it—all the symbols and supports of an elegant, rich, distinguished life.

"You say one would only have done—done what I did— the secrecy, the—the calculation of it all—for somebody one loves?"

Nigel nodded.

"You wonder why I should do so much to protect poor Finny?"

Nigel nodded again. He could hardly have spoken a word, so breathless had the atmosphere become in the square, shining room. Janet Seaton's voice was a harsh whisper.

"Finny is my child," she said.

CHAPTER EIGHT

RENNELL TORRANCE REVEALS

M<small>RS. SEATON</small>'s child! Oh well now. Extraordinary. Could you believe it! Inexperienced girl, no doubt. Unfortunate lapse. Best-regulated families. Most disconcerting. Oh well now, what next, I wonder."

Superintendent Blount, as was his way when events sprang a surprise upon him, fell into the idiom of Mr. Jingle, and repeatedly patted the dome of his bald head.

Nigel, who felt a dim atavistic unease at discussing the case with Blount under his host's roof, had compromised with the summerhouse. They were sitting there in deck chairs, facing the garden and the old tithe barn.

"I'll leave you to elicit the details from Mrs. Seaton," said Nigel.

The Superintendent looked unhappier still. "I suppose I shall have to. Vairy distasteful. Oh dear me," he complained, unprofessionally. "And it doesn't help us at all. Unless the puir wee dwarf did it. I suppose she's afraid he did? Is that all she told you about—e'eh—her relationship to him?"

Janet Seaton, in a stony, broken voice, had gone on to tell Nigel that Finny's father was a cousin of hers, later killed in the First World War. She had been seduced by him at the age of eighteen. She had gone down to a lonely cottage outside a village in Dorset, where she was unknown to anyone but her old nurse, who lived there. When the child was born and its abnormality became painfully clear, she left it in the nurse's charge. The nurse herself had died ten years ago; and Robert Seaton, to whom she had confessed the episode before their marriage, said they must look after Finny. During their honeymoon, spent in a village some distance away, Robert had gone over, Janet not daring to show herself, and found Finny in a bad way, living from hand to mouth, persecuted by the village hobbledehoys. They had brought him back to Plash Meadow.

"So you understand why Robert—why I dared not have any children again," Janet had ended.

Nigel now passed on this information to Blount, who presently commented,

"I doubt it's strange she should take him back after all that time, and get fond of him. You'd think it was the last thing a proud woman like her could bear—having him about the house."

"It was Robert's doing, chiefly, I presume. If it's true. With the two chief witnesses dead, you'll find it difficult to corroborate her story."

"But why should she make up such a humiliating story? Unless, of course—"

"Exactly," said Nigel. A shrewd look was exchanged between them.

"Well, we've found the head now. What about the clothes? Have your people checked up on the luggage Lionel Seaton took away that week end?" Nigel asked.

"He left here with one large suitcase. The gardener, who drove him to the station, confirms that. And he arrived with one large suitcase."

"Very helpful," said Nigel.

"I've been thinking about those clothes. Look here, Strangeways, supposing you've got a bloodstained suit on your hands, pair of boots, underwear, all the doings. And

112

suppose you're too fly to bury them or put them in the river, or try and burn them, or send them to a cleaner's, what'd you do?"

Nigel gave the subject his attention for a minute. "Wrap 'em all up in a parcel and post them off to some total stranger," he answered.

"Too risky. Chances are the recipient of a bloodstained suit would take it to the police, and then there'd be the postmark to give you away."

"Post it from somewhere else, then."

"But none of the family except Lionel Seaton has left the neighborhood since the murder."

"Well, Lionel had a *big* suitcase, you say. And for a short week end too."

"That's true enough. But the recipient would still take them to the police. Or would he?" Blount paused expectantly in the manner of a schoolmaster prompting a brilliant pupil.

"I see what you're hinting at. A recipient who needed clothes so badly that he'd not make a fuss about a few bloodstains."

"Capital, capital!" The superintendent, vigorously massaging his head, beamed upon Nigel.

"A displaced person. Someone abroad. A German."

"Lionel Seaton was in the Army of Occupation in Germany for a short while."

"So he might have addressed the parcel to someone he knew out there?"

"Or handed it to one of the relief organizations. We've started inquiries on those lines. No results yet."

"If that turns out to be the explanation, Lionel is the murderer; or else he got rid of a parcel, in all good faith, handed to him by someone else. But, you know, there's a simpler solution," said Nigel slowly.

The superintendent cocked his head. "What's that?"

"Finny found a heap of clothes where he found the head, and took them off to another of his hiding places."

"I got Robert Seaton to take me round to all the old caches he knew of. We drew a blank."

"Damn it, Blount, you seem to think of everything. Still, it's not decisive. Finny might have made a new cache."

"That's what worries me. I wish we could find him. It'd no' be healthy for him, wandering about with that secret in his head."

"Surely you needn't worry now. The clothes were disposed of, presumably because they'd give a clue to the victim's identity: otherwise they'd have been deposited in the river with the body, or never taken off it. But once the head was found, there'd be no point in the murderer's killing Finny to keep the secret of the clothes."

"But the best part of a night elapsed between Finny's disappearance and the discovery of Oswald Seaton's head. And Robert Seaton and his son were out hunting for Finny some of that time. They started out together: then they parted company, Robert going over the grounds and the meadow out yonder, Lionel along the river bank. That's their story, anyway. Hello! There's Dolores looking for me."

The bearer of this exotic name was the village girl who came every morning to clean the house. Blount had evidently established good relations with her.

"Well, Dolores my lassie, so you can't keep away from me!" he exclaimed as the slatternly creature approached the summerhouse.

"Saucy! You're wanted on the telephone. Or shall I bring it out for you?"

The superintendent lumbered off toward the house, exchanging elephantine badinage with Dolores. Nigel lay back in the deck chair and closed his eyes. His mind played around the interview with Janet Seaton this morning; the confession which had told so much and explained so little: he kept recurring to the crucial question—the question which, as it happened, he had never asked her.

"That was Gates," said the superintendent when he returned. "He's found a witness at last who saw Oswald Seaton the night he was murdered. Farm laborer. Lives in a cottage about a mile out from Chillingham. Been on the booze, fell into a ditch and decided to stay there till he'd sobered up, his wife being a bit of a termagant. Incidentally, that's why he's not come forward till now—wife told him to have nothing to do with the police. Anway, he saw a chap walking fast away from Chillingham. Shortish mackintosh, no hat, same height and general description as Oswald Seaton. Not much doubt it was he. Farm laborer didn't hail him. Surly chap. Looked at watch, though. Time was 11:15. So we can take it as fairly certain our man arrived on the 10:58 from Bristol. Which narrows down our search to Bristol and a few intermediate towns where that express stops."

"Was Oswald Seaton carrying any luggage?"

"Apparently not. Why?"

Nigel was frowning in concentration. "I wish you'd find out from the station check room at Chillingham Junction if they've any unclaimed articles left over from that night. A cheap suitcase possibly. Though why should he deposit it at the station? You see, if they haven't, it means that Oswald turned up here with nothing but what he could carry in his pockets—shaving tackle, toothbrush, etc."

"Just so. But—"

"Don't you see? That means he was expected. It means he knew somebody here would look after him, rig him out. And how could he know that, if this somebody hadn't been in communication with him? Judging by past history, he'd have had every reason, otherwise, to expect to be chucked out on his ear."

"You may be right," said the superintendent cautiously. "But why should anyone at Plash Meadow want Oswald back? I don't know the legal ins and outs of it; but when the original owner of a property, presumed dead, is found to be living, it'll likely make things vairy awkward for the present owners, to say the least of it."

"Even if they've still got the same hold over him which compelled him to disappear originally?"

"Aye, there's that, to be sure. But it was your own idea that something had happened—maybe his seeing that picture in the old society periodical—which gave Oswald the all-clear to come back to this country."

Nigel's eyes were fastened upon a spider hauling itself up its own thread in a slant of sunlight at the summerhouse door. "What it boils down to, Blount, is this," he said slowly, "Find someone here to whose advantage it would be for Oswald to return from the dead, *when he did*, which implies someone who knew he was alive, which probably means someone who was instrumental in Oswald's disappearance ten years ago, in the fake suicide, and—"

"And you've found the murderer?" asked Blount, with a quizzical glance at his friend.

"Oh dear me, no. You've eliminated one suspect. But you've also begun to crack the case open."

They talked for a few minutes longer. Then the superintendent rose to go. Nigel walked pensively toward the garden-close of the old tithe barn, where Rennell Torrance was asleep with a newspaper over his face. Mara had just gone indoors, Nigel noticed, presumably to prepare lunch. It seemed a good opportunity for a private talk with the painter.

Nigel shook him unceremoniously by the shoulder. Torrance grunted, heaved up in his chair. The paper slid off his face.

"Eh? What's that? Oh, it's you."

"Sorry to wake you up. But I've an urgent message for

you from the superintendent. He wants to see you when he comes back this afternoon. About half-past two."

A flicker of apprehension came and went in the man's eyes. "Wants to see me? What the devil for? I've told him everything I know about—"

"I doubt if you have," said Nigel cheerfully.

"Are you suggesting—?"

"You misunderstand me. In a police investigation, as new facts crop up, fresh questions arise. So the witnesses have to be interrogated again. Over and over again sometimes." Nigel gazed placidly at a feathery white cloud in the sky above Torrance's head. "Absolute terror, old Blount is, once he gets his teeth into a case. Probes away, you know, like a dentist with a drill."

"The metaphors are rather mixed," said Torrance, laughing wheezily, "but I see what you mean. Have a drink, old man."

Nigel took the gin and lime which Torrance handed him, and resumed his scrutiny of the cloud. A silence fell between them, which Nigel had no intention of breaking first. A bee hummed a light tenor against the distant bass of the weir.

"What's he after now?" said the painter at last. Nigel lowered his eyes, taking in the man's shabby, dissolute face, the pudgy hand which trembled as it raised the glass, the unconvincing air of impersonal interest.

"Blount? Oh, Oswald Seaton's past, of course. His supposed death. Who profited by it. Who stood to lose by his return. That sort of thing."

"He can't need me to tell him the answers."

Nigel spread out another silence, like bait. Torrance could not refrain from taking it, after a little.

"Well, I mean to say, of course nobody who knows Robert and Janet could imagine for a moment that they'd—but, as a purely academic point, it was they who profited by it. Robert did come in for the property. *And* he needed it."

"And they'd be highly embarrassed by Oswald's resurrection? It isn't really so academic, is it? And then there's yourself."

"Me? Don't be absurd, old man. I'd nothing to lose." The phrase touched a spring of self-pity in the painter. "I've not got a reputation, like Robert: or Janet's insane *amour propre*. I'm a failure, by the world's standards." He gave a creditable imitation of what novelists call a hollow laugh. "Not that I'd choose to be anything else. I've no use for these cheap successes. In the arts, success always corrupts. What matters is integrity. By that standard, my work is bound to survive—oh yes, in fifty years' time, when I'm safely under ground, the dealers will be putting their fancy prices on it. And—"

"And, in the meantime, you starve in your attic," said Nigel, gazing into his gin and lime.

The painter gave him a sulky look. "That's rather uncalled for. One can be starving for other things than food: for a bit of recognition, for instance. And no one likes living on another man's charity."

"Well, there's something you had to lose by Oswald's return. Or would he have allowed you to stay on in the old barn?" asked Nigel, bringing Torrance firmly back to the point. Equally firmly the painter grasped it. Raising his voice, he exclaimed:

"My good Lord! One doesn't do murder to maintain one's tenure of a charming piece of old-world brick and mortar. At least," he added, with a singular glint of malice in his eyes, "at least *I* wouldn't."

"Don't you be so sure, Rennell," came a gentle voice from behind him. Robert Seaton had approached unobtrusively, raising his pipestem in salutation to Nigel, he sat down cross-legged on the grass beside them.

"But I am. Quite sure. I've lived hard before, and I could again."

"Same here," murmured the poet. "Though I'd rather not."

118

There was an appeased, detached, floating-in-air look about him, a look of delightful exhaustion which Nigel had noticed often enough before during this last week: the poem was evidently still going well.

"What are you two talking about?" he asked.

Nigel said, "Artistic integrity."

"Oh, that. Dear me." The poet waved it away with the stem of his pipe. The effect on Rennell Torrance was positively embarrassing. His slack, heavy body stiffened with the rage of some long-suppressed emotion. Was it pure jealousy? Nigel wondered: or was it fear, finding a safe outlet here?

"That's absolutely typical of you, Bob," Torrance said. "You've made a name. You can afford to lie back on your bed of laurels and be amused at the idea of integrity. Or you think you can. But by God! at least I do produce some work. I may be living on charity, but I've not been corrupted by luxury, not been atrophied. The artist lives the life of a *bourgeois rentier* at his peril, and you damned well know it. One of these fine days you'll be asked to account for your talent. And you'll have to answer, 'I buried it, Master— buried it under a heap of roses.'"

The tirade continued bitterly for some time. When it was ended, Robert Seaton said,

"How you do fuss, Rennell! I don't believe in all this fussing about integrity and the proper life for the creative artist. It just uses up energy that ought to go into one's work. There's only one thing people like you and me need to pray for—" the little figure on the grass was oddly impressive "—patience. Patience. And an Act of God. We can do something about the former: the latter—that's His worry."

"Oh phooey! And He moves in a mysterious way, you'll say next. He's certainly taken a long time to—"

"He does indeed," remarked the poet, a queer little ripple of humor passing over his face. "A very mysterious way indeed. However, we must take Him as we find Him."

Nigel could feel, like an emanation, the poet's authority. No, it was not exactly authority: it was a supreme inward confidence, which made him, for the present at any rate, intact and inviolable. No wonder he exasperated Rennell Torrance beyond measure. There was no getting at Robert Seaton just now. Nigel said,

"This is all very interesting. But I came here about a different kind of mystery."

"The bloody old murder," said Rennell Torrance, who had been refreshing himself once again from the bottle. "Very sordid. Not at all the sort of thing we Laceys are accustomed to."

"What the police will ask you," pursued Nigel, using his convenient formula, "is why you were so extraordinarily disturbed by the head."

"The police are damn fools then. Who wouldn't be disturbed when a head falls out of a tree right at his feet?"

"I don't mean that head. I mean the clay head your daughter did. Before she altered it. While it still bore the expression of a fiend. Of Oswald Seaton."

"Ah yes. It certainly did give me a turn. The expression on it, I mean. Queer girl, Mara," said her father.

"But a clever bit of modeling doesn't give one a heart attack. Unless—"

"Unless?" interrupted Torrance pugnaciously.

"Well—I'm only telling you what the police will think—if you'd killed Oswald Seaton the week before, and removed his head, and then were confronted by the living image of it in your studio, that would account for—"

"What utter bunk! I—we all had Oswald on our minds just then, quite naturally, and—"

"Oh no. There was no reason, at that time, for anyone to dream that the murdered man was Oswald Seaton. Anyone but the murderer, that is," Nigel cut in swiftly.

"Look here, this is outrageous! Who the devil are you to

come pestering us like this? A bloody nosy-parker, setting your piddling little verbal traps!"

Rennell Torrance clawed himself out of his chair and loomed unsteadily above Nigel. He was almost beside himself with anger: but it was the anger of a frightened man; and well it might be, thought Nigel, after such a slip.

"Don't get so fussed, Rennell. Strangeways is only telling us what our behavior looks like from the police point of view. We should be grateful to him," said Robert Seaton, who had been listening to the previous exchanges with the birdlike, intent attitude, which was becoming familiar to Nigel. "The most trying thing about a business like this is that the innocent and the guilty are equally in the dark. The police pop in and out, asking everyone the most prosaic, drab questions—it's like a bad play, really; you've no idea what goes on in the characters' minds when they're off the stage."

If Robert Seaton had been talking to gain time for Torrance to recover his composure, he was successful enough.

"Trying, you call it? It certainly is. Though *you* don't seem to turn a hair," grumbled the painter. He sat down again, poured himself another drink and turned to Nigel. "I'll tell you why Mara's head upset me. The last time I saw Oswald, he did look just like that. Quite literally, his head was the last I saw of him."

Robert Seaton unexpectedly chuckled. "Rennell has a great turn for the macabre," he remarked, with childlike appreciation.

"Oswald was walking away over the dunes," Torrance continued. "Scrambling down the far side of one of them, he turned round. I saw his head over the top, looking back. His body was cut off by the line of the dune. Quite prophetic."

"When did this happen?" asked Nigel. "You don't mean—?"

121

"Yes. It was ten years ago. The evening he—er—disappeared. I was probably the last person to see him."

"We were all there," said Robert Seaton. "In the neighborhood, I mean. Oswald had asked—"

"Just a minute," Nigel interrupted. "This never came out at the inquiry, did it?"

Rennell Torrance replied, "My seeing him? No, it didn't."

Nigel had found himself extraordinarily disconcerted by this revelation. He had an odd impression, too, that Seaton and Torrance were not just stone-walling; that they were stealing quick runs, and for the moment at any rate there was a close understanding between them. Or could it be that, to change the metaphor, they were shortening their front? Was one important position being surrendered, the better to defend some key point?

"Why not?" he asked, rather feebly.

"Why didn't it come out? Because I wasn't asked about it, I suppose," said the painter.

Robert Seaton knocked out his pipe on the leg of Nigel's chair. "I think you should be a bit more forthcoming, Rennell," he said.

"Well, then. All the evidence pointed to Oswald's having committed suicide. There was a farewell letter and so on. If I'd said I was on the dunes, too, and had seen him, well, it might have been misunderstood, produced unnecessary complications."

"You mean, you might have been suspected of doing away with him?"

The painter nodded curtly.

"The police would have discovered you had a motive for killing him?"

"Everyone who knew Oswald had a motive for killing him," said Torrance, rather theatrically. "He was a running sore on the face of humanity, if you don't mind my saying so, Bob."

"So your motive would have been one of pure social hygiene?" Nigel commented. "Oh well, if you're determined to be evasive—"

"I'm sorry, but—oh, damn it all, it's not my secret only! It affects other people."

Nigel got the impression that the painter, though he studiously avoided looking at Robert Seaton, was really addressing him—whether in appeal or in challenge, Nigel could not be sure. He heard Seaton gently murmuring,

> He had done most bitter wrong
> To some who are near my heart.

"I think we'd better stop talking in rhymed riddles," said Nigel irritably. "But first, may I have all the facts about your brother's fake suicide? There seems to be quite a lot that didn't come out at the inquiry, or didn't get into the papers anyway. What were you doing there, for instance?" Nigel asked Torrance.

There was a marked silence. So the run-stealers are a bit rattled, thought Nigel; they'd like to have a few private words with each other between the wickets; but they won't, if I can prevent it.

At last, Rennell Torrance took up the parable. The story as he told it, calling on Seaton for corroboration from time to time, or led on by a question from Nigel, and as Nigel himself wrote it down shortly afterward for Blount to have checked by Inspector Slingsby, the officer working on that end of the case, ran as follows:

The Torrances had first met Oswald Seaton while on a caravan holiday in 1937. He had allowed them to camp in the Plash Meadow fields and supplied them with milk and water. The following summer he invited Rennell and Mara to stay at his holiday cottage in the Quantocks, half a mile from the sea. The other members of the party were Robert Seaton, Janet Lacey and her mother.

123

It was in the second week of this holiday, the last week of August, that the "suicide" occurred. Two days before, Mara, then aged fifteen, was taken seriously ill with what seemed to be a kind of nervous breakdown. She had been nursed by Janet Lacey: but, according to Rennell, it was chiefly Robert Seaton's care and solicitude for the girl which finally restored her to health. Janet Lacey, who was going through a Christian Scientist phase at the time, had persuaded Rennell not to call in a doctor.

Oswald Seaton himself had been very much on edge the previous week. It was his first holiday from the business since the death of his father, two years before; but he seemed unable to keep his mind off it, was continually ringing up the Redcote factory, complaining to Robert about the strain of the work, the severity of foreign competition, etc., and was subject to alternations of irritability and extreme depression. These were aggravated by Mara's illness—he had taken quite a fancy to the girl and used to spoil her with presents; indeed she was the only member of his house party who had seemed able to raise his spirits. When Mara fell ill, Janet Lacey had her hands full: for, as well as looking after the girl, she had also to minister to her host, Oswald having got it into his head that he was responsible for Mara's illness, through having kept her out too long in the fierce heat of the previous day, and allowed her to get sunstroke. However that might be, he had turned to Janet in this new trouble, and when she was not at the girl's bedside, she was usually with him.

After dinner on the evening of his disappearance, Oswald had seemed half distraught. He said to his brother, "I can't stand this bloody house another minute. I'm going for a walk. Don't let anyone wait up for me." Robert went upstairs and read to Mara for an hour or so, then went to bed. Old Mrs. Lacey had already retired. Janet, who was sleeping in Mara's room, went to bed soon after Robert had left the girl. Rennell Torrance had gone out for a walk when dinner was over. No doubt he had dined heavily. He fell asleep in a pocket of the dunes, a hundred yards or so away from the sea. Awaked by the sound of feet scrunching the sand, he had seen in the last of the daylight Oswald Seaton walking seaward, away to his left. Oswald turned round once, before disappearing behind the last ridge of dunes: whether he had noticed Rennell Torrance, the latter could not be sure. A sea mist, which had been hovering over the Channel, was now beginning to drift inshore. Rennell heard the scrape of a boat being launched from the secluded cove beyond. He assumed Oswald to have gone fishing, as he occasionally did late in the evening.

The next day, fishermen had found Oswald's dinghy anchored in the Channel, a mile from shore. It was empty, but for his clothes and, pinned to the coat, a letter for Robert. Oswald was known to be a very poor swimmer. Tracks of footprints offered by the dunes and the muddy foreshore proved that nobody had accompanied Oswald in the boat. The police had no doubt made exhaustive inquiries as to the possibility of Oswald's having transshipped from his own boat to another. Four factors had weighed heavily in their final decision to accept the disappearance as a suicide, and in that of the probate court when later it gave leave to presume Oswald Seaton's death:

First, Oswald's farewell letter, which was indisputably genuine.

Second, the testimony of the members of his house party as to his disordered state of mind during the previous days, the way his business affairs had been preying on his mind, etc.

Third, the fact that he had not drawn any large sums out of the bank in the preceding weeks, which he would certainly have done if he was planning a disappearance.

Fourth, the fact that within the last three years the bodies of two holidayers drowned off this stretch of coast had never been recovered.

The crucial point, as Nigel and Blount agreed when they were discussing Rennell Torrance's information later in the day, was the third one. Clearly Oswald Seaton could not have got out of the country without money. He had withdrawn no large sum from his own bank: therefore he must have been financed. A considerable amount of money would have been required, for, apart from Oswald's personal expenses, it seemed pretty certain that he must have been taken off his own dinghy by some local fisherman or boatman and landed further along the coast under cover of the sea mist that night, and this man would have to be paid a lot of money to keep his mouth shut during the subsequent inquiry.

"A fairish outlay of cash," said Blount. "Two or three hundred pounds at least, I'd imagine. The question is, whom did it pay to lay out such a sum?"

"Robert Seaton. On the face of it. But it's not as simple as all that. In the first place, he was very poor still, as far as we know. Where'd he raise the money? Secondly, I just don't believe he's the kind of man who'd organize a conspiracy of this kind in order to get hold of his brother's property."

"That's a matter of opinion. Besides—look here, Strangeways, it was your own theory that Oswald was persuaded or compelled to disappear by some person or persons who knew a guilty secret of his, knew he'd committed some criminal offense which so far had been kept dark. Isn't that so?"

"Yes."

"Well, then, Robert Seaton is a quixotic character, you say. And I got the impression myself, talking to him this afternoon, that in spite of everything he'd had a real feeling for his brother—there was a sort of bond between them. Don't you think Robert might have helped his brother to fake the suicide, not for what he'd get out of it himself, but simply to save him from worse—from imprisonment, from ruin and total disgrace?"

"Ye-es. Yes, I do think that's possible," said Nigel slowly.

"And it would account for the Torrances being his pensioners. Rennell Torrance was there at the time. He'd every opportunity to discover that some hanky-panky was going on. We've only his word for it that he saw the last of Oswald Seaton on the dunes that night. He may have followed him down to the foreshore and heard him being transshipped later. At any rate, he's been living in comfort here since 1945. And you can't account for the Seatons' tolerating a slob like him about the place, except on the theory that he discovered the conspiracy of Oswald's 'suicide,' and has been cozily blackmailing Robert ever since. *Can* you?"

Nigel looked worried. At last he replied, "Well, I could. Though I mightn't be right. There's more than one kind of blood money . . . I wonder. I really shall have to have a talk with young Mara now. I've put it off too long."

But the talk was fated to a further postponement. That same evening, at six o'clock, just as Nigel was walking across the court toward the old barn, he heard the galloping of hooves. It was Vanessa Seaton, on Kitty. She tore into the courtyard, her hair streaming behind her, reined up the horse near Nigel and excitedly announced,

"I've found Finny!"

CHAPTER NINE

FINNY BLACK TURNS UP

Taking the horse by the bridle, Nigel led it and its fair rider out of earshot of the house. Vanessa dismounted, rather cumbrously, slung about as she was with a variety of impedimenta—haversack, field glasses, water bottle, camera case and an ancient bandolier—so that she resembled some intrepid pioneeress of covered-wagon days.

"You'd better tell me about it while you unsaddle this animal," said Nigel.

"He's in the church. I saw him from Meldon Hill. On the tower. Has he taken sanctuary, d'you think? What's the rule about that nowadays? Can the police drag him from the altar, or must they get the vicar's permission first?"

"Just a minute, begin at the beginning. You can take Kitty's saddle off while you talk. My word, she's been sweating."

"Yes, I galloped all the way back. Janet would be furious if she knew. You won't tell her, will you?"

"No. But she's bound to have heard you. You sounded like the charge of the Heavy Brigade. Well, you were on Meldon Hill—"

"Yes. It's just over there." Vanessa pointed at a cobweb on the stable ceiling. "I saw him through my field glasses."

"What were you doing on the hill?"

"I was Developing my Initiative. Lieutenant says that

tracking is one of the best ways of developing your initiative. She says that the Mothers of the Future must be Fearless and Self-Reliant, and of course truly Womanly. You know?— Steel-true and blade-straight—that's how Englishmen like their mates, isn't it?"

"Well, some do, no doubt," replied Nigel cautiously. "But—"

"I don't see, myself, how tracking makes you blade-straight, since you're bent double half the time—oh, damn this buckle!—Where was I?"

"On Meldon Hill."

"Oh yes. As a matter of fact I've been tracking Finny ever since he disappeared. In my spare time. I thought he was a gargoyle at first."

"A gargoyle?"

"Yes. There's one at each corner of the tower, you know. So when I was raking the countryside with my powerful glasses and saw his head, sort of resting on the coping of the church tower, I thought for a moment it was a gargoyle. Poor Finny. He's ugly enough for one, isn't he?"

"Did he move? I mean—"

"Oh, he's not dead. I went to see."

"Did you indeed?"

"Yes, I galloped down the hill and up the spiral staircase in the tower—I left Kitty outside the church of course. But he wasn't there any longer. Expect he heard me coming. Guess what I found, though."

"I can't imagine."

"Crumbs," announced Vanessa, in a bloodcurdling whisper. "Here, help me off with my accouterments. . . . Thanks awfully. I put them in one of the pocket things of the bandolier. Detectives always seem to carry envelopes about with them to put clues in: but I hadn't—oh, here it is."

She hooked out with her middle finger a few morsels of cake.

"Do you recognize these crumbs?" she demanded.

"Well, no, I don't think—"

"*I* do. I'll *swear* they're from the cake I helped Mrs. Fitch to make the other day. I bet you Finny's been getting into the house at night and taking things from the larder. What are you going to do about it?"

"There was no sign of him in the church?"

"Only these crumbs. I found them in such a funny place too. Guess where."

"In the pocket of the vicar's cassock."

"No. Have you been in our church? Well, there are some effigies of the Laceys, kneeling at sort of stone prayer desks. In a chapel over the vault. And the crumbs were on one of the desks. Just as if this crusader Lacey was saying grace after eating his tea."

"Did you call to Finny when you were in the church?"

"No, of course not. I was tracking him, I told you."

"Have you told anyone else? As you went through the village, for instance?"

"No."

"Good. Now I want you to do two things. First, find out tactfully from the cook if she's missed any food out of the larder during the last two days. Second, don't tell her or any-one else that you've seen Finny. *Nobody* must know. O.K.?"

"Not even Lionel?"

"Not even Lionel. It's *very* important."

"Well, I'll try," said Vanessa dubiously. "But Li always seems to know when I've got a secret, and he worms it out of me somehow."

As soon as Vanessa had left him, Nigel made off to the vicarage, which stood beside the church at the other end of the village. He introduced himself to the vicar, whom he had not met before, as a friend of the Seatons; the telephone at Plash Meadow was out of order, he said—might he use the vicar's?

130

After two ineffectual calls, he got Blount at the Redcote police station. He told him of Vanessa's discovery. He asked Blount for two men to be posted unobtrusively, one in the church, one in the churchyard, by dusk. No, they were not to look for Finny: he would keep till tomorrow morning. Yes, he could guarantee that Finny would not make a break for it. No, he had not been into the church yet himself, but he had a pretty good idea where Finny was concealed. Yes, that was the idea—either Finny would emerge to steal some more food from Plash Meadow, in which case one of the watchers could follow him; or someone at Plash Meadow would be bringing food to the church under cover of darkness, in which case—no, he didn't know who it was. Yes, he was pretty sure that, if anyone at Plash Meadow was concealing Finny Black, that person would show his hand tonight.

Blount said he would attend to the matter himself, in company with Sergeant Bower. Would Nigel arrange for the vicar to receive them about 9:30 P.M.? They could wait in the vicarage till darkness fell.

Nigel rang off and returned to the vicar's study, feeling more than ever a snake in the grass, if that reptile can be supposed to entertain qualms of conscience. He reminded himself that all he was doing, at the moment, was to safe-guard Finny's life. Or was he? In a sense, there seemed no necessity to do so. If Finny were a danger to X., and if X. knew where Finny was, X. would not be so officiously keeping him alive. But perhaps the food had been brought by Y. Perhaps there was a Y. who had arranged for Finny to lie concealed in—

"I believe you have some remarkable effigies in your church, sir."

"You are an antiquarian, sir?" asked the vicar, a waffling and well-nigh senile man.

"I am interested in the Lacey family."

131

"You must let me show them to you. Very fine twelfth-century stonework. Can you spare ten minutes? . . . No trouble, I assure you. I do not have my supper for half an hour yet."

They stepped into the small, musty church. A greenish light filtered through the window, half-obscured by ivy, of the little chapel in the southeast corner. The chapel was chock full, like a box room, with relics of mortality. Tablets, urns, recumbent figures; enough miscellaneous stone legs and arms, detached from their original trunks, to have fitted out, it seemed, a whole dynasty of Ozymandiases: and, against the south wall, six figures in pairs, husband and wife, kneeling each at a *prie-Dieu*.

"Observe the chiseling of the baldric," quavered the vicar enthusiastically. "These are probably the finest examples of—"

But Nigel was observing a small door, let into the thickness of the great stone plinth upon which the effigies knelt: three steps led down to it from the east side, and there were footprints in the dust that lay thick upon them.

"—the normal practice of the stonemasons of the twelfth century," the vicar was saying. His dim eye became aware of a certain inattentiveness on Nigel's part, who was in fact trying with his little finger the keyhole of the vault door.

"Ah, you are interested in the family vault. Note the coat-of-arms, subscribed with the motto *'Quis Lacey Lacesset?'* Who dares provoke, or perhaps better, challenge, a Lacey? The homophone, or play on words, can hardly be rendered in our own tongue. A most historic family, the Laceys." The vicar groped at the back of his mind, like a shortsighted man for a lost collar stud, and produced, *"Si monumentum requiris, circumspice"*—which seemed to Nigel, under the circumstances, something in the nature of a truism.

"Do you have a key to this door?" he asked.

"I—er, yes. But it may not be opened, of course, without

132

the authorization of Mrs. Seaton, or her legal representatives. No doubt, should you wish to inspect, to—er—examine the vault, she would lend you her own key. It has not been opened since her dear mother was laid to rest: some six or seven years ago, that would be."

Nigel privily rubbed a stain of oil off his little finger and professed himself satisfied.

At dinner, an hour later, Vanessa studiously avoided his eye. It was apparent to him that she had not been able to keep the secret. Which was what Nigel had counted on.

Lying awake, soon after midnight, he heard footsteps cautiously approach his door and stop. He breathed louder and slower, mumbled to himself as if in sleep. The feet moved away. Nigel pulled the bedclothes closer and composed himself for genuine sleep. It was up to Blount now. . . .

The next morning, Vanessa entered his bedroom, looking sullen and mutinous.

"You're to have breakfast in bed," she announced, still avoiding his eye. "There's a flap on downstairs."

"Finny?"

She nodded dumbly; then burst into tears. "It *wasn't* my fault," she sobbed. "I couldn't help seeing him on the tower —and telling someone—telling you. Li is furious."

"You told him the secret too? Last night? Oh, Vanessa!" said Nigel gently.

"He heard me asking Mrs. Fitch if she'd missed any food. You know how you have to bawl at her. Then he dragged it out of me."

"And had she missed any?"

"Yes. Oh, I hate all this," she desolately exclaimed. "Why should it happen to us? I'd been so looking forward to these holidays. And now everything's gone wrong. Everyone's trying to keep things from me, and snapping my head off if I ask questions, and Daddy's been too busy to talk to me like

133

he used to and go on expeditions. And Lionel—why is everyone so different? Oh, I do feel miserable! They ought to be glad I found Finny for them. But—" she choked, and burst into tears again.

"Look, Vanessa—come and sit on the bed a minute. There. I know it's absolutely foul for you. But you've just got to live through bad times like this. Everyone does. They come to an end, sooner or later, and you find you're still alive, and you can look back at them and understand what they were all about. At your age, it's difficult to believe they won't go on forever, isn't it? It's like one of those dreams, when you dream you're lost, and you know you're dreaming, yet you can't wake up. But you always do wake up." Nigel stroked the girl's hair. "My wife was killed in the war. She was driving an ambulance through a blitz: refused to get out and take cover. Well, I thought that was the end of *my* life. You understand? She was rather like you, in some ways. She was extremely brave: an explorer. Perhaps you'll be one, when you grow up. Her explorations made her a famous woman. I remember her telling me once how she'd got lost in a wood, quite near home—she was about thirteen then. Just about your age. She got into an absolute panic, worse and worse, she told me, and went tearing round in circles bashing into trees: well, really, it was as if the trees were bashing into her, and the branches deliberately whipping her face, and the brambles tripping her up. She was quite lost. Everything seemed against her. And soon it would be night. Do you know what she did?"

Vanessa shook her head, glancing up at him sideways through her tumbled hair.

"She sat down with her back against a tree, and made three resolutions. First, always to carry a compass with her in the future: second, to remember that no wood goes on forever: and third, to go to sleep for a bit. And that's what she always did afterward, when she became an explorer and got a bit panicky."

"And what happened that time, in the wood?"

"Oh, she went to sleep, and woke up an hour or so later, and walked slap out of the wood as easy as pie."

Vanessa gazed at him a moment with tear-brilliant eyes. Then she flung her arms round his neck, kissed him heartily, and ran out of the room.

Three hours later, as Nigel was walking in the orchard to clear his head before the meeting Blount had fixed for mid-day, he came upon Vanessa Seaton. Her back was against a tree. Tiptoeing up, Nigel perceived she was peacefully slumbering, a small pocket compass on her lap. "Pleasant dreams," he murmured, and retraced his steps. Poor Vanessa! —she would have need of them before long. "Yes, we found him all right," Blount had said hurriedly when they met an hour ago. "He came out of the vault—had a key in his pocket. *And* we found Oswald Seaton's clothes there. A lot of bloodstains on 'em. Why didn't Gates think to look?— Why didn't I, for the matter of that?"

"Not a churchgoing generation," Nigel offered.

"Pish! And who should turn up in the middle of it all? Robert Seaton. Out for one of his nocturnal perambulations, he said. No food on him, anyway. Heard a noise in the church. You bet he did: I was trying to get a grip on the wee dwarf—he fought like a demon: then Seaton came in and called out to him and he went quiet as a lamb."

So now, Nigel apostrophized the calm face of Plash Meadow, so now what have you got in store? How many more tricks up your sleeve, you charming illusionist? And when will you cease pulling wool over my eyes?

What Plash Meadow had had in store for him, thought Nigel as he entered the dining room a few minutes later, appeared to be a Board Meeting. Robert, Janet and Lionel, Rennell and Mara Torrance sat round the table, fidgeting, muttering or impassive, each according to his temperament. At the head sat the Chairman of the Directors, impersonated by Blount. A little behind Blount, notebook open on knee, the confidential secretary, Sergeant Bower. The eyes of Henry Lacey gazed bleakly down at them from above the mantelpiece: the Company is not what it was, they seemed to be saying, when I was Managing Director.

"Ah, there you are, Strangeways," said Blount. "Sit down. I thought you had all better be present when I questioned Finny Black. As you know, we found him last night. He'd been hiding—" Blount coughed primly "—or hidden, in the family vault. He's none the worse, I'm glad to say, for his— e'eh, immurement. Of course, one of you must have given him the key that night he ran away after attacking Mr. Strangeways, and kept him supplied with food. It'd save a lot of trouble if that person would now come forward."

The Board of Directors shifted their feet, muttered, avoided one another's eyes, in the awkward pause that followed. How absurdly guilty they all look, thought Nigel— particularly Robert Seaton, with that angelic expression of innocence, like a dear little choirboy bluffing it out on the vicar.

"Surely it's possible that Finny took the key himself and stole the food out of our larder at night," suggested Janet Seaton.

"I'm afraid not," Blount replied. "He'd have left his fingerprints. And there aren't any. As to the key, now— But, if no one will volunteer the information, I'll have to ask Finny himself. Bower, will you—?"

"I will not have Finny bullied," said Janet with strong emphasis.

Blount replied suavely, "You are all here to see that he is not."

"I think," began Robert Seaton. His son interrupted him:

lounging back in his chair, eyes on the ceiling, Lionel Seaton said coolly,

"Oh well then. I hid Finny and acted as his supply line."

Mara Torrance's hand flew to her mouth, stifling a cry. Janet knitted her thick brows at her stepson.

"You? But Lionel, why?—"

"I hid Finny and brought him food," Lionel repeated more loudly. "I—"

"Damn it, Bower, come back! We don't want him yet," Blount exclaimed to his sergeant, who had moved to the door just now, in smart anticipation of his superior's command, and opened it. Finny Black, a uniformed policeman close by, was sitting outside.

Blount turned upon Lionel when the door was shut again. "You realize you were obstructing the police in their duties by what you did?"

"I suppose I was," the young man equably replied. "I'm sorry. I just wanted to give him a chance."

"A chance to do what?" asked Blount, manfully refraining his exasperation.

"Oh, get his second wind, pull himself together. He was scared stiff after what happened that night. I found him quite soon, near the river. I thought he might be going to chuck himself in. So I told him to go to the church and wait for me. Then I came back here. And later that night I slipped out again with some food and the key of the vault. I told him to pop into the vault if anyone came along. He thought it was a new sort of game."

"It was an odd hiding place to think of, Mr. Seaton."

"I suppose it was," said Lionel. "But poor Finny wouldn't mind a few Lacey skeletons, you know. And I did hate the idea of his being chivvied all over the countryside by the constabulary."

The superintendent unmasked a battery. "Had you not already used the vault as a hiding place? Wasn't that why it occurred to you at once as the best place to conceal Finny Black?"

"I don't get you."

"Was it not you who put the bloodstained clothes of Oswald Seaton in the vault, where I found them last night?"

"The bloodstained—? Well I'm jiggered!"

The whole company rocked visibly at this blow. Rennell Torrance's eyes bulged. Janet's hand went to her throat. Robert pursed his lips as if to whistle. Mara was staring desperately at Lionel, who alone seemed, after his first exclamation, to be taking the thing in his stride.

"Now this won't do at all," he said. "In the first place, if I'd murdered Oswald, I'd never be so dim-witted as to hide Finny in the very spot where I'd hidden my victim's clothes. And secondly, if I'd murdered Oswald, I wouldn't have hidden Finny at all; not alive, anyway. Finny'd be much too dangerous to have about the place. I'd have pushed him into the river—he can't swim, you know—or locked him up in the vault, dead. Wouldn't I now?" The remarkable young man gazed blandly at Blount. "I'm assuming," he added, "that all this fuss about Finny is because you think he knows who murdered Oswald."

Nigel had a sudden conviction that this performance was partly for Mara's benefit. The girl was certainly gazing at Lionel now as if she saw him in a new light. So, for that matter, was Superintendent Blount.

"Very well then," he said. "I'll come back to you later. Bring in Finny Black now, Sergeant."

The scene, as always happened when the dwarf appeared on the stage, took a grotesque turn. What was it now? A midget being interviewed for a key post? An oracle being consulted? No, thought Nigel as the uncouth mannikin climbed on to a chair beside Superintendent Blount and sat there, his legs sticking out straight in front of him, his square mouth gaping like a box, a patch of red on each cheek, thi

138

is the ventriloquist's act. The illusion was increased by the mechanical way in which Finny's head turned to Blount at every question, and by the bizarre grunts and cluckings that came from his lips.

"Now you understand, Finny, that you must tell us the truth, don't you?" Blount was saying. "Mr. Seaton wants you to tell the truth. Isn't that so?"

"Yes, Finny must tell the truth," said Robert Seaton.

"I'm going to ask you questions," Blount went on. "You can nod for 'yes' and shake your head for 'no.' If you don't know the answer, put up both your hands. If you don't understand the question, put up one hand. Do you follow me?"

Finny gurgled, nodding vigorously.

"Good. Now, Finny, you've been asked some of these questions before. Never mind that. You know that a man was murdered here?"

Finny nodded.

"Did you kill him yourself?"

Finny, gibbering, shook his head so violently that it seemed as if it might fly off his neck.

"Did you see this man, alive, the night of the thunder-storm?"

Shake.

"Did you find his head and climb up the chestnut tree with it and hide it there?"

Finny looked puzzled, put his hand over his face with a smearing movement; then tentatively held up the other hand.

"You don't understand my question?"

"I think he's confused between the two heads," suggested Robert Seaton.

"Ah yes. Finny, I'm not talking about the clay head, the model one of Mr. Seaton, which you took just before you ran away. I'm talking about the real one—" Blount had a grisly inspiration "—the one with blood on its neck."

Finny's face lit up. He nodded cheerfully.

"You took that head and hid it up the tree?"

Nod.

"Did you find it—e'eh—in the house somewhere?"

Shake.

"Out of doors?"

"Oh for God's sake!" Mara Torrance exclaimed, almost whimpering. "Must we listen while—it's like a game of Twenty Questions. I can't stand—"

"Be quiet, Miss Torrance! Compose yourself!" said the superintendent very firmly. "Did you find this head, the bloody head, in—e'eh—in the dairy, perhaps?"

Finny clucked and nodded, bouncing a little in his chair.

"The dairy. Just so. Was the head in a net?" Blount made a sort of conjuror's movement, and held a net shopping bag up to Finny. "Something like this?"

The dwarf nodded.

"When you found the head in the dairy—we'll go out presently and you can show me just exactly where you found it—did you see the man's body too?"

Shake.

"You didn't. Was the light on in the dairy? The electric light?"

Finny shook his head, but looked troubled. He made a writing movement. Blount at once put paper and pencil before him; and Finny, tongue in cheek, laboriously scrawled a word.

"Oh, I see. 'Lantern.' There was a storm lantern there, already lit?"

Nod.

"Vairy good, Finny. You're doing fine. Have you any idea what the time was when you found the head?"

Finny put up both hands.

"Do you remember, was it raining when you went into the dairy?"

140

Finny's big head rolled on his neck. He began to put up both hands. Then he startled the audience by standing upright on the chair, and doing a little pantomime. His eyes winced; a growling sort of bark issued from his throat.

"Lightning and thunder," said Lionel Seaton.

"Capital, Finny! Excellent! There was lightning and thunder when you went to the dairy, not rain?"

The dwarf nodded, beamed hideously all round, chuckling and clapping his hands at his own cleverness. Then he resumed his seat.

"When you found the head, did you also see a heap of clothes?"

Nod.

"Did you take those clothes away and hide them somewhere else?"

Shake.

"You're quite sure, Finny? It wasn't you who put them in the vault, in the church, where I found you last night?"

Finny Black shook his head vigorously. A hissing sigh was heard from Rennell Torrance.

"You didn't touch that heap of clothes in the dairy at all?"

Shake.

"Very well. Now, Finny, when you went out that night, and into the dairy and hid the head, and then went for a little walk by yourself, did you see anyone else about? Anyone you knew?"

Not by the faintest change of intonation did Blount betray the urgency of this question. The figures round the table might have been turned to stone. Bower's pen was poised above his notebook. Finny looked exceedingly troubled. His eyes flickered toward Robert Seaton, as if in appeal.

"You must tell the truth, Finny," said the poet gently.

Finny gobbled and grimaced a little, jigging uneasily in his chair. Then, with an eeny-meeny-miny-mo gesture which recalled for Nigel a similar one made by Mara at the tea

141

party in June, the dwarf's arm and outstretched finger moved slowly round the company and stopped at Rennell Torrance.

The painter sprang to his feet. "That's a lie!" he roared. "He couldn't have seen me. I was—"

"Sit down at once, Mr. Torrance, and don't interrupt again, or I'll have to ask you to leave the room," said Blount sharply. He turned again to Finny, who was cowering away from Torrance's outburst, and resumed his patient, quiet questioning. He elicited the information that Finny had seen Rennell Torrance standing just outside the French windows of the old barn: this had happened when he returned from his "little walk"; and Robert and Janet had already testified that Finny had come back "drenched to the skin" about an hour after they'd gone out to look for him—that is, about two o'clock.

"Very well," said Blount, "we'll return to that presently. Now, Finny. Did you see anyone else that night?"

The dwarf shook his head, but rather uncertainly. Then, after a hesitation, he pointed to his ear.

"Oh, you *heard* someone, but didn't see who it was? Splendid, Finny. We're getting on fine, aren't we?"

The gruesome game of question and answer went on. Finny, it appeared, had heard someone walking up toward the house from the direction of the river. This, as far as he could satisfactorily make it known, seemed to have happened not long after he'd come down from the tree, while he was wandering about at the end of the orchard nearest the river. It proved impossible to fix the time more precisely: nor could Finny say whether the footsteps he had heard were a man's or a woman's. The dwarf was clearly tired by now. His hand smeared more frequently across his face; and his brain, such as it was, showed signs of becoming confused.

"I've only two more questions, Finny," said Blount, mopping his brow. "You've been very good. But, you know, some

142

of these things I've been asking you about—well, you could have told us before and saved us a lot of trouble. Why didn't you? Did someone tell you not to answer the police questions?"

Finny nodded, a last flicker of intelligence—or was it gratified self-importance?—in his eyes.

"Who was it?"

Finny pointed, without hesitation, to Janet Seaton.

"Oh, Finny!" she murmured, in a deeply wounded voice. "Oh Finny, how could you?"

"And my last question—who gave you the key of the vault and told you to stay hidden in the church?"

Finny's eyes went wild, staring in a sort of agony of inarticulateness at the side of the table where Robert, Janet and Lionel were sitting together. Foam appeared on his lips. Like a ventriloquist's dummy he folded up and fell off his chair.

CHAPTER TEN

MARA TORRANCE REMEMBERS

I CAN'T make out what everyone's playing at here," remarked Blount gloomily that afternoon, as he and Nigel sat down on the river bank near Hinton Lacey. "Young Seaton, for instance. He sticks to his story. Well, I ought to run him in, I suppose. But what'd be the use? It wouldn't solve the problem of this crime. He had the nerve to tell me he'd no objection to a spell in quod—couldn't be worse than the army, he said."

"We're getting old, Blount. We don't understand the younger generation."

"Do *you* think it was Lionel Seaton who hid Finny?"

"I doubt it. That's why Finny passed out this morning. He has a very primitive, very loyal mind. You handled him beautifully, by the way. But, you see, Robert Seaton had told him he must tell the truth: on the other hand, Finny had heard Lionel declare it was *he* who'd supplied the key and the food—your sergeant conveniently opened the door just when Lionel was making this confession."

"Damned fool, Bower!" muttered the superintendent.

"So a conflict of loyalties was set up in Finny's mind, and he passed out. Which suggests it was not Lionel who'd been hiding him."

"Well, why on earth should he say he was, then?"

"Protecting his father, I fancy. But the really fascinating question is, why should Finny have been allowed to survive at all?"

"A damned waste of our time! We might have had half the Oxfordshire police chasing after him for weeks if young Miss Seaton hadn't spotted him yesterday."

"That's just the point," said Nigel. "Someone is playing for time. Is it the murderer? If so, why not have killed Finny and put him in the vault? It'd serve the same purpose, and get rid of a damnably dangerous witness. If it was not the murderer, then what's he playing for time *for*—whoever hid Finny?"

"Search me."

"Time for repentance. Time for tea. Time, you old gypsy man. Time present and time past. Time for—"

"Oh do stop burbling! Why, what the devil's up with you now?"

"Oh, my good Lord!" muttered Nigel. "I believe I've got it."

"Got what?"

"The right time, so to speak. D'you ever listen to the B.B.C. programs at week ends, Blount?"

"Och, you're just havering. No, I do not."

"I bet all those highbrow yokels at the Lacey Arms do. You just ask them. And if I'm right," Nigel went on meditatively, "we may be in for another crop of Mysterious Occurrences at any moment."

"Uh-huh? Such as?—"

"Oh, I don't know. Disappearances. Kidnappings. Anonymous letters. Can't say. Just you wait and see though."

"And what am I supposed to do about them?"

"Take my tip, Blount, and ignore 'em. Don't let 'em rattle you."

"You're in a strangely freevolous state of mind today. I'll leave you to it. Must go and ring up Bristol."

A quarter of an hour later—he was still lying near the river bank—Nigel heard the puttering of an engine from downstream. Presently Vanessa's head, tawny and disembodied, could be observed gliding smoothly as if on rails above the level of the water meadows away to the right, where the river bent backward in a long loop. Then, round the bend, came a motor canoe, Vanessa sitting upright in the stern, Lionel and Mara lolling side by side on the cushions amidships. As they approached, Nigel sat up and waved. Vanessa spun the wheel at her side; the canoe careened over, making direct for Nigel. The girl tugged at a lever, the craft shuddered like a fever victim as the engine went into reverse, then rammed the bank at Nigel's feet with a violent impact.

"Well done, Fatty!" said Lionel.

"I miscalculated," replied Vanessa, picking herself up from the floor of the canoe. "Are our bows stove in? Prepare to man the pumps!"

"Prepare to hop out and walk home, Love," said Lionel. "Mara and I want to have a talk with your Mr. Strangeways. In private. Buzz off now, there's a good girl."

Reluctantly Vanessa climbed ashore. "They've been holding hands all the way up the river," she remarked treacherously to Nigel as she turned to go. "Soppy things. At their age, too."

Nigel moored the canoe and climbed down into it, noticing that Mara had altered her sprawling posture on the cushions for a more decorous one.

"Where did you get this beautiful canoe?" he asked.

"Just been lent it by some friends at Shelford—three miles that direction." Lionel jerked his thumb over his shoulder, pointing downstream. "No objection, I hope."

"Don't be an ass."

"It's the trouble about your being identified with the po-

146

lice now," said Lionel equably. "One tends to read a sinister meaning into every remark you make."

"Yes, I suppose so." Nigel sighed. A cloud, passing over the sun, turned the river's face from blue-gray to olive-green. The water lisped against the bank. Nigel found himself wishing that Mara would take off the sun glasses which hid her eyes: and, as though she had read his thoughts, she removed them that moment.

"Look here," she said, "what side *are* you on?"

"How many sides have you?"

"I'm serious."

"So am I. It's not just a question of Rex v. Plash Meadow and the Old Barn, you see. There are so many conflicting interests among you all. Among the suspects."

"Such as?" asked Lionel, his keen young eyes fastened intently upon Nigel's face, as though it were the pressure gauge of some powerful and dangerous engine.

"Well, take Mara. She is torn between love of *your* father and a rather dim sense of loyalty to her own. Her position is further complicated now by her feeling for you: she's obviously taken to you since she saw the lengths you'd go to in protecting your father—taken to you, I mean, in a big way, not just the old cat-and-mouse line—"

"*Well!* I *must* say!" Mara raised her hands in pleased consternation.

"And on top of that," Nigel pursued, "she's got her own worry. Suppose *she* killed Oswald?"

"We won't suppose that," Lionel said, with dangerous calmness.

Mara put her hand on his. "Yes, we will. Why should I kill Oswald?"

"You told us the motive at tea, that day in June. You said there was only one thing you'd murder for. Revenge."

As if he'd knocked the breath out of them both, they faced him, openmouthed and speechless. In the silence that fol-

147

lowed, the plop of a water rat diving startled like a depth charge.

"Revenge? But why on earth should Mara—?" said Lionel at last.

So you *don't* know about it, thought Nigel. Well, I won't be the one to tell you. He said lightly,

"Oh, Mara's always had it in for—she's the kind who must take it out of people. You should know," Nigel went on vaguely. "But, going back to your first question, if you put it like this—which of you all would I most hate to be hanged for the murder of Oswald?—I'll tell you straight away. Robert Seaton."

He noticed Lionel's tense form relaxing. "Well, that's something," the young man said. "Not that there was any danger, I suppose, of—" his voice trailed away.

"I'm afraid there is, though. Your father had a stronger motive than anyone, except your stepmother, for doing it. And—"

"But he was out for a walk. He wouldn't—"

"Wouldn't go for a walk if he'd been expecting Oswald? But he might have gone to meet him. He went out on the road to Chillingham. He'd forgotten that Oswald wouldn't know the short cut through the wood had been wired up. He'd expect him to come along the road."

The expression of misery was deepening upon Mara's face. Her white fists lay beside her like tear-soaked, crumpled handkerchiefs. Nigel went on,

"If the police find out where Oswald stayed when he reached England, at Bristol or wherever it was; if they find anything to connect him with Robert—a letter, say, from Robert inviting him to come along to Ferry Lacey, to come secretly—well, it'll be very awkward for Robert indeed. You can see that."

"But my father *didn't* meet him on the road," said Lionel. "So—"

148

"There's no *proof* that Oswald was murdered at Plash Meadow. No proof he ever reached it."

Mara Torrance put her right hand slowly into the water. The Thames was not boiling, but the gesture unaccountably reminded Nigel of a medieval ordeal. She said,

"It would help if—if someone had seen him, Oswald, at Plash Meadow that night?"

"It might. Depends." Nigel studied her averted face. "But perjury never helps, not in the long run," he added.

"Don't be a fool, Mara," exclaimed Lionel, with a suddenly hostile glance at Nigel. "You can't trust him."

"I can't trust anyone," she replied drearily. "You'd better leave me to talk to Strangeways, darling. Go along. I must talk to him alone."

"No. I think it's a mistake."

"Go away. *Please.* I'm asking you."

"Oh well, if I'm not wanted—" Lionel sounded, for once, very young. Sulkily, he began to get out of the canoe.

"One thing before you go," said Nigel. "I've been meaning to ask you for some days. You said you slept right through the thunderstorms that night. But the night Finny Black set on me, and I shouted for help, you said it woke you up, and you came running out of the house at once. The statements don't seem to correspond."

Hands on hips, Lionel Seaton gazed down from the bank. His face was hard. "I can only suggest," he said, "that thunder doesn't wake me up, and shouts for help do. Make what you like of it." He turned on his heel and strode off across the meadow.

"You don't think?—" began Mara.

"It may be the simple truth. He was a soldier."

A silence fell between them. Now they were alone, Mara seemed to find it difficult to begin. Nigel studied the lank black hair, that had a gloss on it now, the pasty-white face with dark smudges like bruises under the eyes, the violent red of her mouth.

"Are you in love with him?"

The girl came out of her abstraction. "That's not the point." She patted the cushions beside her, giving Nigel a bold, delinquent-child look. "Come and sit here. Oh, it's all right," she added impatiently, "I shan't seduce you. Why is everyone afraid of me? I can't talk to you while you're looking at me like a mental specialist across a desk."

Nigel moved over to her side. "That better?"

"Mm. Nice, kind Uncle Strangeways." As if involuntarily, she had crept closer to him. He could feel the whole length of her leg pressed against his. She began to talk very fast, looking away. "I suppose I am. In love with Lionel, I mean. I'd like to go to bed with him, of course. It seems about all I'm good for—to go to bed with people. But he wants me to marry him. And I daren't. I'm no good, you see, I'm hopeless. I wouldn't care, if it was just Lionel—I'd risk it. But—"

She dried up suddenly, like the brief shower that is a precursor to the deluge.

"But you're afraid of hurting Robert Seaton, through his son?" Nigel prompted.

She nodded dumbly, wrenching hard at Nigel's hand. From the deck of a passing river steamer, three lads whistled and catcalled.

"You see? It's taken for granted I'm a tart."

"That's absurd. They'd whistle at a Salvation Army lass with spectacles."

The waves from the steamer's wake lifted the canoe, jostling them together. Nigel felt her breast against his arm. She flinched away, as if something had scorched her.

"I don't know where to begin," she said, breathing hard.

"I should begin at the beginning," said Nigel gently. "With Oswald. That day in the Quantocks. When you were fifteen."

Mara's body had gone rigid beside him, as if gripped by

150

lockjaw. A lark sang its strident song interminably above the meadow. At last she muttered,

"So you knew?"

"I guessed. It was the most likely explanation. He—?"

"Oh yes, he raped me," she said bleakly. "Damn that lark. There was one singing when—"

"And you got ill. And Robert pulled you through it. And Oswald had to vanish. Well, it was all a long time ago. Hasn't the account been paid? On both sides?"

Mara gave him an oddly furtive look. "On both sides? You think I killed Oswald?"

"That's not what I meant. But never mind. So Robert got rid of Oswald, organized his 'suicide?'"

"Robert was—I can't describe how wonderful he was to me. He never put a foot wrong: I can see that now. Gentle and bracing, each at just the right time. Can you understand? It wasn't his fault that I'm—what I am. He stayed with me nearly the whole time. All day, for days after. And at nights—Janet was sleeping in my room—but I used to wake up screaming, I had awful nightmares, and Robert was always there in the next room to come in and soothe me down. Janet was no good. And my father—" She shrugged her shoulders with an ugly movement.

"They are the only people who know about it? Not Lionel?"

"I've never dared tell him."

"Which means you *are* in love with him. Well, I think you've been repressing all this far too long."

"Repressing? Oh, I don't believe all that Freud stuff—it's out of date," she said, with a return to her old, brittle manner.

"You don't quite understand me." Nigel, gazing at the fleecy clouds overhead, said very carefully, "Do you know why you're so unhappy? It's not because of what *happened* to you then. It's because you half-liked it."

"No! No! No! No!" The cries came out of her mouth like

blood pulsating from a severed artery. Her hand writhed in his, the nails drove into his palm.

"*Yes*," Nigel said firmly. "And why in heaven's name shouldn't you? Nothing unnatural about that. Nothing to be ashamed of. *Yes*."

"No," she whimpered. "No. No."

Nigel's voice went steadily, soothingly on. "That's why your head of Robert went wrong, and the figure in that bit of wood carving you did. You wanted it to be Robert. But Oswald came up out of your unconscious and pushed Robert aside, and took possession of your artist's hands, and made the clay head in his own image. It wouldn't have happened if you'd been altogether unwilling, if you'd altogether hated it—what Oswald did to you. It happened because part of you liked it, and the rest of you was terribly shocked and ashamed by it. Think, my dear. Remember back. Be absolutely honest with yourself. There was a lark singing. Remember? Don't be afraid of it. It's a bogey—a phantom of guilt you've kept battened down all these years. It's been poisoning your life, don't you see?"

"Yes," said Mara at last, after minutes of silence. Her voice was quite different. For the first time, Nigel dared to turn his head and look at her. Tears were streaming down her face, which was calm, drained, almost happy, as if she had been listening to great music. "Yes. You're right. It's quite true. I remember now."

"Listen," said Nigel urgently. "How did you get this conflict? Did anyone say, at the time, you were a wicked girl? Your father?"

"Oh no. It was kept from him. Till after Oswald had disappeared."

"You're sure of that?"

"Certain."

"Someone else, then?"

"Need I talk about it any more?" she asked childishly.

152

"Yes. Just this one thing, my dear."

Mara sobbed weakly for a moment or two. Then she said, "After it happened, I ran away from him. Back to the house. Janet was there. I didn't want to talk to her, but she took hold of me; she dragged it out of me. I was frightened—she looked so angry when I told her. She kept on asking questions. Horrible questions. Details. Yes, she somehow made it seem as if it had been my fault. She made me feel I'd done something abominable. I think I'd have gone mad there and then if Robert hadn't come in. He stopped her. He was kind to me, like you've been. . . . Oh, listen! The lark has stopped singing!"

"He's done his work for the day. And a very good day's work."

"With some help from Mr. Strangeways." Mara grinned at him: a simple, impudent grin—not a trace of the delinquent-child look any more. "Oh dear, I suppose I'm working up to a crashing transference—isn't that what you call it? You'd better watch out!"

"Good Lord, this hasn't been a course of deep psychoanalysis, my dear! You did it yourself. We just chose the right moment, and you had the courage to call out a ghost and stand up to it."

"Yes," she said after a long silence, "I do love Lionel. Perhaps it'll be all right now. I'm going to bathe." She stood up in the canoe, stripping off her dress. There was a bathing suit beneath it. "After all, it must happen to thousands of people—adequately sexed girls anyway." Standing there before him, the glow of the late afternoon sun mellowing her white skin, she had never looked so un-self-conscious, or so sexless. She climbed down into the water and swam away.

"Of course," murmured Nigel, wearily shutting his eyes. "And good-by to a promising sculptor, maybe."

Presently Mara clambered out on to the bank. She asked Nigel to hand her towel and dress up to her. When, dried

153

and clothed, she was back in the canoe, he asked what it was she had wanted to talk with him about privately.

She picked at a button of the velvet cushion. "It's all very difficult," she said irresolutely. "I'm not strong on filial feeling, but—" She took a deep breath and, turning her eyes away from Nigel, said, "Well, I think you ought to ask Rennell who he was talking to downstairs that night."

"The night Oswald was murdered?"

She nodded. "You said it might be important if someone else—if someone had seen him at Plash Meadow."

Gradually Nigel drew the facts from her. She had gone to bed at half-past eleven, leaving Rennell over a whisky bottle: he was well oiled, but not incapable. At about a quarter-past twelve, having been waked by the start of the thunderstorm, she heard voices from the studio below. All she could be sure of now was that they were men's voices and that one was her father's. They were speaking in low tones, not angrily. She assumed at the time that the other man was Robert Seaton. Afterward, when she knew Robert had been out walking, she thought the visitor must have been Lionel: but when she asked him, Lionel denied it. She had then asked her father, who laughed it off, saying he must have been talking to himself under the influence of drink. She had thought no more about it till the police investigation opened, several days later. The voices had stopped after five minutes, and she had thought she heard the French windows being opened and closed.

"Did they both go out?"

"No. Rennell didn't. At least, I presume he didn't. I heard someone moving about below, grunting a bit, like Rennell does, after the window was shut."

"But he didn't go up to bed then."

"No." Mara picked nervously at the button again. " wouldn't have told you this if there seemed any real chance of its getting him into trouble. I mean, if the visitor *was* Oswald, he certainly left the studio alive."

"But Finny Black saw your father standing *outside* the French windows at about two o'clock."

"Well, *I* didn't hear him go out. And I was awake till—till after Finny found the head in the dairy. Besides, why should Rennell want to murder him?"

Nigel raised his eyebrows.

"To avenge my honor?" Mara laughed harshly. "Oh dear me, you don't know him if you think that. Besides, he could avenge it just as effectively by handing Oswald over to the police."

"Why didn't he?"

Mara looked rather confused. "It all happened so long ago. Of course, Rennell blustered a lot at the time. When he'd been told. But—"

"But he was making a good thing out of it? Free board and lodging?" said Nigel, with deliberate hardness.

The girl grimaced. "I suppose so. But, don't you see? Even taking that view of it, now that Oswald had reappeared, it was to Rennell's interest to keep him alive."

"Putting it bluntly, he could extract the hush money from Oswald instead of Robert now? Assuming that Oswald would get back the estate?"

"Yes. Does it seem awful, talking about one's father like this? He's not a bad sort really—just weak and lazy. And not a genius. Honestly, I don't think he blackmailed Robert. It was just that Robert felt he must make restitution for his brother."

Nigel offered no comment on this. He was trying to work out the implications of Mara's story. It would have been possible for Oswald to have reached Plash Meadow by a quarter-past twelve that night, or a little before. But why should he go first to the old barn? Either because Rennell had made an appointment with him, or because somebody else at Plash Meadow had done so and failed to keep it, or because at the last moment Oswald funked going straight to the house and decided to try out his resurrection on Rennell first. There was a fourth possibility—that the murderer had instructed Oswald to go to the old barn, in order to implicate Rennell Torrance.

The first explanation seemed the simplest. But it implied that it was Rennell whom Oswald had apprised about his return to England. And there were obvious snags about this.

"Look here, Mara, you've got to do some more remembering."

"It's getting cold," she said. Her eyes rested on him with misgiving.

"It was about half an hour after you heard the voices downstairs that you saw Robert and Janet cross the courtyard?"

"No, a quarter, more likely."

"But it was quarter to one when—"

"Oh hell, I've got so confused about the time. I honestly thought it was half-past twelve striking when I saw them. But the superintendent said someone saw Robert walking through the village fifteen minutes later, so it must have been quarter to one."

"But it seemed more like quarter than half an hour between the two things?"

"Well, yes, I must say it does."

"I wish to God we could get this timetable definite. However, you saw them by a flash of lightning. You're certain it *was* Janet?"

"Of course."

"Think hard. How was she dressed?"

"She had on a mackintosh, and a dress underneath it."

"How do you know there was a dress underneath?"

"Why, I could see it. Quite a bit of skirt showing below the bottom of the mackintosh."

"And Robert? What was he wearing?"

Mara knitted her brows. "I couldn't see him very well, because he was on the far side of Janet, and he's smaller than she is. A dark suit, I think."

"Not a mackintosh."

"No. I remember now thinking she must have borrowed his. I saw his arm swinging. Sort of dark cloth look. But I couldn't swear to it."

"Did he have a hat on?"

"I didn't notice."

"Hmm." Nigel became lost in thought, his unseeing eyes fixed upon Mara Torrance. Presently she said,

"I'm still here. And I'm getting colder than ever."

"What? Oh, yes. You must go back. There's absolutely nothing else you can remember about that night? However trivial it may seem? No mysterious sounds, movements, will-o'-the-wisps? Nothing?"

"No. . . . Yes! How silly of me! It was such a familiar sight, though—it never occurred to me—Robert was carrying a storm lantern. Your 'will-o'-the-wisps' reminded me. In the blackness after the lightning flash it showed for a moment—a faint glow: then they went out of my sight."

"Toward the dairy?"

"No. They were visiting Kitty's loose box, don't you remember?"

"Of course. And you stayed at the window for some time after that?"

"Yes."

"But you didn't see the storm lantern again?"

"No. I—oh!" It was a little wail of dismay. Mara bit her knuckles, staring at him with affrighted eyes. "Finny said there was a storm lantern in the dairy, lit. But that needn't mean anything bad, need it?"

"You go back now, my dear," said Nigel gently. "You can work this canoe?"

"Aren't you coming?"

"Not yet. I must walk over to Hinton Lacey. Would you be an angel and tell them I'll not be in for supper?"

Nigel climbed out of the canoe, and untied the mooring rope. Mara was sitting motionless, gazing in front of her. When she spoke, it was not what Nigel expected.

"Ought I to tell Lionel?" she asked, childishly.

"About the storm lantern? Well—"

"No, no! Damn the lantern! *You* can chase after that will-o'-the-wisp, if you like. I mean, about Oswald and me."

"Yes. But not yet. You don't want him to marry you out of pity, or to get it into his head that he's to be a sort of male nurse from now on. Wait till you've got quite accustomed in your own mind to what you've discovered about the Oswald incident today. There's bound to be a pretty severe reaction. You can't deny the truth to yourself all these years and expect everything to be straightforward once you've admitted it."

Nigel had been making a noose with the free end of the painter. He tossed it neatly over Mara's head and shoulders, then gave the canoe a push with his foot. When the girl had disengaged herself and knelt down by the starting handle, she looked up at him.

"You'll make it all right about the storm lantern, won't you?" she said, trying to smile . . .

Twenty minutes later, Nigel was talking with superintendent Blount. He gave him a résumé of Mara's information.

"So that's how they got Oswald out of the country," said Blount. "Compounding a felony. Hah!"

"Not so much of your 'they,' Blount! If Miss Torrance has given me the facts correctly, her father wasn't told about Oswald's nasty deed till after he'd 'committed suicide.' I'm pretty sure now he was not involved in the conspiracy of Oswald's disappearance. He may have suspected some hanky-panky about it: but I don't believe he had evidence on which he could blackmail the Seatons."

"You may be right. But the Seatons are in it, up to the neck, anyway."

"I disagree. My bet is that Janet Seaton arranged the whole thing, singlehanded. And you're safe to tell your chap down there—Inspector Slingsby, isn't it?—to concentrate on her now."

"How d'you make that out?"

Nigel ticked the points off on his fingers. "First, Robert was a poor man and couldn't have had the necessary cash. Second, I believe he's an honorable man, and it would never have occurred to him to exploit Oswald's crime for his own benefit. Third, Oswald's 'suicide' would need a good deal of time, as well as money, to arrange. Now, from Mara's evidence, Robert was with her nearly all the time after the horrible thing happened, till Oswald disappeared. Janet was only with her at night. And Rennell Torrance told me that Janet had been pretty thick with Oswald those days—'ministering to him,' is how he put it. Putting the screws on him, I should call it. Fourth, it all fits in with what we know of Janet. She'd set her cap at Oswald and been rejected. Then she finds out what Oswald has done to Mara: salt in the wound, Blount. It's highly significant that she should have taken a violently censorious and nastily inquisitive line with the poor child that day. We won't labor the morbid psychology point—it's obvious. And, on top of that, she was a strong-minded, ambitious woman, with a monomania about her ancestral home. If Robert could come in for the property, *she* could get her hands on Robert, easy as pie. *And* she would. *And* she did. Q.E.D."

Blount vigorously massaged his bald head. "I've a mind to go down to Somerset tomorrow. I'll leave you and Bower to look after things here."

"Thank you very much."

"You'll not be up to any games?" said Blount, glancing at him severely. "That storm lantern, now. It looks bad."

"I presume you'd asked Robert Seaton how it came to be in the dairy?"

"He said he'd left it by the mare's loose box when they went out to look at her."

Nigel raised his eyebrows. "Well, perhaps he did. Somebody else may have used it later. The murderer. Or Oswald. Fingerprints?"

"It's been cleaned. Nothing suspicious about that, necessarily: Mrs. Seaton likes things kept kenspeckle. It's a queer thing about this case, incidentally, there being no fingerprints of the victim anywhere. Gates tried any number of likely surfaces early on, as you know. But—"

"It's all part and parcel of Oswald's caution. One keeps on forgetting that he was a criminal. He'd take damned good care not to touch anything, in case someone here ratted on him and he had to make a bolt for it again."

Superintendent Blount moved heavily across the room, sat down on the window seat and looked out at the evening sky. "There are times," he announced with a sigh, "when I find myself wondering if that laddie ever existed at all."

"Oswald?"

"Uh-huh."

"I know what you mean."

"A body. A head. And a dirty story. That's all he seems to amount to. If only we could trace his movements—fill in the picture a bit."

"You've not done badly, you know."

"It's the way, apart from the little matter of his head and body, he vanished without a trace. He gets out at a railway station, walks through a wood—and p'ff." Blount flicked his fingers.

"Good Lord!—One thing I quite forgot to tell you. Mara

heard her father talking to a strange man at a quarter-past twelve that night."

Before Blount could speak, the innkeeper put his nose through the door to say that the superintendent was wanted on the telephone. Two minutes later, he returned. He said,

"That was Rennell Torrance. He wishes to make a statement."

CHAPTER ELEVEN

LIONEL SEATON OVERHEARS

THE superintendent was not going to take Rennell Torrance's statement till next morning. "The reducing process" he called this. If Torrance was the guilty man, whether he intended to confess or to spin a yarn, the night's delay would get on his nerves: if not, the apparent negligence with which Blount had treated his message would be calculated to make him all the more forthcoming tomorrow, in an effort to impress the superintendent. Blount dispatched the long-suffering Sergeant Bower, however, to keep an eye on the old tithe barn during the night, just in case Torrance should change his mind and decide to make a run for it. He asked Nigel, on the general principle of keeping everyone on the jump, to let it be known at Plash Meadow, when he returned, that Torrance was making a statement next day.

"If any of 'em have a bad conscience, it'll stir 'em up," he said.

"Let's hope Bower stays awake then," remarked Nigel. "You'd look pretty silly if Torrance was liquidated tonight."

"I've every confidence in Sergeant Bower," said Blount, a little stiffly.

After he had left the superintendent, Nigel decided to look in on Paul Willingham. He found his friend sitting, elbow-deep in paper, at the parlor table.

162

"Homework," said Paul. "Give me ten minutes. There's some beer over there. And a bottle of Hollands, very expensive, very good for the liver."

Nigel poured himself a glass of Hollands, borrowed a sheet of paper and set to work on a timetable. He had already spent a lot of time trying to work out the movements of people on that Thursday night, but every timetable seemed to have more gaps and question marks than the last. However, with what he had heard from Finny Black and Mara today, a few gaps might be filled in.

Farmyard noises strayed agreeably through the open window as he worked. Presently Paul muttered,

"Now for P.A.Y.E. Then I'll be finished."

He flipped through the tax tables and set to working out the weekly deductions for his farm hands. When he had finished, he put down the Biro pen with which he had been making the entries, took out a checkbook and rummaged among the papers on the table.

"What are you looking for?" asked Nigel.

"My dip pen."

"Biro run out?"

"No, but I want to sign a check."

"I don't get you."

"Well," said Paul abstractedly, "I was going to sign a check with the old Biro at a travel agency last year, and the bloke asked me to use another pen. It was the agency's checkbook. He said the old Biro left an impression on the check below the one you're actually writing on; so a criminal type could come along and ink in your signature on the next check form and draw himself a few hundred or thousand smackers as the case might be. Ah, here it is! So, seeing as you're in the room, I thought I'd better be on the safe side."

"You make life very complicated for yourself."

Paul Willingham put check and deduction cards into an envelope and sealed it up.

"Well, how's your murder going?" he asked, pouring beer into his tankard.

Nigel gave him a brief synopsis, leaving out Mara Torrance's private affairs.

"What do you think?" he said at the end of it.

"Obviously the work of a gang," was Paul's cheerful comment.

Nigel buried his head in his hands and groaned.

"A gang of mysterious Orientals, I suppose?"

"No, no. I'm quite serious. I've been giving the matter some thought. It's like this, Nigel. Let's agree for the sake of argument, that Oswald was carved up in the dairy. Now, look what had to be done. First, he had to be got into the dairy: then his throat cut: then his clothes removed: then his head to be severed from his body: then a net bag provided to put the head in, with the idea of carrying it away and hiding it somewhere: then the body had to be wrapped up in his mackintosh, conveyed to the river and presumably towed some way downstream by a strong swimmer: then the bundle of clothes had to be hidden in the church vault, and the dairy sluiced down. Not necessarily in that order, of course. Have I left anything out?"

"I don't think so. You might have been there yourself."

"Plus a few oddments—going through the pockets of the clothes to see there was nothing incriminating in them; cleaning the tools and putting 'em back, or hiding 'em. All took time, old man. More time than any one person could afford. Besides, who kept *cave*? Can you see anyone going through all those motions, even at night, even if he'd planned every detail beforehand, without another chap to keep watch? The risk'd be appalling. That's why I say it was a gang."

"Yes, the thought of two people being involved had occurred to me."

"And then," said Paul, warming to his work, "have you considered the significance of the blood trail?"

"But there wasn't a blood trail."

"That's what is so significant, old boy. I don't believe one man could cart a recently decapitated corpse from the dairy to the river without leaving blood spots, even granted that the top of the mac was well buttoned over the neck."

"The rain might have washed the blood spots away, you know. And anyway, the corpse wouldn't have been bleeding any more by then. But I agree, it'd have been much simpler if there had been two people to carry the body."

"Good-oh! I'm glad you've come round to my way of thinking."

"But *what* two people?" asked Nigel, a worried look on his face. "There aren't many possible permutations and combinations at Plash Meadow. I can't conceive any two of them planning such an elaborate affair. Robert and Janet? Lionel and Mara? Rennell and Robert? Lionel and Janet? Mara and Rennell? And so on. Take your pick: but none of the possible partnerships makes sense to me."

"You're obsessed by the number two, old boy," said Paul, waving his pipestem airily at Nigel. "Why shouldn't the whole lot of them have organized it? This Oswald was a menace to 'em all, in various degrees, wasn't he?"

Nigel nodded.

"Well then? The whole squadron was laid on for Operation Oswald. And a very good job they seem to have made of it—or would have, if Finny hadn't gone skirmishing out into the middle of it. And very sorry I'd be to see any of 'em taken up for the job."

"No, no, Paul. Don't let's make the thing more fantastic than we need. People don't commit murder in a shoal. Other crimes, yes. But not murder."

"I expect you're right," said Paul, a faraway look in his eyes. "But isn't murder always unreal? You remember Robert

165

talking about the flash point, that day we went to tea? Well, either you've planned your murder in fantasy, brooded over every detail beforehand, thought of your alibi and so on, or else it's unpremeditated—a moment of madness. But, in a way, they're both the same. There can't be degrees of murder, because there's no such thing as a cold-blooded murderer. There's only a different flash point. The chap who plans a murder never really means to commit it. Generally he never gets further than the planning: there must be thousands of murders committed in fantasy every year. But just now and then the point is reached where the fantasies take charge and push the bloke over the edge. What I say is, this bloke is no more responsible for his action than if he'd struck down a total stranger in a moment of blind rage."

"I don't agree with you. But it's very interesting."

"That's why I say all murder is unreal. Or put it like this—every murder is a case of possession: instantaneous or gradual doesn't matter. The murderer is possessed by something not himself—by a stranger within—which compels him to do violence to himself no less than he does it to his victim. And afterward—do you know, I can imagine myself having murdered someone and a year later genuinely not being sure whether it was a dream or a reality. Once the wound caused to myself by the self-violence had healed over—and nature'd do that quickly enough—I'd go about my affairs as innocently as any other citizen."

Nigel was pondering Paul Willingham's words as he walked back to Ferry Lacey. He had had supper at the farm and arranged that Paul should invite Vanessa Seaton to stay there if affairs at Plash Meadow took the ugly turn which Nigel feared. Paul had been talking through his hat, of course, he reflected now. But he had indirectly put his finger, once again, on a crucial point.

Premeditation or not? Assume that Oswald Seaton's murder was premeditated. What follows? First, the killer must know some little time before that Oswald is alive and back in England. Second, if the killer knows about the Oswald-Mara affair, he can be sure that Oswald will conceal his own identity out of self-protection. Now the only people at Plash Meadow who did not know about that affair were Finny Black, Vanessa and perhaps Lionel. Vanessa could be eliminated: Finny would be mentally incapable of planning a murder: Lionel would have no motive for it *unless* he had discovered the Oswald-Mara secret. Thirdly, a killer acquainted with this secret would have, so to speak, the ideal victim—a man believed to be dead years ago, a man who dare not reveal his own identity. Then *why*, it struck Nigel now with irresistible force, *why murder him at Plash Meadow*, the one place in the world where there would be a danger of the "body of an unknown man" being associated with the Oswald Seaton of ten years ago? It seemed to follow, with the most unassailable logic, that because Oswald was murdered at Plash Meadow, his murder could not have been premeditated.

At once the whole complicated and unsatisfactory mosaic of the case showed a different pattern to Nigel. A premeditated crime had been unthinkable, unless motivated by the desire either for security or for revenge on the murderer's part. But an unpremeditated one opened up new possibilities —a sudden quarrel, for instance, or an accident; or even, it strangely occurred to Nigel, sheer fright—the shock of seeing, on that lurid, storming night, one whom the killer might have every reason for believing a ghost . . .

At ten o'clock the next morning, Nigel strolled across to the old barn. He had waked early, to find a certain phrase ringing in his head almost as if it had just been spoken into his sleeping ear. "We all had Oswald on our minds just then." Rennell Torrance had given this as an explanation for the horror he had shown when confronted by Mara's clay head of Robert. As Nigel had pointed out, much to Rennell's discomfiture, this statement did not make sense, because it had not been known at the time, except presumably to the murderer, that the murdered man was Oswald. Now, if it turned out that Rennell had seen Oswald on the fatal night, his alarm at the likeness of the portrait head would be explained. But, "we all had Oswald on our minds just then"— was that "all" merely a defensive turn of phrase? or could it by any chance be the truth, supporting Paul Willingham's absurd suggestion that everyone at Plash Meadow had been in a conspiracy to remove Oswald?

No, thought Nigel, this won't do: I convinced myself last night that Oswald's murder was unpremeditated. Well the *murder* might have been, but the elaborate effort to conceal it could still have been a communal one. Lack of premeditation does not imply that there was no conspiracy. How many of them, then, were accomplices after the fact? It must have been pretty soon after the fact, too. "Oh bosh, it's fantastic," he muttered to himself, remembering the pleasant family breakfast he had taken only an hour ago—Lionel and Vanessa mildly chaffing each other; Janet Seaton discussing plans for the day, for a picnic up the river; her husband, at the head of the table, smiling at his children, talking to Nigel about Paul Willingham, then leaving his coffee half finished to slip upstairs and resume work on the poem which impatiently awaited him. None of them seemed apprehensive, or even curious, about the statement which, as Nigel had told them the previous night, Rennell Torrance was to make this morning. Their only worry appeared to be the weather, which was clouding over and threatening the projected picnic. As Nigel entered the old barn, a few drops of rain began to fall.

Superintendent Blount was already there, with one of Inspector Gates' men who had come to relieve Sergeant Bower. Blount had cleared a space on one of the littered tables in the studio. Rennell Torrance, slumped in a basket chair, pointedly ignored Nigel as he entered. The sound of a vacuum cleaner could be heard from upstairs, Rennell's flamboyant and shoddy canvases blushed hotly on the walls, relics of a misspent life.

"We'd better begin," said Blount, and administered the official caution.

It was like a major operation, thought Nigel, so masked and impersonal was Blount's method, so tense the atmosphere, so like an anesthetized patient's the flaccid, dead-white face of Rennell Torrance. A surgical operation to extract a piece of truth which had been poisoning the patient's system. "On the night of Thursday the ——" The "statement" proceeded, question and answer, question and answer, with infuriating deliberateness.

Rennell Torrance had been sitting up late that night, Mara having gone to bed. About ten minutes after midnight he heard a light tap at the French windows: they were not locked: they opened and a man came in. For a moment he did not recognize him—Rennell admitted he'd been a bit fuddled with drink, and besides, he'd never seen Oswald Seaton without a beard before. No, he'd not been expecting Oswald: why, damn it, how could he, when to the best of everyone's knowledge, Oswald had been dead these ten years? No, he had not been in communication with him. You could have knocked him down with a feather when Oswald had appeared.

"Yes, it's me," were Oswald's first words. "Back from the dead. Quite a nuisance for everyone, I reckon. What about a drink? I've had a long walk."

"Help yourself. But where the devil did you spring from?"

Rennell noticed that Oswald did not take off his gloves as he poured out the drink.

"As you know very well, I did not commit suicide," Oswald had proceeded. "I knocked around the world a bit, changed

169

my name, was working in Malaya when the Japs came in. Prison camp for three years. I'm not all that afraid of prison now, Torrance. I suggest you and I let bygones be bygones. You won't find me less charitable than my dear brother. I'll rely on you to keep—what's her name?—Mara quiet."

Nigel noticed that by an eerie coincidence, the sound of the vacuum cleaner overhead stopped at this instant. Gazing through the French windows, he saw that the rain had begun in earnest: Janet Seaton, in a long dark-blue mackintosh, was walking down the drive away from the house. Nigel turned his eyes back to Rennell Torrance.

"I realized," he was saying, "that Oswald was convinced I'd known all along his suicide was phony, and believed I'd been blackmailing Robert ever since."

"Was there any truth in that?" asked Blount.

"Good Lord no. Ask Robert if you don't believe me. Mara told me last night she'd talked about Oswald to Strangeways. So you know why he left the country."

"What happened next?"

"I told him he'd a bloody nerve to come in here, and he'd better get out double-quick before I gave him the soundest thrashing of his life. I said he'd ruined my daughter's life and I'd a good mind to hand him over to the police straight away."

"Why didn't you?"

"Well, I didn't like the way he put his right hand in his mackintosh pocket at that point. I was afraid he had a gun in it." The painter's heavy body shifted uneasily.

"Did he actually threaten you?"

"No. Not exactly. But—"

"But he pointed out, perhaps," Nigel put in, "that his return—even if you did inform the police about what had happened to Mara—would kill the goose that laid your golden eggs? Robert would lose the estate."

"Well, he hinted something of the sort," muttered Rennell at last, with very bad grace.

It dawned upon Nigel that Oswald had come first to the old barn in order to have a witness of his existence. He might also have hoped to strike a bargain with Rennell Torrance: but the main point of his visit was that he should be able to say in effect, if he ran into bad trouble later at Plash Meadow, "Keep your hands off me, don't think you've got the perfect victim for a murder, somebody else knows I was here, alive, at a quarter-past twelve tonight." He had preferred the risk of being exposed by Rennell, whom he obviously despised, to the risk he might incur from—from whom? Who was the X. at Plash Meadow that this dangerous and desperate man so feared? Or was it just in Oswald's nature to mistrust everyone?

"Did he suggest to you why he'd come back to England at all?" Blount was asking. "Did he say who'd invited him?"

"No, but he seemed cocky enough. I couldn't make it out. As though he were sitting pretty, somehow."

"What gave you that impression?"

"Well, after I'd ordered him out, he said 'O.K. But I'll be seeing a lot of you from now on, if things go right.' Then he paused a moment, and then he said, 'Robert always was a bit soft: he'll be glad to see me, even if you aren't. Blood's thicker than water.'"

Superintendent Blount now took Torrance back over the ground, trying to discover fragments of information he had overlooked. But the result seemed entirely negative. Oswald had said nothing more to Torrance about where he'd come from, or why he'd returned to England when he did. The painter had obviously been three-quarters crocked, what with drink and fright; and Oswald had only stayed in the studio, he reckoned, seven to ten minutes.

As Blount plugged away, Nigel's attention wandered again. Framed in the French windows, the west corner of

Plash Meadow looked—there was only the French word for it—*morne*. The slanting rain, the tattered clouds drifting low overhead, the wind nagging at leaves and roses: summer was going, the garden wept inconsolably. The fairy-tale house, so unreal when first he had seen it, was still less real today: then it had been the fabulous exuberance of its roses, the trance of high summer; now it was as if Plash Meadow, having drunk too deep of horrors, suffered from a blighting hangover.

Abruptly Nigel checked his thoughts. Ridiculous. That damned house seemed able to impose its moods upon one. But the real truth of the matter was that, like the poet working away now under its roof, it had the knack of intensifying, of illuminating whatever mood one happened to be in, of adapting itself to each different personality. Which of its Protean selves had it offered to Oswald Seaton that night, Nigel wondered. But Oswald himself was still a hopelessly unreal figure; nor did Rennell Torrance's statement help in the least to bring him alive. It was likely enough that Rennell was telling the truth now: but the truth was not enough— not his kind of truth, anyway, thought Nigel, scrutinizing the painter's flabby, defeated face, the body slumped in the chair like a sack from which all meaning had leaked out long ago.

Something was fidgeting at Nigel's mind, like the wind teasing the tarnished roses outside. Through the web of question-and-answer, question-and-answer that Blount and Torrance were interminably spinning, Nigel became aware of a silence. Somewhere in the background, like an attentive eavesdropper holding his breath, stood this silence. Well, of course, the vacuum cleaner stopped some time ago. But surely Mara had not finished her housework then? Surely one ought to be able to hear her moving about overhead? Or, if she has finished upstairs, why has she not come down? —there is only this one staircase, leading down from the

172

minstrel gallery. Well, thought Nigel, she's probably up there, listening to what we're saying: no great harm in that.

"So then he left this room," Blount prompted. "Did you see him out?"

"Not exactly. I didn't like to go too near him. But, when he'd stepped outside, I went to the French window. I shut it behind him and stayed looking out for a few moments."

"Did you see where he went?"

"He must have walked over to the house. At least, I saw him once again. There was a long shake of sheet lightning, and I noticed him quite near the courtyard door over there."

"Did you see who let him in?"

"No. But I assumed he must have got into the house somehow, because when the next flash of lightning came, he wasn't visible any more."

" 'Not visible any more,' " muttered the constable who was taking it all down.

"Very well. What did you do then?" asked Blount, keeping his stride like a tireless runner. Rennell Torrance mopped his forehead: his head rolled wearily and jerked upright again, as if he'd been on the verge of sleep.

"I locked the windows, sat down again, had some more drink. Felt I couldn't go to bed yet. I was uneasy. I wanted to puzzle things out. To tell you the truth," he went on in a sleepwalking kind of voice, "I began to wonder after a bit if I hadn't dreamed it all. I simply couldn't get used to the idea of Oswald being alive."

"And then?"

"Well, after a bit I went to bed," Torrance replied lamely.

"How do you account, then, for Finny Black's statement that he saw you standing outside the French windows at—" Blount deliberately thumbed through a sheaf of papers "—at about two o'clock?"

Torrance seemed too exhausted even for a spurt of righteous indignation. Wearily he said,

173

"I went to bed *after* that. I just wanted a breath of fresh air. That's all."

"Did you go for a walk?"

"No. I stood outside the window for a few minutes. I told you all this last time."

"Just so. But you didn't tell me last time I questioned you that Oswald Seaton had paid you a visit." There was a slight edge on Blount's voice. "Have you—e'eh—remembered anything else since? Anything you forgot to tell me then?"

"No."

It was the first time that Nigel got the impression Rennell was keeping something back. His denial came too pat—a trace of defiance in it. The same idea must have occurred to Blount, for he treated Rennell to a prolonged, steady stare and a silence that positively bristled with incredulity. As he waited for this treatment to take effect upon the painter, Nigel, lying back in his chair, idly cast his eyes upward.

He was sitting just below the edge of the gallery. His eye caught a dark metal object protruding from between two of the banisters which supported the rail of the gallery, at its far end. It took Nigel three full seconds to realize that this object was the muzzle of a revolver. During that space, Rennell Torrance burst out in weak exasperation, "What d'you want me to say?"—and the muzzle up there tilted down so that it seemed to be pointing at the back of the painter's head.

"I just want you to tell the truth. Did you not see anyone moving about as you stood outside the French windows? Did you see Mr. and Mrs. Seaton, for instance, searching for Finny Black?"

"Well, as you ask me—"

"Stop!"

"Stop!"

Fantastically, Nigel's warning shout was echoed by a fierce command from the gallery above. Superintendent

174

Blount was on his feet. Nigel sprang into the middle of the studio, and stood between Rennell Torrance and the long-barreled Mauser pistol which Lionel Seaton, lying flat on the gallery floor, his face visible between the bars, was sighting at the group below.

"Don't be a young fool!" said Blount sharply. "Put that gun down at once!"

Lionel Seaton ignored him. "I'm talking to you, Torrance. You've said enough. D'you understand me? Quite enough. I've been listening. If you say a word more, now or at any time, I'll come back and knock you off."

Involuntarily Nigel had moved a little away from Rennell's chair. The painter, gray faced and shaking, had screwed his head round when Lionel began to speak: now he had slid off the chair and was groveling behind it. Lionel Seaton's eyes blazed at him from between the bars. He spoke again,

"You see that bloody awful picture over there?"

Four pairs of eyes switched in the direction pointed by a wave of the Mauser in Lionel's hand—a self-portrait by Rennell Torrance, hanging on the wall to the left of the French windows.

"Now look, Torrance. This is what will happen to you if—"

There was a stunning explosion. Lionel Seaton had hardly seemed to take aim at all; but a black hole appeared in the dead center of the greenish-white forehead of the self-portrait. Rennell Torrance whimpered.

"Now!" exclaimed Blount, and dashed heroically for the foot of the staircase, followed by the constable. Nigel, hard on their heels, suddenly checked himself. Whipping round, he saw Mara Torrance at the French windows. Before he could get there, she had opened them, withdrawn the key and locked them from outside. Nigel ran out of the studio, catching a glimpse as he went of Blount falling over a heavy chair which Lionel had bowled down the staircase at him.

The front door of the old barn had been locked from the outside too. The pair had planned it pretty well. Mara had, no doubt, climbed out of her bedroom window down a ladder, locked the front door, then waited for Lionel's signal—the revolver shot—to lock the French windows while the attention of those in the studio was concentrated on Lionel.

"Silly young asses!" muttered Nigel as he went upstairs. "Are there any duplicate keys?" he called to Rennell over his shoulder.

"No. Afraid not. Look here, what on earth is Mara up to? You've got to stop her."

Upstairs, Blount and the constable charged Mara's door. The lock splintered and they tumbled into the bedroom. The window was open. A ladder lay on the ground below. Lionel could hardly have had time to climb down it. He must have jumped, and then pulled the ladder away from beneath. But Lionel had been trained to this sort of thing as an officer in the Airborne Forces: neither Blount nor the constable could risk a twenty-foot jump.

They ran out, colliding with Nigel in the doorway. As they got to the French windows, a car whirled past down the drive. Lionel Seaton waved gaily. Mara Torrance was beside him. By the time Blount had borrowed a chisel and forced the lock of the French windows, they were well away.

"They won't get far," said Blount grimly. "I'm going across to telephone. Wait here for me."

Five minutes later, he was back. "Now then, Mr. Torrance," he said, "we'll go on from the point where we were —e'eh—interrupted." He cocked an eye at the constable, who turned to his notebook and unemotionally recited.

" 'Did you see Mr. and Mrs. Seaton, for instance, searching for Finny Black?' . . . 'Well, as you ask me—' "

In the interval, Rennell Torrance had put down a couple of strong whiskies, and his nerve was somewhat restored. He began to bluster.

176

"Look here, Superintendent, this is outrageous! I'm threatened by a young lunatic with a pistol; my daughter runs away; and the best you can do is to—"

"One thing at a time, Mr. Torrance. You were about to tell us that you saw suspicious movements at two o'clock that morning, weren't you?"

A look of bleary cunning came over the painter's face.

"You're trying to catch me out, eh? Don't care for your methods. It was at *one* o'clock, wasn't it, that Robert and Janet went out to look for Finny? So how could I have seen them at two o'clock?"

"Whom did you see then?"

Rennell's eye wandered to the self-portrait on the wall, with the hole in its forehead.

"I didn't see anyone. I can't see in the dark, you know. The lightning had stopped by then."

"You should take no account of Lionel Seaton's threats. If it proves necessary, we shall give you protection." Blount loomed formidably over the painter. "And I must warn you that you're already in a very awkward position for having withheld this evidence about Oswald Seaton. I should strongly recommend you to conceal nothing more."

"But I'm *not* concealing anything," Rennell answered in the tones of a pettish child. "I was going to tell you, when we were interrupted, that I *heard* something. I heard footsteps crossing the courtyard away to my left, from the direction of the orchard; then I heard the door of the servants' quarters open and shut. Presumably it was Finny Black I heard."

Rennell Torrance stuck on this, and nothing Blount could do would shift him. Nigel found it impossible to decide whether he had told the truth or not.

Presently Nigel and Blount were chatting in the shelter of the summerhouse.

"I'd like to know what that young fool is playing at," the superintendent growled. "He's scared the daylights out of Torrance, anyway, blast him!"

"What are your ideas?"

"Well, I suppose he silenced Torrance at that point either to protect himself or somebody else. And the exhibitionistic way he chose to do it could only draw suspicion on him. No I fancy he thought Torrance was just going to let out something about Mr. and Mrs. Seaton. Maybe he was, too."

"There's a third possibility. All that play acting—if Lionel wanted Torrance to keep his mouth shut, he could surely have found an opportunity to threaten him, on the quiet, last night or early this morning. What I think is that he's playing for time: he wants to divert your mind from—"

"Damn it!" exploded Blount. "Is this what you were hinting at yesterday afternoon? 'Another crop of mysterious occurrences'? Nothing mysterious about those two holding us up with a pistol. Time for what, anyway?"

"Time for verse, Blount."

"Now look here, Strangeways, this case is crazy enough already without your—"

"I'm quite serious. The most important thing in this household is Robert Seaton's poetry. Recently he has begun writing something which, for all we know, may be his masterpiece. We've got to think in terms of values utterly different from the normal man's, while we're dealing with this case. The Seatons—and Mara too, I believe—are people for whom art is infinitely more important than any police investigation. More real, if you like. For Robert's poetry, they will go to any lengths and be prepared to sacrifice anything."

"You're not telling me Oswald Seaton was murdered for the sake of his brother's poetry? I can't swallow that."

"It's not impossible. But my point is this: young Lionel may or may not have reason to suspect that his father was involved in the murder; but he knows that, sooner or later

178

there'll be a showdown, and he wants to postpone it as long as possible, so that his father may finish the work he's engaged on. So Lionel stages this diversion in force. He wants you to waste time and suspicion on him. That's why he told us it was he who'd hidden Finny Black in the vault and kept him supplied with food."

"All I can say is, if you seriously believe that, you'd believe anything. People don't behave like that in real life. Why, it'd be the vairy lunacy of quixotism!"

"The young are quixotic, sometimes, to the point of lunacy. And it's not pure quixotism on Lionel's part. Mara's whole attitude toward him changed when she began to suspect he was putting himself in danger on Robert's behalf: and she'd do anything for Robert herself. Incidentally, Blount, if you want to find them quickly, I suggest you warn all Registry Offices." Nigel's eyes strayed over the entrancing lines of Plash Meadow. "You talk of real life, Blount. Look at that house. Don't you wonder sometimes if it won't vanish, like a dream, between one moment and the next?"

"No," said Blount. "Frankly, the notion has never occurred to me. But I'll bear your other suggestions in mind."

"Hurrah for bonny Scotland!"

Blount's mouth twitched with faint amusement. "Will you hold the fort here? You'll have to tell Mr. Seaton about his son. I must away to Redcote to see Gates. Then I may go down to Bristol for a night. I'll be leaving Bower here."

"So you're *not* going to chase Lionel and Mara all over the countryside in a fast car?"

"Och, there'll be no trouble pulling them in," said the superintendent—a prediction which was to prove curiously wide of the mark.

CHAPTER TWELVE

NIGEL STRANGEWAYS INQUIRES

IT WAS typical of what Plash Meadow stood for, thought Nigel as he walked upstairs toward Robert Seaton's study, that he should feel a strong reluctance to interrupt the poet's meditations with the mere announcement that his son was a fugitive from justice. However, he tapped on the door and marched bravely in. At his desk, Robert Seaton was bending over one of the little black notebooks, in a pose so rigid, so attentive that Nigel almost expected to see some jeweled flower or insect come fabulously burrowing up out of the blank page before his eyes. The poet sat for a minute or two, as if hypnotized by the white sheet: then he wrote a few words, paused, altered one, altered it again, turned back to the previous page and crossed something out; then sat back with a sigh.

"I'm terribly sorry to break in like this," said Nigel, "but something has happened."

Robert Seaton's eyes encountered him at last. They seemed to have some difficulty in focusing him. Nigel got the impression of a gaze which had been embracing vistas infinitely far above and beyond him, now essaying to pinpoint a tiny object somewhere in the vast panorama. Words of an old jazz song came absurdly into his head: "You can't see a fly upon a mountain, The distance interferes with the view."

"My dear chap, come in, sit down," said Robert warmly. "I must apologize for being so inattentive. What were you saying? Something happened?"

Nigel told him. The poet sat there, a worried frown upon his face, raising his eyebrows when Nigel came to the bullet hole in Rennell's self-portrait.

"Oh dear me," said Robert at last. "He shouldn't have done that." The intonation was precisely that of a person gracefully accepting a too-expensive present. He ruminated for a few moments. "Have you told my wife?"

"She went down the village. I'll tell her when she comes back. Unless you'd rather."

"Please do. Very good of you. . . . Well, I'll be jiggered! And Mara too? I say, d'you think those two are going to hit it off now?" The poet gleefully rubbed his hands, then clasped them again on the desk.

"I shouldn't be surprised. If a spell in quod doesn't cool them off."

"Oh poof! A boyish escapade. Surely—I say, Strangeways, it's not going to put any foolish ideas into your superintendent's head, I hope?"

Nigel was accustomed by now to the Plash Meadow style of reference, as though Blount were some large dog over which Nigel had only imperfect control.

"Even Blount's patience is not unlimited," he replied. "And he can't just ignore it when Lionel terrorizes a witness at the crucial point of his evidence."

"No, I suppose not. But your superintendent's an intelligent man. He must realize that no murderer would behave like that," said Robert Seaton with admirable good sense.

"Blount would tell you, from long experience, that it's quite impossible to predicate anything about the ways of murderers."

" 'Predicate.' Good. How refreshing it is to have someone in the house with a wide vocabulary. D'you know, Strangeways, I read the Oxford dictionary every day. The only book a poet really requires."

"Still going well, is it?" asked Nigel, with a glance at the open notebook.

"Pretty well, thanks."

"How much longer will it take?"

The poet gave him an odd look, half-questioning, half of complicity. "Ah yes, that's the point, isn't it? It's turned into a sequence, and there never seems any reason why a sequence should stop—" he grinned delightfully "—though there's every reason why some sequences should never have been started. Yes. Tell you the truth, I've never written so fast in my life. Extraordinary." He peered dubiously at the notebook. "But it seems all right. . . . How much longer, you asked? Well, how much longer have I?"

Nigel found his breath quite taken away by this last remark. He positively gaped at Robert Seaton, whose eyes were fixed upon him now with an expression of singular sagacity.

"What I mean is, sooner or later something'll have to be done about poor Oswald's death, won't it?"

Nigel swallowed convulsively, and suggested that quite a lot was already being done in this matter.

"Yes, yes, of course. But even if it turns out that none of us here is implicated in the murder, there's still going to be a shocking schlemazel, I'm afraid, about his original disappearance—you know, when he was supposed to have drowned himself. I don't know what the position will be about this property. But, once all that has blown up, I can't see myself writing any more for a long, long time. It'll be very hard on poor Janet if we have to leave."

Nigel gave it up. "You wouldn't read me some, would you?" he asked.

"Why not?" Robert Seaton opened a drawer. "Here's my

fair copy. Mm. This passage, perhaps. Yes, I think you'll like this. . . ."

After the poet had stopped reading, Nigel sat in silence for a little, the tears drying on his cheeks.

"Good? My word, it is! It's—it's worth everything."

It was good. It was the tongue of men and of angels.

Nigel went away to his own room, where he sat for quarter of an hour, seeing nothing, Robert Seaton's angelic verse still ringing in his head. "Glory be!" he muttered at last; then, sighing, took out the timetable he had worked on at Paul's last night, made a couple more entries in it, and pored over the result.

1. 10:58	Train from Bristol arrived Chillingham	Stationmaster
2. 11:15	Oswald seen by drunk on road 1 m. from Chillingham	Drunk
3. "Not long before midnight"	Oswald seen by Jack Whitford in Foxhole Wood	J. Whitford
4. "Soon after midnight"	Thunder*storm* begins. Janet goes to Finny's room; finds him asleep.	Mara *et al.* / Janet
5. 12:10	Oswald turns up at old barn	Rennell/Mara
6. 12:20	Oswald walks across to Plash Meadow	Rennell
7. 12:30 (?) 12:30	Thunder*shower* begins Janet and Robert cross courtyard	Mara/Gardener Mara/Janet and Robert
But 12:45 approx.	Expectant father sees Robert walk down road	Expectant father

8. 12:55	Robert and Janet seen crossing courtyard again "after thundershower."	} Vanessa
9. About 1:00	Second thunderstorm	Gardener
(?) 1:00	Half hour after Robert's return; Janet finds Finny is missing: she and R. search for him.	} Janet and Robert
10. 1:05-1:20	A heavier thundershower begins. R. and J. go in again	} Gardener R. and J.
11. About 1:20	Second thundershower ends	} Gardener
12. 2:00 approx.	Finny turns up "drenched to skin."	} Janet
	He has just seen Rennell outside French windows	} Finny

The old problem remained—what time did Robert Seaton get back from his walk? Nigel stared at the contradictions, so sharply posed by his timetable. Mara had at first been sure it was 12:30 when she'd seen Robert and Janet cross the courtyard: they had confirmed this time themselves. On the other hand, the evidence of the expectant father put Robert's return at 12:45; and Mara admitted she might have been wrong about the quarter the clock had just struck. Then again, there was the discrepancy between items eight and nine. Vanessa had looked at her watch when she'd seen her father and mother outside, and it was 12:55. According to *their* evidence, they had gone out to look for Finny about half an hour after Robert's return: if he had not returned till 12:45, this would put their search at 1:15, and there was

184

surely too great a discrepancy between this and Vanessa's 12:55. But, if Robert had returned at 12:30 you only needed to make his "about half an hour" into twenty-five minutes, and the time of the search for Finny fitted with Vanessa's evidence; also, Mara's first statement would be vindicated.

The weight of evidence seemed to be on the side of Robert's having returned at 12:30. Yet Nigel was not entirely satisfied. Since there was no knowing when Oswald had been killed, it is true a quarter of an hour one way or the other seemed to make no difference. But Nigel couldn't rid his mind of the statement made by the expectant father, for this witness was the only disinterested one—Robert, Janet and Mara *might* have a reason for falsifying the time of Robert's return. Well, then, said Nigel to himself, let us take the hypothesis that Robert did not get back till 12:45—what conceivable reason could he have for asserting that it had been 12:30? And Janet and Mara for backing him up?

Nigel racked his brains, but in vain, for a good ten minutes. Then he turned back to the other problem raised by his timetable. What time had it been when Finny Black found the head in the dairy, hid it in the chestnut tree and soon after heard footsteps coming up from the river? Oswald was still alive at 12:30. Supposing even that he'd been killed the next minute, after entering the house—but no, that wouldn't do, Gates and Blount were certain he had not been murdered there. Well then, he had to be persuaded into the dairy, his throat cut, his clothes and head removed, his body taken down to the river. It did not seem possible that all this could be done in much less than half an hour. Say, then, 12:50 as the earliest Finny could have found head, bundle of clothes, but no body in the dairy. All he himself could say was that there had been thunder and lightning, but no rain, at the time; and it seemed reasonable to assume that the footsteps he had heard were those of the murderer returning from putting the body in the river. The first thundershower had begun at 12:30 and was over before 12:55, when Vanessa had noticed the glass gleaming wet "after a shower." The second thunder*storm* had begun about one o'clock and five to ten minutes later a heavier thundershower had followed. It looked, then, as if Finny had made his discovery somewhere between one o'clock and ten after one. But in that case it was perfectly possible that the footsteps he heard might be those of Robert and Janet searching for him.

Finny Black's evidence was, in fact, perfectly useless. But, according to Janet, he had returned about two o'clock "drenched to the skin." On the theory that the murder was unpremeditated—an act of sheer fright, perhaps—might not Finny have done it after all? Might he not have been drenched to the skin because he had been towing the body out into the river? No, that wouldn't do: Lionel Seaton had categorically stated that Finny couldn't swim. Of course, he might have been lying. But why? It could easily be verified, anyway.

Nigel's eye wandered despondently to the window, where beads of rain were sliding down. And at that moment, all unprompted, an answer to his first question came. At first sight, it was an answer so shocking and so bizarre that his imagination rejected it with a sense of outrage. But it would not be denied. The longer he examined it, the more stringently he tested it against the whole body of evidence in the case, the stronger its claims appeared. After half an hour's concentrated thought, Nigel was finally convinced that he knew why Robert Seaton asserted he had returned to Plash Meadow at 12:30 on the fatal night.

But there was still something missing—a link which would complete the chain of reasoning. Nigel knew he had been given this link, perhaps without recognizing it; now he had mislaid it. Something had happened during Blount's examination of Rennell Torrance this morning—was it something heard? or seen?—which would clinch the whole theory. But, try as he would, he could not recapture the elusive thing. And ruefully he admitted to himself that his failure to do so must spring from a deep repugnance for the truth which had forced itself upon him. Desperately, like Jacob wrestling with the angel, his mind struggled to throw off the grip of this overmastering truth. But it was no good. . . . No villain need be. Oswald Seaton was a villain, though. And villainy breeds villainy; corruption corrupts, no one is safe. That's not the point, though—how does it go?—

> 'Tis morning: but no morning can restore
> What we have forfeited. I see no sin:
> The wrong is mixed. In tragic life, God wot,
> No villain need be! Passions spin the plot:
> We are betrayed by what is false within.

But what words are there for the tragedy of one betrayed by what is true within? for the predicament of one destroyed by the war within of two good causes?

The door opened, and Janet Seaton came in, to stand over Nigel's chair like a dark, accusing angel of judgment.

"What's this I hear about Lionel?"

"You've heard? Did Robert tell you?"

"It's all over the village. Surely you could have prevented it?"

"Well, we tried. But—do sit down, won't you?"

Mrs. Seaton ignored it: Nigel had got up and was standing by the mantelpiece. He described briefly what had happened in the old barn.

"I suppose it might have been worse. The talk in the village is that he shot Mr. Torrance and wounded a policeman. We shall never live this down. What could have possessed the boy to behave like that?"

"The police would naturally conclude that he wished to stop Rennell Torrance from uttering some damning piece of evidence about him, or about someone he wished to protect."

187

Moving to the window, Janet Seaton said over her shoulder, "And did he? Afterward, I mean? I presume the police pressed him about it."

"No. He didn't give anyone away. He said he'd nothing more to say, except that he'd heard footsteps when he went outside at two o'clock. He supposed it was Finny returning."

Mrs. Seaton sighed and sat down in the armchair. "It's all very mystifying," she remarked in a vague, hostessy manner. "Surely the police must have formed some theory by now?"

Nigel offered no comment. Janet went on, with an irritable gesture.

"It's most unfortunate. Mara's being concerned in this. She's an unbalanced girl, I'm afraid, and I do not consider her at all a good influence on Lionel. To be quite frank with you, Mr. Strangeways, I should not be surprised if she'd concocted the whole thing—led him on to this escapade, I mean."

"I know all about Mara."

"You—?"

"About her and Oswald Seaton."

The unbecoming flush stained Janet's cheeks. "Do you mean to say she *told* you?" she exclaimed in a tone of outrage.

"Yes. I led her on a bit, of course. I'd guessed it some time ago."

"You can understand, then, why I don't care for Lionel to be too closely associated with her."

"Difficult to avoid, when you have the Torrances living here," said Nigel suavely.

"That was my husband's doing. I never approved of it."

"A young woman is not necessarily—er—undesirable, because she was the victim of a criminal assault ten years ago."

"It depends in what sense you use the word 'undesirable.'" Janet Seaton's mouth snapped shut like a miser's purse, but there was a glint of grim humor in her eyes.

"I can quite understand," said Nigel after a pause, "that

188

you found it undesirable to have Oswald about the place after what had happened."

Janet Seaton, who never lounged in chairs, seemed to sit more bolt upright than ever. Her large-knuckled hands gripped the arms. But if Nigel had sought to flurry her, it was a failure.

"Are you suggesting that I engineered his disappearance?" she asked with dignity and composure.

"Somebody did. He couldn't have managed it by himself. You realize, of course, that the police are investigating that aspect of the case now?"

"What the police may be doing is no business of mine. But do you seriously think I would connive at the escape of a man who had—had behaved so abominably to a young girl in my charge? Really! The imputation is quite disgraceful!"

"Well, you and Robert hushed it up between you, surely. Why wasn't Oswald Seaton given in charge straight away?"

"It was not convenient." Janet might have been talking about a social engagement. She frowned at the quirk of amusement on Nigel's face. "It's not an unheard-of thing for family scandals to be hushed up, is it, Mr. Strangeways? And there's a considerable difference between hushing this one up and engineering Oswald's disappearance."

"Oh yes, I grant you that. If it was just a matter of locking the cupboard door on a skeleton—but you must see that the police are interested in the benefits you and your husband derived from Oswald's presumed death."

"I wish you would talk straight and not in these underhand hints," she exclaimed with a flare of anger. "You mean Robert and I got Oswald to disappear so that Robert could succeed to his property? We are accused of blackmail now, are we? The next thing, I suppose we'll be accused of—of doing away with Oswald here at Plash Meadow. Really, it's intolerable!"

Nigel gazed at her admiringly. "Talking of that," he said,

"was Robert wearing his mackintosh when you and he went out to look after Kitty?"

For the first time, Janet seemed disconcerted.

"His mackintosh? Why? What an extraordinary question! I don't see the connection."

"I wondered. It had just begun to rain, hadn't it? And you were wearing a mackintosh. Did you borrow his, perhaps?"

"No, of course not. Why should I?" replied Janet rather sharply.

"I only mentioned it because Mara believed he hadn't got a mackintosh on when she saw you two cross the courtyard. Can you remember if Robert was wearing his when he came back from his walk?"

Janet Seaton made an odd little ducking movement with her head. Her voice was a bit flustered.

"How stupid of me! I'd quite forgotten. Yes, he was. He came in. He said he thought he'd heard Kitty kicking in the loose box. So we went out immediately; the rain was just beginning, but it wasn't bad yet. So I slipped on Robert's mac—it didn't seem worth while fetching my own. Yes, I remember now."

So that was that. Nigel eyed the handsome, harassed woman sitting bolt upright before him, her hands clasped in her lap, the prominent eyes downcast now. So she might have sat, he thought, if she had decided at last to visit the specialist and reveal the disquieting symptoms which for long she had been stoically enduring or desperately trying to ignore.

"Rennell said that, when Oswald left him, he saw him walk over here. It was about 12:20. You were sitting up. You didn't hear anything, I suppose? It seems odd that Oswald should come to this house—get this far—and then go away again without trying to see anyone."

"He would not want to see *me*," said Janet darkly, staring

down at her hands which lay like two rocks in her lap. "That's why—" she broke off.

"Yes?"

"I think I can explain it. I didn't tell the police because it went out of my head; and afterward, when I remembered, it seemed too trivial: besides, I assumed at the time it must have been my imagination."

"Yes?"

"Well, it was about ten minutes before my husband returned from his walk, I thought I heard the door open—the courtyard door. I was sitting in my boudoir. I went to the boudoir door and called quietly, 'Is that you, Robert?' I was expecting him back, you see, any moment. But there was no reply. So I naturally thought I'd been mistaken. How horrible! Do you suppose that man actually tried to get into the house?"

"It's an explanation. He recognized your voice, didn't want you to know he was here, and slid off again."

"But I can't understand it. Whom did he want to see? What did he come here for at all?"

"We've not much choice, have we?" said Nigel gently. "He'd hardly have come to meet Lionel, or Vanessa."

Janet's prominent eyes opened affrightedly. Then she closed them and at last lay back in the chair, her fists clenched on the arms of it—the pose of a flogged boxer in his corner at the end of a punishing round. She said faintly,

"Not Robert. I won't believe it. I *won't* believe it. Robert wouldn't be so insane as to invite that man to the house. There must be some other explanation."

And after all that, a day passed, another, two more, with a deepening sense of anticlimax for Nigel. The case seemed to hang fire. There was no news from Blount. Inexplicably Lionel and Mara were not found: they had disappeared as thoroughly as if spontaneous combustion had seized them. Sergeant Bower kept Nigel in touch with events. The car

191

was discovered, the morning after their flight, in Foxhole Wood: it had been driven off the road, down one of the drives deep into the wood, then tastefully camouflaged with fern and branches, and abandoned. The police theory was that the fugitives had lain up in the wood till darkness came, and then set off on foot. A watch had been set on the roads and railway stations in the area and the station staffs warned, within half an hour of their leaving Plash Meadow. Understaffed though he was, Inspector Gates had at once set on foot inquiries at the houses of all their friends in the neighborhood. Nor, this time, was the church vault forgotten. But no report came in from any station along the main or branch lines; no cars had been hired or stolen; not a trace of the fugitives could be found for four days. Inspector Gates could only suppose they had thumbed a lift on a lorry that first night. Investigation at Plash Meadow showed they had taken with them two haversacks, some toilet necessaries and food for about three days.

On the fourth day, Blount telephoned to Gates from Bristol, suggesting he should call off the search locally. Lionel and Mara were posted in the list of "wanted persons" in the *Police Gazette*. Apart from this, which meant that the eye of every policeman in England would be lifting for them, no more time was to be wasted on the couple.

On the fifth day, a young man with an incipient beard and a tramplike appearance, but otherwise answering to the description of Lionel Seaton, was spotted in the market town of the next county. He leaped on a bicycle standing by the pavement, evaded the constable who had challenged him, and got away again in spite of the hue and cry that was raised. As Bower said, "Those young chaps trained for the Airborne and the Commandos, they're a proper bastard to lay your hands on." It seemed pretty clear that the pair had separated; in Nigel's opinion, Lionel was putting on an Elusive Pimpernel act intended to have nuisance value only.

However this might be, Nigel now believed that the young man's escapade—if it were only an escapade—had been aimed at impressing his father no less than Mara. Robert Seaton was a being, no doubt, of sweetness and light. But a towering, deep-rooted genius must overshadow all lesser growths around it, and impoverish the soil for them: the children of a man so consecrated, so self-sufficient could not be altogether normal; the stronger the parent stock, the more violent and eccentric would be their efforts at times to assert their own personality. When the father was loved, as Robert was, these efforts would tend toward impressing him, not rebelling from him. What Lionel Seaton had in effect been saying, when he "confessed" to the hiding of Finny Black, when he did his Wild West turn in the old barn, was, "Look, father, I'm a man too, *I* can do something for *you*." And his reward, could he have heard it, was in the tone of Robert's voice, disconcerted, fond and admiring, when he had said, "Oh dear me, he shouldn't have done that."

On the sixth day, Blount returned to Ferry Lacey. The superintendent looked grave, but triumphant.

"We found it at last," he said to Nigel. "Where Oswald Seaton lay up when he got to England. And we found a letter, inviting him to come down here. Aye, I reckon the case is over."

"A letter? From whom?"

"From Robert Seaton."

CHAPTER THIRTEEN

ROBERT SEATON EXPLAINS

Nigel Strangeways examined the sheet of writing paper which Blount had laid before him.

"There is no question of a forgery," said Blount. "Our handwriting experts have been onto it."

"Oh no, it's his writing. I should know it by now."

"And you see it's cheap thin paper, torn off a block; not the stuff they generally use here, headed with the address. He was trying to safeguard himself—just in case."

The letter certainly had neither address nor date on it.

DEAR OSWALD, *This is an incredible surprise to me. Of course I shall make no difficulties. But why didn't you write long ago to let me know you were alive? By all means let us meet. There is a train from Bristol that gets to Chillingham Junction at 10.58 P.M. Travel by this on Thursday. I'll leave the courtyard door unlocked and be waiting for you in the drawing room—don't enter the house unless or until you see the drawing-room lights are out—I'll try to get J. to go to bed early, though. You realize she would not welcome your presence, and might make things very awkward for you. I shall not mention your return to her, therefore, till you and I have had a good talk. You must have your rights, I agree: but the matter is very ticklish because of that affair ten years ago. I would try and talk J. over; also Rennell and M. But in the meantime we must go very cautiously. So it is essential that you should destroy this letter and not advertise your arrival here. I rely on you to follow these instructions.*

Your affectionate brother,

ROBERT

"Will you walk into my parlor?" said Blount, as Nigel finished reading the letter.

"It looks bad, certainly. I don't wonder Oswald took all the precautions he did."

"He didn't take enough, though," Blount grimly replied. "Except to keep Robert Seaton's letter. And that didn't save him."

"How did you find it?"

According to the superintendent's account, Oswald Seaton had arrived at Bristol the Saturday before he came to Ferry Lacey. He had worked his passage on a tramp steamer from North Africa under the name of Roger Redcote: he must have been living under this name for some time, since his papers were all in order. On arrival at Bristol, he had taken a room in a house of very dubious reputation: its landlady was already on bad terms with the local police, and this was why they had had no success at first in their efforts to trace him. Finally, however, through the belated evidence of a young person who was one of this landlady's clients, the presence of "Roger Redcote" in the house, for several days before the murder of Oswald Seaton, was revealed. Blount interviewed the landlady: she was soon induced to part with a suitcase, belonging to Roger Redcote, which she had been keeping in lieu of her unpaid bill; she also told Blount that her lodger had received a letter (Oswald had evidently told Robert to write to him under his alias) on the Wednesday, and had disappeared the following evening.

On forcing open the suitcase, Blount had found the letter from Robert Seaton in the pocket of a coat.

"And what else did you find in the suitcase?" asked Nigel.

"Besides the jacket, there was a pair of trousers, two pairs of socks, a shirt, some cheap underwear, a copy of *No Orchids for Miss Blandish*, a pair of slippers, pajamas, a rough towel, a tie—all pretty shabby." Blount reeled off the list as if he had learned it by heart.

"Was that all?"

"That was all."

"Ah."

"Exactly," said Blount, with a keen look at Nigel.

"Yet Oswald was clean shaven at this time?"

"Just so."

"He expected to be fitted out when he got to Plash Meadow. He wouldn't bother to bring his worn-out old clothes. But he didn't leave his shaving things behind at Bristol, or his toothbrush—supposing the horrible creature used one."

"This girl who blew the gaff—she told us he used a cut-throat razor."

"Well, there's your weapon," said Nigel. "No doubt he was carrying it in his pocket."

"You're taking it all very calmly, I must say."

"Do you want me to give a war whoop? I'm very fond of Robert Seaton. No doubt he said to Oswald, as the thunder rolled and the lightning played, 'Could you lend me a razor just a moment, old chap? I left mine in the house by mistake.'"

The superintendent looked hurt. "Oh come now, Strangeways, you're not being very co-operative."

"I only want you to tell me how the murderer managed to get hold of Oswald's razor—that's all: remembering that Oswald didn't trust a soul here."

"Presumably Oswald took off his mac at some point and Robert found the razor in the pocket."

"That seems to me very lame. And it suggests that the murder was unpremeditated—that Robert didn't think of it till he happened upon the razor. But this letter doesn't incriminate Robert unless it was part of a *plan* to get Oswald here and kill him. You can't have it both ways."

"Well, if you can give me any other reason why Robert, who had everything to lose by his brother's resurrection, encouraged him in it—damn it, Strangeways, he could just have ignored Oswald's letter! Oswald wouldn't have dared to appear here, with that criminal charge hanging over his head. Yet Robert writes back to him, 'Of course I shall make no difficulties.' How d'you explain that?"

"You'd better ask him. But, if my theory is correct that it was Janet who blackmailed Oswald out of the country ten years ago, and that Robert had had no suspicions about her share in the proceedings, until Oswald reappeared, then his recent behavior makes sense."

"You mean, he just wanted to make honorable restitution?"

"Partly that," said Nigel. "And partly to protect his wife. He'd soon realize that Oswald could make things as hot for Janet, because of her complicity in his 'suicide,' as she could for Oswald. I suggest Robert's idea was to get everyone round a table and discuss how a compromise could be reached. At any rate, he'd want to make sure that Oswald didn't intend to blow the gaff on Janet; and, in return for Oswald's silence about this, he'd promise that no action would be taken over the Mara affair—and possibly throw in some hush money as well. Didn't you and Slingsby find out anything in Somerset?"

"We did. And it supports your theory. But it's vairy inconclusive."

Blount summarized the results of this part of the investigation. Inspector Slingsby, following a ten-year-old trail—

and one which had petered out to nothing when the police originally followed it, after Oswald's disappearance—had interviewed scores of people in the Somerset village where Oswald's seaside cottage was situated. Having talked to everyone who had been living there at the time of the disappearance, and discovered nothing inconsistent with the findings of the original investigation, Slingsby then set out pertinaciously to trace various individuals who had left the village since. His diligence was finally rewarded when he hit the trail of a certain Eliza Hanham. This woman had moved to a village near Bridgwater after the death of her brother in 1942; this brother, a R.N.R. man, recalled to the navy at the beginning of the war, had been killed during a dive-bombing attack upon a convoy in the Mediterranean. Eliza Hanham herself had died a few weeks ago: but in her cottage there had been discovered a hoard of money—nearly £150 in notes of small denominations. Both she and her brother were notoriously close; and the brother had owned a small motor fishing boat, which Oswald and his guests used sometimes to hire. Further investigation disclosed that Eliza Hanham had bought her cottage with the money accruing from the sale of her brother's boat, and that she had no source of income apart from the pension which came to her after his death. It proved impossible to account for the notes found in her cottage, except on the theory that they had been given to her brother in return for services to Oswald, ten years ago, and kept hoarded ever since. At the time, the police had interviewed this John Hanham; but he and his sister both said he had slept at home on the night of Oswald's disappearance: asked to account for Janet Lacey's visiting his cottage two days before it—a visit reported to the police by some neighbors—John Hanham explained that she had come to discuss a fishing trip for Oswald's house party. The police had naturally kept an eye open, for some time after Oswald's disappearance, in case any of the local boatmen started flinging money about in a suspicious way. But John Hanham had been much too fly to do that.

So far, the evidence was pretty negative. Brother and sister being dead—and a couple who in life had kept themselves to themselves—the source of Eliza's hoard could be confirmed neither by questioning nor through gossip. However, Slingsby had then started at the other end and sought for corroborative evidence in the bank accounts of Oswald Seaton, Robert and Janet Lacey. Here at first he was met with a blank wall. The original investigation had covered this ground and Slingsby found nothing to contradict its conclusions—that none of the three had withdrawn a large sum just before Oswald's disappearance, and none of them had a private account elsewhere from which the money could have been withdrawn. Superintendent Blount, turning up at this point, had suggested that Slingsby should inquire next into the affairs of old Mrs. Lacey—Janet's mother. This was the only point which, as far as he could tell from the police records, had not been satisfactorily covered. Slingsby set to work again, tracked down the man who at the time had been manager of the Redcote bank where old Mrs. Lacey kept her account, and after consultation with him and the present manager, had come upon a very significant fact. It appeared that, two days before Oswald's disappearance, the Redcote branch received a telephone call from Mrs. Lacey in Somerset. The old lady appeared to be panic stricken about the imminence of war, and asked for all the money in her current account, £300-odd, to be sent her in notes. The manager tried to persuade her that, even if war did come the next week, her money would be much safer in the bank than in a stocking under her bed; but she was an obstinate old lady; so after the bank had received a letter of confirmation from her, the money was sent.

Once again, the evidence could only be called circumstantial. Old Mrs. Lacey was dead. There was no proof that her

£300 had played a part in the conspiracy which got Oswald Seaton out of the country. But Oswald *had* been conveyed away, John Hanham *had* been approached by Janet Lacey just before, and his sister *had* come into possession of an otherwise unaccountable £150. So it seemed reasonable to suppose that someone, perhaps Oswald himself, more likely Janet, had preyed upon Mrs. Lacey's fear of war, induced her to take out her money, then "borrowed" or stolen it, to pay John Hanham and to provide Oswald with some ready cash. Blount conjectured that the old lady had been kept quiet, once Oswald's "suicide" took place, by the assurance that she would benefit from Oswald's estate when Robert, now engaged to marry her daughter, came in for it.

"Well," said Blount at the end of it, "we've got to have a showdown now."

"With Mrs. Seaton?"

"With her husband. The matter of the conspiracy can wait. I'm going to clear up the murder first."

"D'you mind if I sit in?"

"Please yourself. But no funny business. If Seaton wants help, he'll have to get his solicitor along."

"One thing, Blount, I wish you'd ask him or Janet." Nigel explained the point about the mackintosh. "It seems odd that a woman who fusses over her husband's health, as Janet does, should have allowed him to go out with her, just when a thundershower was starting, without his mackintosh."

"She says she borrowed his, eh? Well, I'll mention it: but it doesn't seem to me of any significance."

Five minutes later they were in Robert Seaton's study. Sergeant Bower, sitting at the poet's desk, to one side of which was pushed the little black notebook that held Robert's immortality (the poem had been finished two days ago), licked his pencil. Nigel was perched on the window seat. The superintendent, beside the desk, faced Robert and Janet Seaton: he was, Nigel knew, at his most formidable;

yet, such were the presence of Janet and the innate dignity of her husband, that even Blount's burly form seemed to shrink. He might have been just the local bobby come to enlist their help for a police fete or to examine a gun license.

"In view of certain new evidence, Mr. Seaton, I am going to ask you to amplify your previous statements to the police. What you say will be taken down, and may be used in evidence. You are under no compulsion to answer my questions. And you are entitled to have a legal representative present, if you wish."

"I don't think there's any need for that," said Robert.

"Very well then. Will you tell me under what circumstances you wrote this letter to your brother, Oswald." Blount moved bulkily over to Robert and held the letter in front of his eyes for a few moments.

"So the silly fellow didn't destroy it after all?" the poet murmured. "All right, you needn't hold it in front of me. I've got a good memory."

"You admit you wrote this letter?"

"What *is* this, dear?" asked Janet.

"Yes, of course I did."

"But you concealed the fact from Inspector Gates and myself? Why?"

"Oh come, Superintendent! That's not a very intelligent question," replied Robert lightly. "Once it had been established that the dead man was Oswald, things would obviously look bad for me if I'd told you I'd written inviting him to come down here."

Janet Seaton gasped. "Robert! What could have possessed you to?—You *invited* him here?"

Her husband looked a bit sheepish—not guilty so much as apologetic and stubborn at the same time: it might have been some social arrangement he had made, knowing it would incur her displeasure, yet convinced he was right to make it. The hypnotic atmosphere of Plash Meadow once

201

again began to creep over Nigel. Here was the crucial point of a murder investigation: and here were the two chief suspects behaving as though nothing was at stake but the disposition of an unwelcome guest.

"Why did you, Mr. Seaton?" asked Blount softly.

"Invite him? Oh well, he was my brother after all."

"I don't quite mean that. This letter makes it clear that you realized his presence here would be unwelcome to Mrs. Seaton. So why didn't you go to Bristol to see him? Wouldn't that have been a more natural thing to do, under the circumstances?"

"Natural?" Robert Seaton seemed to hold up the word in the air before him, examining it from every angle, as if it had been a possible epithet for a line of verse. "Ah no. That would only have been to postpone things. I wanted to force the issue, you see."

"Will you explain that, please."

"Oswald would have to have the estate back. But my wife would resist this, I knew. Besides, there were Rennell and Mara to consider: they might have brought up the old affair against Oswald."

"You mean his criminal assault upon Miss Torrance?"

"Yes."

"And when you said in your letter, 'Of course I shall make no difficulties,' you meant no difficulties about his getting back the estate?"

"Yes."

"You were prepared to give up everything, to go back to poverty, to deprive your wife and children of all this—" Blount made a semicircular gesture with his hand "—without a murmur?"

"I daresay it wouldn't have been as bad as that. Oswald might have looked after us. But I had to do what I thought was right."

"Hmm. So, by 'forcing the issue,' you meant inviting Oswald down here and compelling your wife and friends to accept the situation?"

"More or less."

Blount leaned forward suddenly. "Then why all the secrecy? Why those elaborate plans to smuggle him into the house, by night, without your wife's knowledge? If you wanted to force the issue, wouldn't it have been more—e'eh —more effective to have announced that Oswald was alive, and that you intended to make restitution? To discuss the matter with the others *before* you invited him here? Surely you would first have sounded Mr. Torrance, for instance, as to whether he was prepared to drop the old charge against your brother?"

"One doesn't always do what is most effective." Robert Seaton's fine eyes levelly returned Blount's somewhat pugnacious stare. "I wanted to have a private talk with him first —discover the lay of the land—before making it public. What you call 'the secrecy' was just a precaution for Oswald's sake."

"Whom did you suppose he had to be protected from?"

"Why, I've just told you—"

"It was not in your mind to protect him from—well, from your wife, for instance."

"From Janet? But my dear fellow—"

"You did not know that your wife had arranged Oswald's fake suicide ten years ago—"

"Superintendent! How dare you suggest—" exclaimed Mrs. Seaton.

"—and that she was thus liable to a very grave charge of conspiracy? And that Oswald, the only living witness to this, was a menace to her therefore?"

Janet Seaton rose formidably to her feet. "Superintendent, I insist on an explanation of this extraordinary charge."

"I am afraid it is you who will have to do the explaining, ma'am. As for instance, the three hundred pounds withdrawn from your mother's account a couple of days before Oswald's disappearance, and the large sum of money handed over to John Hanham in return for his services."

Mrs. Seaton sat down as abruptly as she had risen, her face rigid, glaring at the wall before her. Robert was studying his clasped hands: his small body seemed to have dwindled. The superintendent turned to him again.

"Do you claim to have known nothing, suspected nothing, about your brother's 'suicide'? You were quite unaware, till now, that your wife had engineered it so as to get his estate into your hands and hers? And that the lever she used was the Mara Torrance affair—blackmail, in fact?"

"I cannot answer that question." The poet looked small and sick.

"He does not need to answer it," put in Nigel. "The first sentence of his letter to Oswald is the answer. 'This is an incredible surprise to me.' If Mr. Seaton had known the truth about his brother's disappearance, it would be gratuitous and pointless for him to pretend surprise when Oswald reappeared. What Mr. Seaton may have suspected later is quite another matter."

Blount shrugged his heavy shoulders. "Let us go back to your letter, then. It was in reply to one from your brother. Have you kept his letter?"

"No. I destroyed it."

"Just so. Can you remember exactly what he said?"

"Not word for word. He said he was at Bristol; gave me a name and address to write to; asked me what I was going to do about it."

"Did he—e'eh—make any threats?"

"No. Unless you call that last remark a threat."

"He said nothing about his 'suicide'?"

"No."

"He assumed you knew the truth about it, then?"

"I've no idea what he assumed. It was a brief letter, anyway—only a few lines."

Blount hunched himself in his chair. "Now this is important, Mr. Seaton. Could anyone else here have known you had invited your brother down? Did you leave your reply to him lying about before you posted it, for instance?"

"No. I wrote back to him the same day I received his letter. In any case, no one but Finny—and, of course, Janet—comes into my study." Robert chuckled. "It's a *sanctum*, in the strictest sense of the word."

"Did you post the letter yourself?"

"Yes."

"May I ask one question?" said Nigel. "Did you use your Biro to write it?"

"Why, yes, no doubt I did."

"But you didn't use your ordinary headed notepaper."

"No." Robert gave Nigel a look as much as to say, 'You at any rate will understand this.' "I—it would have been in rather bad taste somehow. Rubbing in the fact that I was the occupier of his own property."

"I fancy such refinements of—e'eh—sensibility would be wasted upon Oswald Seaton," said Blount dryly. "However. Having carefully arranged for him to arrive secretly, at night, when your household had gone to bed, you then decided not to wait for him here after all. You went for a walk instead. What explanation can you give for this change of plan?"

"I changed my mind at the last minute; thought I would go a little way to meet him. It never occurred to me that he'd take the short cut."

"I see. And when you did eventually meet him—after you'd got back here again—"

"Oh, but I didn't. You mustn't lay these traps for me, Superintendent," remarked Robert Seaton mildly.

"You would be prepared to swear, on your oath, in a court of law, that you never saw your brother that night?" asked Blount with impressive solemnity.

Nigel noticed that Janet Seaton's eyes were tight shut,

205

her head pressed back against her chair, as if at the peak of an ordeal.

Robert Seaton gazed levelly at Blount, an expression of boyish, almost cherubic innocence on his face. "I am willing to swear, on my oath, that I never saw Oswald alive after that day, ten years ago, when he disappeared."

"But you saw him dead, eh?" asked Blount sharply.

"I had to—er—view the body, as you know. And I was present when the head was found."

Blount allowed a silence to protract itself, like an evening shadow, over the room. Janet lay back in her chair, inert as a corpse. Briskly rubbing his hands, the poet glanced up toward Blount, then to Sergeant Bower whose pencil was poised at attention.

"Very well," said Blount at last, a little wearily. "You returned from your walk. You were still expecting your brother to arrive. Yet you went out twice into the courtyard with Mrs. Seaton, within the next half hour, although Oswald might turn up at any moment. How do you square this with your intention to keep his arrival a secret?"

"It was very awkward, I agree. But Janet was restless that night—wouldn't go to bed—the storm, you know. So I had to risk Oswald running into us the first time. But I calculated he would avoid Janet if he saw her: that's why I took out the storm lantern—a sort of danger signal. And the second time, when we went to look for Finny—well, I imagined something must have prevented Oswald coming, it was so late by then."

Nigel had to admire the stoical way in which Blount took this blow to his case: yet another article of suspicion, the storm lantern, had been naturally, credibly disposed of. It began to dawn upon Nigel that, as things were going, there simply were not adequate grounds for arresting Robert Seaton, and that Blount realized this too.

"When you went out of the house the first time, with Mrs.

Seaton, it was raining and she borrowed your mackintosh?" asked the superintendent.

"Yes."

"Tell me now, Mrs. Seaton—you allowed your husband to go out into a heavy thundershower—"

"It was only just across the courtyard, and my own mackintosh was upstairs."

"Your *only* mackintosh, did you say?" put in Nigel.

"I didn't. But, as you ask, I have only the one."

"The long one I saw you wearing the day Lionel and Mara went off?"

"Presumably."

Robert Seaton was at last looking really worried. "What is the point, Nigel? You're not suggesting that this was the mackintosh found upon the body, are you? I only possess one myself, and that's hanging up in the hall."

"No, I had something else in my mind. Did you have your mac with you when you were out for your walk?"

"I—yes, I think I did." Robert answered with something less than his usual crispness. A frenzied ringing of a bicycle bell came to their ears from the courtyard below.

"You see," Nigel went on slowly, his eyes fixed upon Robert's, "it would explain everything—how that chap down the lane saw you at quarter to one, how Oswald was killed, and why, and *by whom*—oh, everything, if—"

Feet were galloping up the stairs. A voice cried, "Daddy! Daddy!"

"If what?" asked Robert Seaton, more intent than Nigel had ever yet seen him.

"If it wasn't your mackintosh that—"

Before Nigel could finish the sentence, the door was flung open as if by a mighty, rushing wind, and Vanessa, pink cheeked, hair flying, breathlessly announced,

"Daddy . . . I've found . . . Mara!"

CHAPTER FOURTEEN

FAREWELL TO THE ROSES

A FEW minutes later, Blount had swirled off in his car to Hinton Lacey. Vanessa's story was that she had bicycled over there earlier in the morning, to fetch a couple of chickens which had been ordered from Paul Willingham. Waiting for them to be dressed, she had been left alone in the parlor. She was sitting in a big armchair there and counting her money, when she found a sixpence was missing. She thought it might have fallen into the chink between the seat and the side of the chair. She pushed her fingers in, and pulled out, not the sixpence, but a woman's handkerchief, which she recognized at once as Mara's. Paul Willingham, coming in that moment, took it from her rather unceremoniously, saying that Mara must have left it behind during her last visit. Vanessa asked when this had been, and Paul said a fortnight ago. But Vanessa knew this handkerchief had only been bought a couple of days before Mara's disappearance, for Mara had shown it to her then.

Vanessa, at once bitten by intense curiosity and the detective urge, kept her head. She took the chickens, paid for them, put them in her bicycle basket, and pedaled away. But she went no further than the village inn, where she left her bicycle; then, summoning up all her resources as a tracker, returned to the farm and cautiously reconnoitered. She had instantly jumped to the conclusion that Paul Willingham must have made away with Mara, and concealed the body somewhere on the premises. But while peering round, from the cover of an outbuilding, for signs of freshly dug earth, she noticed that the curtains of a spare bedroom in the farmhouse were drawn. This struck her as curious, since Paul normally kept all the curtains open during the daytime: so she settled down to keep the window under observation; and after half an hour she was rewarded by the sight of the curtains being cautiously parted and the face of Mara Torrance appearing for a moment at the window.

"So I deduced that Paul had been hiding Mara and hadn't murdered her after all," Vanessa concluded, a faint note of disappointment in her voice. "Or perhaps he's keeping her a prisoner, for felonious reasons of his own."

"Well done, lassie," said Blount. "I must ask you all to stay in the house till I return."

Robert Seaton passed his hand wearily over his face, when Blount had left the room. "There's got to be an end to this," Nigel heard him mutter.

Janet rose. "Where are the chickens, Vanessa?"

"In my bicycle basket still. Shall I give them to Cook?"

"Yes. And please understand, Vanessa, there's nothing to be proud of in spying upon people."

Vanessa gazed at her stepmother, her face drained white with shock. Then tears filled her eyes, and she rushed from the room, slamming the door.

"Janet, you shouldn't have said that. It was unpardonable." Robert's voice was quite impersonal. He looked straight at his wife—a look without love, without even the anger which comes of love abused: Janet might have been a stranger to him, thought Nigel, as he went to his own room. . . .

When he heard Blount's car return, Nigel walked across to the old barn. He found Mara, with her father and Blount in the studio.

"You're a fool, Mara," Rennell was saying as he entered. "It's only a matter of time, the superintendent has told you, before Lionel is picked up. So why not tell us where he is."

"Because I *don't know*," said the girl in an exasperated voice. "Oh, hello Nigel. I wish you'd stop these people badgering me. I don't seem able to make the superintendent understand that I don't care two hoots whether I'm put in prison for obstructing the police in the performance of their duties, or whatever the rigmarole is."

"*You* may not care," exclaimed her father, "but—"

"—But there'd be nobody to cook your meals. It'd be just too bad, wouldn't it?"

"You make me sick! Don't you ever think of anyone else but yourself, and that young thug you've got yourself tangled up with?"

Mara, smiling secretly to herself, ignored it.

"Robert has finished the poem, my dear," said Nigel.

The girl's face became vivid, almost transfigured. "You've seen it?" she asked eagerly. "But I know it's wonderful. It was sure to be." She sighed, relaxing in her chair. "It *was* worth it. Oh, I feel so happy! I don't mind what happens now. I've paid my debt, haven't I, Nigel?"

"Ah yes," said her father, his pudgy face twisted almost out of shape with malice. "As long as Robert can write his piddling verse, nothing else matters. Not even a murder. Well, let me tell you, my girl, he'll not do any more."

"Any more poetry? Why shouldn't—?"

"Any more murder. And therefore any more poetry."

"Father! You're insane! What do you mean?" Mara was standing over him, her fists clenched. Rennell, as if intimidated by the words which naked jealousy had forced out of him, averted his eyes from her and would not answer.

"Come now, Mr. Torrance," said Blount. "It is your duty to tell the police anything you—"

"He doesn't know anything," cried Mara. "Don't believe a word he—"

"Hold your tongue, young woman!" The superintendent lost his self-control for a moment. "Take her out of here, Strangeways; she's made quite enough nuisance of herself."

Mara allowed Nigel to lead her upstairs to her own room, where she flung herself on to the bed, sobbing.

"It's not true! It's not true! He's always hated Robert. Oh God, I—"

"Listen to me, Mara," said Nigel firmly. "Pull yourself together! There's one question you must answer. About what you saw that night."

Nigel asked the question.

Mara's stricken eyes opened wide; her body seemed to be held in a vice. "Yes," she whispered at last. "Yes, it could have been. But—"

"That's all I want to know. No, don't ask questions. Tell me about your own adventures. It was a hairbrained thing to do, wasn't it?"

"I'd do anything for Robert."

Mara's tale was soon told. On returning in the motor canoe to Ferry Lacey, after her conversation with Nigel, she had thought it only fair to let Rennell know about it. A little later she heard her father telephone to Superintendent Blount, saying he wished to make a statement. She had at once sought out Lionel, and they decided they must somehow listen in to this statement: now that Rennell knew the police would be informed of the Mara-Oswald affair, and of Oswald's arrival at the old barn that night, Mara feared that he might try to incriminate someone else. The plan for overhearing what he said to Blount was then elaborated into a scheme for drawing suspicion upon Lionel. Neither of them, Mara now perhaps too urgently insisted, had ever believed

211

that Robert was the culprit. But they did realize he must be under grave suspicion: and it was Lionel's idea that, if he himself could create a temporary diversion, the police would stop pestering his father, who would then have time to finish his poem without distractions.

It was a naïve idea, and a childish plan, as Mara now admitted. However, he had egged her on to play a part in it; not that she required much persuasion—their new-found love made everything they did together seem like a wild, innocent game. Mara would have preferred to follow it out with Lionel to the end, sleeping with him in ditches or hay-stacks, sharing the risks and the gypsy delights of two lovers on the run. But Lionel had been determined that they should separate; it would give him much greater freedom of action, and therefore gain all the more time for Robert. So it was arranged that, if they did make their getaway, they should lie up for one night in Foxhole Wood, and Mara should make her way on foot to Hinton Lacey, before daylight, and ask Paul Willingham to hide her. If he refused to do so, or her presence at the farm was soon discovered, Lionel would still be at large and no great harm done.

Lionel had been in a state of irresponsible excitement, careless of the consequences both to Mara and himself, and to Paul. But Mara was more level headed. When she got to the farm, she spun a tale for Paul Willingham's benefit, say-ing that her father had threatened her with violence when she told him she was going to marry Lionel, and would have kept her locked up in the old barn: she had escaped, and implored Paul to hide her until Lionel returned with a spe-cial license. Whether or no Paul really believed this romantic tale, it would at least provide him with some sort of defense if the police discovered Mara's presence at the farm. He had, in fact, been out when Inspector Gates called there to in-quire about Mara: and the housekeeper, who did not sleep in and had no idea even now—the spare room being kept locked during the day—that Mara was there, had told Gates in all good faith that she had not seen the girl.

After hearing Mara's story, Nigel went downstairs. Blount was about to depart and asked Nigel to drive back to Hinton Lacey with him. Sergeant Bower was left to keep an eye on the inmates of Plash Meadow. The superintendent was very taciturn on the drive. He stopped at the public call box, and spoke for some minutes. At last they were alone in Blount's room at the Lacey Arms.

"Well?" asked Nigel.

"I've asked Gates to relieve Bower as soon as possible. And he's going to tell the newspapers that the police expect to make an arrest very shortly."

"You can't arrest Robert Seaton on your present evidence. It simply isn't good enough."

Blount gave his friend a meditative look. "He'd by far the strongest motive for it, you can't deny that."

"Robert had a very strong motive for murdering Oswald," said Nigel slowly, "but he had an even stronger one for not murdering him."

"Och, I'm too old to be impressed by these paradoxes of yours," said Blount after a pause, since Nigel did not seem disposed to enlarge upon the statement. "No. But I fancy young Seaton will make a move when he sees in tomorrow's papers that an arrest is imminent."

"He'll come tearing back here. That's what he'll do."

"Aye. Mph'm. Just so."

Something in Blount's tone made Nigel look at him sharply. "When you start talking your hideous native lingo, I always know you've got something up your sleeve. Out with it!"

"E'eh, well perhaps we lay our hands on young Lionel. That's something, isn't it? Gates is going to draw a mighty fine mesh round Plash Meadow."

"And you arrest Lionel for carrying arms, for intimidating

a witness, for obstructing the police, and what have you. But all that won't find you the murderer of Oswald Seaton."

"Maybe no. Maybe it will. It depends whether Lionel does come back. If he does, it will be to rally round his father. If he doesn't—" Blount vigorously massaged his bald head "—if he doesn't, then he's our man."

"What on earth do you mean by that?"

"Rennell Torrance has come clean at last. He has just told me that he saw Lionel Seaton, round about two o'clock that night, skulking along beside the dairy."

"Crikey!" Nigel was thoroughly startled. "D'you believe him?"

"I don't know why he should make it up. Or why, if he was making it up, he should wait till now to let it out."

Blount proceeded to outline the case against Lionel Seaton. First, he had claimed to have slept through the thunderstorms of the fatal night: yet he had been awakened by Nigel's shout for help on a subsequent night; and Torrance had seen him "skulking along beside the dairy" at the time of Oswald's murder. Lionel had therefore lied. Had he lied to protect himself, or someone else? Up to this point, there had been a too facile assumption (thought Blount) that all Lionel's actions could be explained as part of a design to protect his father. But suppose the exact opposite were true? Suppose that Robert had seen Lionel—as well he might, having been twice across the courtyard that night—behaving in a suspicious manner? had caught him, perhaps, actually disposing of the corpse? Could not all of Robert's subsequent behavior, the hiding and supplying of Finny Black, for instance, be explained by an intention to conceal his son's guilt?

Nigel agreed that it could.

Second, the simplest solution of Lionel's "escapade" in the old barn was that he had been genuinely afraid lest Rennell Torrance might disclose some incriminating evidence against him. He had therefore threatened Rennell with his pistol: and not unsuccessfully, for Rennell had, in fact, kept silence till this morning. It was a desperate thing to do, certainly. But Lionel may have been a desperate man by then; and he might also have been clever enough to perceive that such a public exhibition of violence would draw suspicion away from him, as indeed it did—would look like the action of a quixotic young man trying to protect somebody else. His later actions—the deliberate brush with the policeman in the market town, for example—would lend color to this picture.

Third, and this was perhaps the strongest point in Blount's theory, Lionel was the most likely of all the suspects from the physical point of view. He was young; he had been trained in the ruthless combat technique of the Airborne troops; only a strong, cunning and ruthless man could have done everything which was done to Oswald Seaton that night. It was difficult to imagine the pudgy Torrance, or the slight-built Robert, let alone Janet, cutting the throat of a man who would certainly be on his guard, then severing the head, then carrying the body to the river and towing it downstream.

Fourth, the motive. This hinged on the question whether Lionel knew what Oswald had done to Mara ten years before. Mara herself, and Robert, had said that Lionel was ignorant of this: but they might well have done so to protect Lionel. If Lionel did know about it, on the other hand, he had a most compelling motive—his love for Mara and his experience of the hideous psychological damage which Oswald had inflicted upon her, to say nothing of the further harm that might be done if Oswald appeared in her life again.

Fifth, opportunity. This was the weakest point of Blount's case, as he freely admitted. To suppose that Lionel had run into Oswald that night, before the latter could make contact with Robert, was to postulate a thumping coincidence.

"Not necessarily," Nigel said.

"But he couldn't possibly, if Robert's evidence just now is to be believed, have known that Oswald was coming to Plash Meadow—couldn't know he was alive, even."

"You're forgetting Robert's Biro. And the thin blockpaper he used for writing to his brother. Paul Willingham told me the other day that a Biro leaves a visible impression on the sheet below the one you're writing on. I tried the experiment later myself, and it's quite true. It's quite possible for Lionel to have gone into his father's study, soon after he'd written it, and seen a facsimile of the letter on the pad."

"So that's what you were after! Well, the murder may have been premeditated, then. At any rate, Lionel might have been on the wait for Oswald, to head him off. But now we come to the next snag. How could he get hold of Oswald's razor. And where is that damned razor? We've pretty well taken the house, the dairy, the outbuildings and the old barn to pieces, looking for it. And why should the murderer have been at such pains to conceal it? He'd only to wipe his fingerprints off, and being Oswald's razor, it wouldn't incriminate him more than anyone else."

"Don't ask me. I haven't the faintest idea. But, going back to premeditation or the reverse—" Nigel looked strangely at Blount "—no, we'll leave that for a moment. Let's go further back still. To Robert's poetry. I'm convinced that his poetry is at the very roots of this case. Now, you suggested that Robert's actions have been dictated by a wish to protect his son, whom he knows or gravely suspects is the murderer. Yet, since the murder, Robert has written a great poetic sequence. Poets can be pretty heartless, inhuman almost, when their work is in question. But I can't see Robert writing merrily away with the knowledge that his son, whom he loves, is a murderer."

"Well, maybe not. But—"

"No, wait a minute. I'm going to spring a mine under you, so hold tight. It's a variant of your own theory. Suppose that Janet, not Lionel, read the impression of Robert's letter: she'd be more likely to, because Robert told us that no one but Janet was normally allowed into his study. She now knows what date and approximate time Oswald will turn up at Plash Meadow. She intends, perhaps, only to gatecrash on the meeting between Oswald and Robert: Oswald won't get the estate back if she has any say in the matter. But, at zero hour, the wretched Robert is missing; out for a walk. Janet hears the courtyard door open. That was her own admission. But she doesn't, as she pretended to me, call out 'Robert': she suspects the visitor is Oswald, she goes down the passage—and Oswald it is! What is she to do? Her instinctive reaction, I suggest, would be to get him out of the house—*her* house. Under some pretext, she persuades him to walk across to the dairy with her."

Blount slapped his head. "Good Lord, man! You mean it was he—"

"Yes, the man Mara saw crossing the courtyard with Janet could have been Oswald. I asked her just now, and she agreed. She assumed at the time that it was Robert, quite naturally. But the man was on the far side of Janet, and Mara had only one lightning flash to glimpse him by; and anyway, Robert and Oswald are about the same build, and not unlike one another in feature. This would explain how the expectant father was able to see Robert, about a quarter of an hour later, walking down the lane toward Plash Meadow. Well then—"

"By the Lord, Strangeways, I believe you've got it!" exclaimed Blount. "She'd lock Oswald into the dairy, or tell him to wait there till Robert turned up. Then she'd get a scunner, maybe, at the idea of a deadly wee fellow like Oswald being about the place. She'd lose her nerve suddenly, and want protection. But Robert was away somewhere, walking. So her natural impulse would be to run along to Lionel's bedroom, and wake him, and tell him what had happened. Lionel gets up and goes across to the dairy alone. Maybe he knows about Oswald and Mara, maybe not. But Oswald draws his razor on the lad, and Lionel wrests it from him, and Oswald gets his throat cut. Aye, it all fits in. And this would explain why Robert was able to write his vairses. He didn't know what had happened at Plash Meadow while he was away. It was Janet who's been protecting Lionel. It was she who persuaded Robert to conceal Finny Black—aye, it'd explain all her actions too—and it's possible that Robert may have been thinking all this time it was Janet who'd killed Oswald—that would account for *his*; but it'd no' interfere with his poetry writing, because he does not care for Janet—not as he does for Lionel and Vanessa."

"Ah, you've noticed that too, have you?"

"It's written on his face; and on hers, forby."

"So now what?"

"We wait for Lionel to come back. If he doesn't, we'll go out after him."

"Lionel. Yes. What a home-coming!" said Nigel, with unusual emotion. "You'll not be able to charge him with the murder, of course."

"Not yet. Not on the evidence we've got, I agree. There should have been clothes of his with bloodstains on them. And there are other little snags. But I'll sort it, when we've got him. It's the most convincing theory of the crime, Strangeways."

"Oh, it's a beautiful theory," Nigel wearily replied. "On paper." . . .

Dinner at Plash Meadow that evening was a somber, uneasy affair. Even Finny Black seemed to feel the weighted atmosphere: he came in and out with the dishes, dragging his steps like a sick dog. Vanessa was obviously hard put to it to swallow her helping of chicken. After dinner, in the drawing room, she suddenly moved across to her father, who sat with his hand shading his eyes, and ran her fingers gently through his hair—a mature, maternal gesture.

"I'll sing to you," she said. "Poor old Saul. David will sing to him. I wish I could play the harp too."

She went to the piano, and accompanying herself in a wooden way that strangely consorted with the pure, small, unwavering tone of her voice, sang *The Queen's Maries*, and *Lord Randal, My Son*. Then she sang *Will Ye No' Come Back Again?* Janet Seaton's face was like stone. Tears trickled through Robert's fingers.

"That was beautiful, my dearest," he said when she had finished. "Thank you. It used to be your mo—it's one of my favorite songs."

"I know what you were going to say," she breathed into his ear as she kissed him good night.

Janet Seaton sat stiffly, like a stranger in the room, containing her agony. She offered her cheek to Vanessa: then, a few seconds after, blindly stretched out her hand; but the door was already closed behind the girl.

"How much longer is this going on?" asked Robert presently.

Nigel said, "I think Lionel will turn up again soon."

"Lionel? But—are the police waiting for that?" Janet's voice was low and harsh.

"Well, yes."

"I suppose they're bound to take a serious view of this escapade of his?" said Robert.

"Yes, I'm afraid so. It might be very serious. If there was a question of his being an accomplice after the fact. Or—"

"—Or what?" asked Janet sharply.

"I must tell you that he's under grave suspicion for the actual murder."

219

"Oh, but that's ridiculous!" Robert's face had the placatory, groping expression of a deaf man who sees others laughing at a joke he has not quite caught.

Janet Seaton's breath came in a shuddering sigh. She left the room abruptly, the keys jangling in her black chatelaine bag.

"I oughtn't to be staying here any longer," said Nigel. "It's not fair to you."

Robert Seaton gazed at him with a pure intensity which Nigel found difficult to meet: it was as if a last veil had dropped from the poet's eyes.

"Do you know who killed my brother?" he said.

"Yes, I think I know everything now."

"Well, don't go yet. Stay on just a little longer, and see us —see us all through it. Will you do that, my dear fellow?" . . .

Nigel did not, in fact, have to wait very long. The following day and night mounted in a crescendo of suspense such as he had never experienced before—and one which he could never afterward look back upon except with pain and dismay.

At breakfast the newspapers announced that an arrest was imminent in the Ferry Lacey case. Robert quietly passed his *News Chronicle* to Janet, his finger marking the paragraph. Then he glanced at Nigel, who at once left the table and put through a call to the inn at Hinton Lacey. The landlord sent one of his children to fetch Paul Willingham.

"Have they arrested you yet, Paul?" asked Nigel.

"As it so happens, not. I suppose there'll be trouble over young Mara. Your superintendent gave me a rocket yesterday about 'harboring her,' as he put it. But I stuck to my story—or rather, her story—"

"Never mind about that. You've got to harbor another female now. We're sending Vanessa to stay with you for a few nights."

220

"Oh, it's like that, is it? I'm sorry. Damn this bloody business! I'll invite my young cousin, Priscilla, to keep her company."

A very subdued Vanessa sat beside Nigel in the Seatons' car, half an hour later. She had shown signs of mutiny at first; but her father had gently persuaded her that she must go—the house would be full of policemen for a day or two, he said, and they wouldn't want her getting in among their large feet.

"Bye-bye, love," he said, as the car was about to depart. "See you soon. Be a good girl, and don't ride Paul's pony too hard." Robert's voice was cheerful and matter-of-fact. He kissed his daughter, waved once, walked steadily back into the house. Nigel felt, looking back on it afterward, that he had never seen a more heroic action.

"It's all wrong!" Vanessa burst out, as the car drove through the gateway. "It's all wrong! I know there's something wrong!" And that was all she said till they arrived at Paul Willingham's farm.

On his return, Nigel was met by Robert Seaton, who handed him a telegram.

"EXPECT ME BACK ABOUT ELEVEN TONIGHT. LIONEL," it said.

"It's just come," said Robert. "I suppose your superintendent has to be told about this?"

"I expect he knows already. They've been keeping a watch on all communications for Plash Meadow."

"Ah well. I hope Vanessa didn't take it too hard?"

"She'll be all right."

"Good. I'm sure she will. If you'll forgive me, I must go and do a bit of writing now." The poet walked briskly upstairs again. . . .

Nigel felt abominably restless. He prowled round the exquisite rooms, peered at their treasures which, glittering or glowing, ravishing the eye still with their precious gifts of color and symmetry, nevertheless appeared to him as ticketed already for the auctioneer's hammer. It was the last, and perhaps the truest, of all the illusions Plash Meadow had beguiled him with—this impression it now gave of a house whose soul was fled, leaving behind a simulacrum of itself soon to be broken up into a thousand sparkling fragments. Unable to endure the atmosphere indoors, Nigel went out into the garden. But there too the shadow lay, mysterious, unmistakable as the "change" on the face of a man dying. The trees, the great chestnut, stood up like a mirage: the hours of the roses were numbered.

Blount's burly figure, advancing down the drive, seemed that of a revenant, one condemned to an eternal repetition of arriving too late for the event which would have explained everything, for the moment of truth.

"That young shaver has a nerve," were his first words. "He's actually sent a telegram to say he is returning about eleven."

"Yes. His father showed it to me."

"He did, did he?" Blount mopped his forehead. "I simply can't understand these people, Strangeways. I don't mind telling you this place has got on my nerves."

The superintendent glared resentfully at Plash Meadow, as though it were some man-eating orchis which had already taken a gulp of him.

"We'll let him walk in," he said, "if that's his idea. But he won't get out again." . . .

Lionel Seaton was as punctual as his word. Eleven was striking that night when Nigel heard the sound of a car turning into the drive. There was a policeman concealed by the gate, he knew; another beneath the chestnut tree; a third in the shadow of the old barn. Inspector Gates had stationed himself in the lobby near the courtyard door. Blount was at the top of the stairs, between the landing and Robert Seaton's study, beneath whose door there showed a chink of light. Three of the police were armed, since Lionel, for all they knew, still had his Mauser.

The next minute was almost delirious anticlimax. Whistling cheerfully, Lionel came up the stairs.

"Father!" he called out, "where are you? Oh, hello, Superintendent, it's you!"

"Lionel Seaton, I must take you into custody on the charge of being in unlawful possession of a firearm, and—"

"Oh fiddle-de-dee! Here it is, anyway."

From the door of his room, Nigel saw the young man politely hand the Mauser pistol to Blount. Lionel had the beginnings of a fine, leonine beard: his clothes were dusty and rumpled: he looked in the most excellent health, an advertisement for the open-air life.

"So you've found the murderer, have you?" he said. "Or was that stuff about an early arrest just your Scotland Yard eyewash?"

"You must realize that you are under arrest," said Blount sternly. "If you wish to make a statement—"

"Oh yes, I'll confess *my* crimes. You shall hear the whole issue. But I want a word with my father first. You can't object to that, surely?"

After a moment's hesitation, Blount replied, "Vairy well: but in my presence."

"Now listen, my dear Superintendent," said Lionel with engaging charm. "Mayn't I talk with him privately? You can stand outside the door. You've got the house surrounded with coppers—or you should have, anyway. What chance could I possibly have of escaping? You can search me, if you like: I've no revolvers, poisons, sharp knives or what not concealed upon my person."

"You may speak to your father in my presence," Blount stolidly repeated.

"Look here, are you charging me with the murder of my revolting uncle, or aren't you?"

"Not just at present."

"Well then," Lionel proceeded with disarming patience, "if I'm not a dangerous murderer, why all this fuss about a few private words with my old dad?"

"I cannot discuss the matter any further."

"Oh, dear, well I suppose that's that." Lionel's rueful tone was drolly reminiscent of his father's. Arms hanging beside him in a dejected attitude, he shifted his feet, scuffing the mat. "I'm sorry about that," he said slowly; then, very swiftly, "and for this," and lashed out a fist swift as a stock whip, which caught Blount on the side of the jaw and knocked him flying.

Before Nigel could move, the young man had darted down the passage into Robert's study. Nigel shouted for Gates, who came pounding up the stairs. They tried the study door: it was locked. The inspector was about to blow his whistle for reinforcements, but Nigel stopped him.

"No. Get 'em to watch the study window. He may try a jump again. And keep an eye on that car of his."

The inspector ran into a bedroom overlooking the courtyard. Nigel could hear his whistle blowing, and orders given. He turned to Blount, who was now on hands and knees, shaking his head to clear it. As he was helping Blount to his feet, Nigel saw the study door opening: he braced himself to tackle Lionel Seaton, but it was Robert who emerged. Nigel ran past him into the room: it was empty; the window stood open.

"The silly fellow jumped out," said Robert from behind him, with a chuckle.

The beams of two electric torches converged upon Lionel, who was standing quite still, as if dazed, on the grass below. The next instant he was off like an arrow. There were shouts: an oath from a policeman who had failed to intercept him;

then the young man was past the chestnut tree and had run out of Nigel's sight.

By the time Nigel emerged into the courtyard, the pursuit was in full cry, torch beams waving wildly like the antennae of some agitated insect, past the outbuildings toward the orchard. Lionel had evidently not attempted to get back to his car. Going indoors, Nigel saw Blount fuming at the telephone: the local exchange was notoriously slow in answering calls.

"I think he's making for Foxhole Wood," said Nigel. "The whole damned county constabulary are after him through the orchard."

"I'll take my car on to the road on the far side of the wood and cut him off, as soon as I've put through this call. Bower's waiting for me in it. Keep an eye on things here, will you? Exchange? Get me Redcote police and look lively, my girl!"

Nigel walked thoughtfully upstairs, back to Robert's study. There he found Janet, fully clothed, at her husband's desk.

"This is for you. But I opened it," she said flatly, reaching out her hand to him with several sheets of paper in it. This is what Nigel read:

"Dear Nigel Strangeways,

"Please pass this on to the police. I don't know if there's an etiquette or legal form for confessions, but no doubt they must be amply documented, so I will try to leave nothing out.

"I killed Oswald Seaton—"

Nigel heard a car moving away into the night. Blount had got off quickly. He read on:

"—and nobody else was involved in the murder, either beforehand or afterward. My motive was a simple one. In my young manhood, I experienced years of grinding poverty and humiliation, which killed my wife and grievously hampered

225

my poetry. When I received Oswald's letter, and realized to my consternation that he, the rightful owner of my property, was not, as I had always believed, dead, I was in despair. I knew that I could not, at my age, face the ordeal of poverty again: I could not bear the thought of Janet, Lionel and Vanessa having to face it; above all, I'm afraid (for poets are bitterly self-centered creatures) I contemplated with utter abhorrence the prospect of returning to conditions so adverse to the writing of poetry—the prospect of becoming once again a harassed, overworked literary hack. The idea was intolerable. So, if I am to be put in the dock, perhaps there should be, after all, an accomplice standing beside me—my dear, possessive, Muse."

Nigel was so absorbed now that he only subconsciously noted the sound of another car engine purring and fading below.

"You remember" [the letter continued] "our talk last June about the 'flash point'? Mine, I found, was a delayed one. When I replied to Oswald's letter, the idea of murder had just flicked across my mind, like the trailing edge of a fantasy, and no more. My plan was to get him here, and talk things over privately—come to some compromise with him by which, in return for giving him back the estate without demur and for keeping silent about the Mara affair, I should receive a decent income from him. I urged secrecy (a) because I believed it was necessary to present Janet with a *fait accompli*, so to say, and (b) because, at the back of my mind, there *was* the notion that if Oswald would not bargain, he must be dealt with in some other way.

"On the night I expected him, I could not get Janet to go early to bed. So I decided to walk some way along the road to meet him. As I told you, the idea of his taking the short cut never occurred to me. I even waited for him outside the village (when I told you I was sheltering from the storm), some time after he should have passed by, thinking his train might have been unpunctual.

"When I did get back to the house, about a quarter of one, Janet was awaiting me downstairs in a very agitated condition. She told me that Oswald had appeared a quarter of an hour earlier, that she had refused to let him stay in the house but agreed to hide him in the dairy till I arrived. She took him out to the dairy—it was he, not myself, whom Mara saw crossing the courtyard with her. She had lit the storm lantern and given it to him to carry, because electric lights switched on in the dairy might bring the Torrances out to investigate. When they got to the dairy, she pushed him in and locked the door, being terrified he might otherwise return to the house."

At this point, Nigel looked up, and saw that Janet Seaton was no longer in the room with him. He bent over the confession again.

"Janet will confirm all this. It became clear to me, at the time, that she was bitterly resentful—and quite naturally so —that I should have invited Oswald to come: he had told her, by the way, that he was here at my suggestion. Janet and I talked for ten minutes or so. Then she suddenly realized that she had forgotten all about Finny. She discovered he was not in his room: so we went out to look for him. Failing to find him, I sent her back to the house, taking the key of the dairy from her and saying I must now have a talk with Oswald.

"As I entered the dairy, the feeling uppermost in my mind was curiosity. What had happened to Oswald? How had he survived when we were all certain he was dead? What would he be like after those ten years? I did not enter the dairy with murder in my heart. Well, of course the poor chap was not in a very amenable frame of mind, after being locked up there for half an hour. I tried to reason with him, tried to suggest

227

a bargain; I even threatened him with the Mara business. But it was no good. He just squatted over in the corner, by the storm lantern, and jeered at me. He knew he had the whip hand, and he was not going to 'turn into a charitable organization' after what he'd been through abroad.

"I began to feel desperate. Then he said something, which I won't set down, about my wife. That was the flash point. For the first time in my life I felt the spurting flame of pure hatred. I went for him and hit him hard in the face. As he fell, something slipped out of his mackintosh pocket and rattled on to the floor. He reached for it, but I got it first— the razor—and before he could grapple with me, I slashed him across the throat. At that instant I experienced a delicious exaltation, a thrill of blind, single-minded, excruciating joy. Then it left me, and my brother was dying at my feet.

"Thereafter, things seemed to happen to me with the compulsive movement of a dream. I acted as if every detail had been planned out by me beforehand. Extraordinary. A clever, cold being took control (my antiself?): whispered in my ear that, if Oswald's features could be obliterated, there would be nothing to connect the dead man with myself and Plash Meadow. I drew the line at battering them in, though. He was quite dead by now, so I severed the head completely, removed all of his clothes, put his mackintosh on the body again, and buttoned it over the neck. Then I fetched the key of the Lacey vault, and a string bag to put the head in—one's compunctions at such times really seem very curious—I revolted from the thought of carrying it about by the hair.

"Then (assisted by my antiself, who gave me preternatural strength) I hoisted up the body, carried it along to the river, swam some way downstream with it and let it go. It was a parcel of spoilt meat; not my brother. I dropped the razor into the river at the same point. I should add that I'd stripped naked to do all this, lest I should get blood on my clothes: fortunately the blood spurt from his neck, when I struck him, had missed me. I had piled his clothes on top of mine in the dairy, which accounts for Finny's seeing only one heap of clothes. Well, when I got back to the dairy, the head was gone: I'd not been able to lock the door behind me, since I was afraid of dropping the body if I did so. I had intended to bury the head, either with Oswald's clothes in the Lacey vault, or somewhere in the orchard, for I reasoned, as to the latter, that the signs of so small a hole having been dug would not attract attention. It gave me a dreadful qualm to find the head missing. But I thought Finny Black might have taken it—I could not imagine anyone else's doing this—so I went through with the rest of my plan: sluiced down the dairy, put on my clothes, took Oswald's to the vault.

"All this, from the moment when I first entered the dairy to talk with O., occupied a little over an hour. On returning to the house, I found Janet in bed but still awake. I told her I had been discussing matters with Oswald all this time, and had finally sent him away, on the understanding that I should pay him an annual sum in return for his not troubling us any further. Janet seemed much relieved by this. We then went along to see if Finny had come back yet, and he did turn up a minute later—just after two o'clock.

"I want to make it quite clear that no one else was implicated in what I did that night. I have reason to think that Lionel was awakened at some point and came out: he may have seen me returning from the churchyard. What Janet may have suspected, after the body was found, I do not know: I had no wish to make her a party to my secret, though I did use her later as an unwilling tool in my scheme to discover if it was Finny who had taken the head—and for this I ask her forgiveness. But neither she nor Lionel can be held as accomplices after the fact."

Nigel heard a step in the passage. Janet came into the study, her face gray and anxious.

"Has Robert been in here? I can't find him anywhere," she said.

"Let me just finish this," said Nigel, and read on:

"I write this confession of my own free will and in my right mind. I should have done so before, seeing what trouble I've made for everyone. But I wanted to finish my sequence first. The most ironic thing of all is that the emotional upheaval caused by Oswald's death should have thrown up this rich vein of poetry. I think I have made good use of it, but I shall not be there to hear time's verdict. Please, my dear Nigel, try to convince the authorities that Lionel's behavior, though foolish, has been innocent. When his mother was dying, she asked him to look after me. He knew I was writing poetry, and he wanted to gain time for me, the dear fellow: he set about this in an ill-advised way, I know, but there was no collusion—I could not take him into my confidence. But everyone, as a certain distinguished lady once said, has been too kind, yourself included.

"I have no wish to stand my trial. So, if Lionel does turn up tonight, and an opportunity arises, I shall slip away. I have a fancy to die where my heart is buried. Little Vanessa is very fond of you: perhaps you could help her through it— I don't scruple to make this last request.

"And now—you remember Dorothy's words?—'The hour is come. . . . I must prepare to go. The swallows, I must leave them, the well, the garden, the roses, all. Dear creatures! . . . Well, I must go. Farewell.'

ROBERT SEATON"

It had not taken Nigel many minutes to read this. Crumpling it into his pocket, he stood up. The momentary indecision cleared from his face.

"What did you say? He's not in the house?"

Janet shook her head.

"We've got to find him. Don't you realize what—?"

"No," cried Janet Seaton passionately. "Can't you let him be?" She held to Nigel's arm with a grip of extraordinary strength, but he managed to shake her off, and hurried downstairs. The car in which Lionel had come was still standing at the courtyard door. Nigel hesitated, then ran across the court to the garage. Its doors were open. The Seatons' own car was gone.

Janet was outside when he returned, a dead, sleepwalker's expression on her face.

"You shan't stop him!" she said dully. "You shan't stop him!"

Nigel put his hands on her shoulders and shook her hard.

"Tell me, where was his first wife buried? You must tell me."

"The sleeping tablets are gone from the medicine cupboard. The whole bottle. What did you say?"

"I said, 'Where was his first wife buried?'"

A dreadful pang twisted her face: then it was stubborn as stone again. "I shan't tell you."

"I'll have to ask Vanessa, then," said Nigel, getting into Lionel's car.

"No! No, I'll come with you. Just let me get my coat."

It seemed an age to Nigel before she returned, carrying her black chatelaine bag.

"It's a village about five miles beyond Redcote," she said. "In the churchyard there. It's where she was born. Great Hammersley."

They tore through the night to Hinton Lacey, across the river bridge two miles beyond it, back along the main road to Redcote. On the far side of Redcote, in a maze of lanes, they lost their way.

"I can't remember," faltered Janet. "It's so long since—"

Nigel stopped at the next village, knocked up the occupants of the first cottage. He was given sleepy, surly directions.

A mile outside this village, the engine spat, hesitated, tried again, then died. Nigel found an electric torch and a map in a sidepocket. The petrol tank was empty.

"Thank God!" muttered Janet Seaton.

"I'll just have to walk. Will you stay in the car till I get help?"

"No. I shall come with you."

They hurried on, in the livid moonlight. The lane seemed all forks and no signposts. There were four miles still to go. Nigel had the choice of making a wide detour by a hamlet which was itself nearly two miles distant and might not have a telephone, a car or a gallon of petrol to its name, and of pressing on to Great Hammersley. He chose the latter course.

Janet Seaton at first went stride for stride beside him, like a man. Later, distressed, she slowed down. Nigel stopped for a moment to study the map. Janet's voice came to him in a rasping breath.

"I implore you! Can't you let him die in peace?"

They were the last words she spoke, until they came to the outskirts of Great Hammersley and saw the squat church tower whitely sleeping in the last of the moonlight.

Then she said, "He may not be here after all. Are you sure that's what he meant?"

"We'll soon know."

"I don't see the car."

"He wouldn't drive it right into the village."

They were already whispering, as if in the presence of death. The long grass of the churchyard, sweetly scenting the night air, whispered at their feet as they brushed through it, and cast brilliants of dew, transient tears, along their way.

I ought to have telephoned to a doctor and asked him to meet us here, thought Nigel: I've mismanaged everything. But perhaps it's for the best.

His torch beam presently found the figure of Robert, lying face down, full length, upon a mound beneath a yew tree in the far corner, his hands stretched out toward the stone at its head, which told that Daisy, the dearly beloved wife of Robert Seaton, rested beneath. A faint smile showed on the poet's face when Nigel turned him over: his cheek was cold with dew: the body felt warm still to Nigel's touch, but the heart had stopped.

"Is he dead?" asked Janet from the other side of the grave.

"I think so. But we must get a doctor at once. Will you find a telephone, please, Mrs. Seaton."

When, a few minutes later, she returned, she knelt down beside the grave and awkwardly touched her husband's cheek.

"I loved him too. I *did* love him." Her voice was uncomprehending, almost querulous. Then she suddenly drew in a harsh breath. "There's blood on my hand!"

"It's only a yew berry. You must have squashed it when you knelt down," said Nigel. "But there *is* blood on your hands."

"On my—? What do you mean? Why are you looking at me like that?"

"I destroyed your husband's confession. While you were getting your coat. You took such a long time."

Janet Seaton, on her knees still, was glaring up at him.

"You *destroyed* it? Why, you must be mad." Her voice seemed to boil up from a deep cauldron of fury. "I don't believe you!"

"I destroyed it because it was not true," replied Nigel implacably. "You know it was not true, because you killed Oswald Seaton yourself."

CHAPTER FIFTEEN

FROM NIGEL STRANGEWAYS' CASE BOOK

I HAD not destroyed the "confession," of course. I still don't know what to do about it. It's one thing to drive your cart and your plow over the bones of the dead, but another thing to rake them up for public obloquy. Such honored bones too. However.

Robert's confession is a masterly document—his last, and by no means his least, piece of imaginative writing. But it was just a bit too imaginative, and there are passages not at all in character with R. as I knew him: for instance, the somewhat artificial trope about his Muse (a girl he never mentioned by that name); but chiefly the analysis of his own sensations before and during the actual "murder," which gives me the impression of a brilliant, highly sensitive man trying to *imagine* himself into the mind of a murderer—there is a fictional timbre about these sentences, "delicious exaltation," "my brother was dying at my feet," and in the picture of Oswald squatting over the storm lantern and jeering at R., which doesn't ring true for me at all. No, Robert slightly overdid the verisimilitude.

These points did not strike me when I was reading through the letter last night: circumstances were not favorable for such fine perceptions. But I did notice, even then, certain

234

things in it which didn't fit the facts or the probabilities. Whether they would get by with Blount, I am not sure. For example:

(a) Is it conceivable that Oswald, who had every reason to be suspicious of Janet, would sit quietly in the dairy for half an hour, raise no outcry, make no attempt to escape? The windows are small and high up, but it could have been managed. Wouldn't he suppose that J. had locked him in so that she might telephone the police and hand him over for the Mara business?

(b) Is it conceivable that R., a quiet, peaceable little chap, so well-balanced psychologically, should be provoked into striking his brother? He was an oldish man, after all, and oldish men don't commonly behave like fighting cocks even if their wives *are* insulted. Moreover, I am sure R. was speaking the truth about himself when, during the tea party in June, he said, "I could never bring myself to facing my victim. It'd have to be one of those long-range murders."

(c) Is it conceivable that R. should have got no blood on his clothes from the wound in Oswald's neck? You have to be standing close to a man to strike him with a razor, and the blood would have jetted out at once.

(d) Could R. have carried the body to the river and swam out with it, unassisted (except by his "antiself")?

The answer to each of these is that it is improbable but not inconceivable: that *all* these conditions should have applied, together, makes for far greater improbability. Add to them (e) that, by Robert's account, he could not have got round to sluicing down the dairy till about half-past one at the earliest, when the second thundershower was over, yet nobody heard the sounds of sluicing; (f) Oswald's own self-defensive measure—his visit to Rennell Torrance; it's most unlikely that, in the course of a long conversation with Robert, he should not have mentioned this, and that R., knowing there was another witness to his brother's arrival at Plash

235

Meadow, should still have murdered Oswald; but, if Janet took O. straight out to the dairy and struck him down there at once, he might well not have had time to mention his visit to Rennell; (g) the crucial point of Oswald's mackintosh; if, as R. says, O. was wearing it when he had his throat cut, why were bloodstains found all over the *outside* of the mackintosh *and* on his clothes?

This mackintosh, together with Robert's poetry, was always the key clue to the mystery.

It was not till his last interview with Blount, two days ago, that Robert decided to make his confession and "slip away." He had finished the sequence several days before that; so his statement that he was waiting to finish it before confessing is invalid. What decided him, at this interview, that the game was up? My question about the mackintosh, my hints that the whole case would be solved, if—

He knew then that I had arrived at the truth.

If what? If Janet had met Oswald and borrowed his mackintosh to walk across the court.

I tumbled to this as a result of Mara's telling me that she had seen Janet's dress showing beneath the hem of the mackintosh she was wearing: then I saw Janet walk down the drive in a *long* mackintosh; and at our last interview she agreed this was the only mac she possessed. Therefore, when she crossed the court that night, she was not wearing her own. At first I assumed she'd put on Robert's: but (a) would she allow her husband to go out into the rain, in her company, without one? (b) how could R. be there at all if the expectant father did not see him walk down the lane till quarter of an hour later?

The rational answer was that Janet had met Oswald first, and borrowed his mac to take him over to the dairy. Whether she had read Robert's letter to him and was expecting his arrival or not, is immaterial. Now, in the pocket of that mac there was a razor. And Janet is a woman of strong physique and a smoldering, ungovernable temper. It may well be that the murder was unpremeditated, that the idea of killing Oswald never occurred to her till she felt the razor in the pocket of the mackintosh.

I am convinced that this was, for her, the flash point. I believe she followed O. into the dairy and slashed his throat at once, perhaps while he was putting down the storm lantern. This is the only theory which would satisfactorily account for there being so much blood on the *outside* of the mac (it spurted on to J. immediately she had struck him), for there also being a lot of blood on Oswald's suit, and for no blood having been found on any of Janet's or Robert's clothing. It also accounts for no outcry having been heard from the dairy, for there was thunder to drown it.

Janet, then, had both means and opportunity. What of the motive? Now, all along, there could be no question that she had by far the strongest motive of all the suspects. She is a highly possessive woman. That afternoon last June, Mara said, accurately and prophetically, "Janet's ruling passion is Plash Meadow. She'd kill anyone to protect it." She had been prepared to marry Oswald himself, and had then married Robert, in order to get back the Lacey property. She doted on Plash Meadow and its contents almost to the point of mania; it, and the family name, were her obsession: I saw it on my first visit in the way she touched the ornaments. But Oswald, as the investigations in Somerset were later to prove, was doubly a menace to her. Not only was he the rightful owner of the property, but he knew—he was the only surviving person to know—the truth about the conspiracy which underlay his "suicide" ten years before. So Janet could not safeguard her property now by handing Oswald over to the police on the Mara charge: for, if she did so, Oswald would at once inform against her for having organized the "suicide" conspiracy, and she would lose the property just as surely as if Robert had himself restored it to his brother.

Robert's "confession" was a brave and remarkably ingenious effort to turn all the points against himself which were in fact pointers to Janet's guilt. Particularly brilliant was his treatment of the first episode: realizing I now knew that it was Oswald who had crossed the courtyard with Janet at half-past twelve, he developed this in a perfectly natural way to consist with her innocence of the crime or of any complicity in it. I think it just possible that his confession might have convinced the police. It was convincing, largely because so much of it was true.

This brings me to the question, why should Robert confess at all to a crime committed by a wife he did not love? Surely he was not a man to carry quixotism that far? I believe there were two reasons: first, Robert was implicated in the murder as an accessory *after* the fact; second, since this was so, and he would be likely to go to the gallows anyway, he decided to try to clear his wife. Moreover, I believe the very fact of his not loving her drove him to this decision: his sense of not having given her the love she required of him would create, in so goodhearted a man, a feeling of guilt and remorse. The "confession" was, in effect, also an expiation.

Nevertheless, it confirmed me in my opinion that Robert had been implicated in the murder—one sentence, particularly, where he says he fetched the string bag because he revolted from the thought of carrying the head about by the hair. For me, that has the ring of pure truth. I doubt if the keenest effort of imagination could have hit upon an explanation so odd, so simple, so natural. Of course, it was possible that Janet had disposed of the body and the head by herself and then confessed to Robert, who later used all the details for his own "confession." But this raises again the very serious difficulty as to the disposal of the body single-handed. Janet is a hot-tempered woman, but not a cold-blooded one. Could she have gone through, unsupported, with all the horrors that had to be gone through after the murder? I very much doubt it.

Robert, in a mood of exalted altruism, *could* have done so. Apart from this, the way Janet's and Robert's stories tallied, at the various stages of the investigation, indicates that there was close collusion between them.

My reconstruction* of the events is as follows, then: Janet takes Oswald out to the dairy, kills him, peels off the blood-stained mackintosh and leaves it and the razor in the dairy, which she locks behind her. The crime was unpremeditated: she is dazed, has lost her nerve. She hurries back to the house to find Robert. When he returns from his walk, she tells him everything—probably says it's all his fault, really, for having invited Oswald to the house. Robert says he will help her to conceal the crime. After that, everything takes place as in his confession, except that the pair of them do it between them. The head was clumsily severed because it had to be done by the light of the storm lantern alone. I should imagine that Robert would undertake the more gruesome jobs, but that they both carried the body down to the river, and while they were doing this, Finny stole the head. The phrases about the "antiself" in his confession are perhaps significant here, in view of Robert's relations with Janet: it's just the sort of mischievous twist he might have given to it—that "assisted by my antiself, who gave me preternatural strength, I hoisted up the body," etc.

Lionel's subsequent behavior is contributory evidence of Robert's complicity. One must take into account what he said to me on the lawn, the first day I was staying at Plash Meadow: particularly his remark that he must "see Vanessa through the present dust-up," and the way he tried to sound me then. Again, if he had not seen Robert behaving suspiciously at some time that night, why should he go to such extraordinary lengths to divert suspicion upon himself? He

* This was later to be substantially confirmed. N.S.

certainly wouldn't have done it for his stepmother, at any rate. And he'd hardly have done it *merely* to give his father for finishing the poem: for, if Lionel had no reason to suppose his father implicated in the crime, then he equally had no reason to fear that the discovery of the truth about the crime would put a term to his father's writing.

To return to Janet's guilt. It was finally proved, to my own private satisfaction, last night in the churchyard. Also, by her attempts to delay our arrival there, which she pretended were for Robert's sake—so that he might not be prevented from committing suicide and compelled to stand his trial, but actually were made so as to insure that he *did* die before he could be questioned about his "confession." But also, in the course of the investigation, she gave herself away more than once. (1) On the day after the murder she was "very queer and edgy," according to Mara; (2) she resisted a police search of the house; (3) during her first conversation with me, she fell into the trap of agreeing that the night of Thursday/Friday was the operative period, though she should not have known, at that time, *when* Oswald was killed; she managed to cover up this slip pretty well; (4) she was extremely discomposed when I first questioned Robert and herself about the unknown man who had lived here all his life and left the village under a cloud nine or ten years ago; (5) she was equally rattled—and indeed contradicted herself—when I asked her whether she had borrowed Robert's mackintosh to wear across the court. Now each of these points is open to a more innocent interpretation—that Janet knew of Oswald's return, suspected Robert of having killed him, but was chiefly worried lest the investigation should reveal her share in the conspiracy of Oswald's "suicide."

But then (6) comes the affair of the clay head. In his "confession," Robert had to skate very lightly over this: he speaks of using Janet as "an unwilling tool in my scheme to discover if it was Finny who had taken the (Oswald's) head." Yet, if

J. was no more than an "unwilling tool," if she did not yet know the identity of the murdered man, why did she provoke Mara to do a head of *Robert*? How could she know that the murdered man bore a strong facial resemblance to her husband and that therefore a clay head of the latter would be most likely to cause Finny to repeat his performance of head snatching? This was the crucial question which I decided not to ask her at the time. But, still more betraying, was (7) Janet's extraordinary admission that Finny was her bastard son. In the first place, the police have found not a trace of evidence to support it. Second, if it were true, it is inconceivable that a woman of Janet's pride should have admitted it, except in a desperate effort to avert some worse situation. She did, in fact, come out with this confession, as a last resort, to give color to her story that the whole clay-head stratagem was aimed at the protection of Finny Black. But I simply could not believe that a woman of Janet's character would make such an appalling admission in defense of Finny, or even of her husband—in defense of anyone but herself. Moreover, on Finny's own evidence, it was Janet who had told him not to "answer" the police's questions.

All this pointed at least to Janet's complicity in the crime. But it did not prove that it was she who struck the fatal blow. On the other hand, I am morally certain that Robert did *not*: so, by elimination, and apart from the evidence of the blood-stained mackintosh, etc., Janet must have done it. I am convinced that Robert, in spite of the strong murder motives he set down in his "confession," had an excellent reason for keeping Oswald alive. So we come to the roots of the case—Robert's poetry.

The main thread was put into my hands that day in June, when I met Robert Seaton for the first time. That oddly revealing little remark about the hens looking "so much at a loose end": the signs of hobbies taken up and dropped: the impression of boredom: the look of misery on his face when

241

Janet referred to the epic of the Great War, which he was supposed to have been at work on for years, but which there was no trace of in his manuscript books: above all, his version of the Sleeping-Beauty story. "Have you thought what really kept her there? Not the thorns, but the roses." And "the Queen took away all the spinning wheels": a perfect Freudian slip: in the real story it is the King who takes them away: Robert was expressing his unconscious resentment against Janet, against Plash Meadow, and everything they stood for, *because they had deprived him of the power to write poetry.* So "the poor girl" (his Muse) "had nothing to do but moon about and admire her own reflection in the roses." What's more, Rennell Torrance, when he made that outbreak of his, said, "One of these fine days you'll be asked to account for your talent. And you'll have to answer, 'I buried it, Master— buried it under a heap of roses.'" Rennell had a pretty good notion that Robert had been for years inactive.

And then Robert went on, "I don't believe in that Prince. He'd never have got through the thorns. It'd take the Beast to do that. Some rough beast." And the Beast did turn up. Oswald Seaton. And Robert jumped at the opportunity: it gave him the chance (with a perfectly good conscience, for Oswald was after all its rightful owner) to leave Plash Meadow, to break the cataleptic trance it had thrown upon his Muse, to return to the conditions under which—however grim they had been—he had in the past produced poetry. To kill Oswald would be to destroy his last chance of freeing the creator in himself.

Yet how could I convince Blount of this? He's an exceptionally able and broad-minded man, but no Scotland Yard officer, no layman at all perhaps, can be expected to understand the motive force of the creative artist—how he is compelled by this unpredictable force to subject himself and anyone connected with him to hardship, to indignity, to apparent

242

caprice or an inhuman routine, so that a few precious drops of immortality may be squeezed out.

I was deceived myself, for some time, by Robert's insouciance about the crime. I took it for innocence: and of course he was innocent of the actual killing. Possibly, being human, he got a certain kick from the altruism of his own conduct in helping Janet conceal her crime. But the great change I noticed from the Robert Seaton of June—the new briskness, vitality, clarity which I felt in him—was the result of his having begun to write poetry again. As he says, this was the ironical effect of Oswald's death; for him, its prime effect. And the fact that, at last, he was re-engaged upon the work for which nature had designed him, and knew it was good, gave him an extraordinary detachment: in his interviews with Blount and myself, he seemed to maintain the attitude of an intelligent but dispassionate observer. Compared with the poem he was writing, the criminal investigation was secondary—a game which he now had enough spare energy to take part in, to play with a certain impudent ease, to relish almost. This culminated in his audacious, yet literally accurate statement, "I am willing to swear, on my oath, that I never saw Oswald alive after that day, ten years ago, when he disappeared."

It would not do to exaggerate this. Robert was not behaving irresponsibly. It was just that, for a while, his social responsibility yielded place to a more urgent one: he had to be about his Father's business. If he seemed to treat Oswald's death, and its inevitable consequences, with a sort of impish disrespect, it was only as a man upon whom sentence of death has been passed finds the ordinary world unreal: he may be excused a certain levity. I am sure Robert knew that the case could, for him, have only one ending. His was a heart of gold. He tried to arrange it so that no one else should permanently suffer for the crime. I can't forget how the editor of the local paper said of Robert's first wife, "It was his poetry, when you

243

get down to the bottom of it, which killed her." Robert must have felt the same about Oswald and Janet: if he hadn't invited Oswald down, with the intention of getting the paralyzing weight of Plash Meadow lifted from his shoulders, Janet would never have gone in danger of the gallows. History had repeated itself: the destructive potentiality in genius was vindicated once again. . . .

Lord, how he would have chuckled at all this solemn stuff! "I've written my confession, so for God's sake get on with it and spare us your pretentious analyses and moralizings!" I can hear him say it. But the "confession" does pose me a difficult moral problem. On the one hand, it's basically untrue, it might quite possibly fail to convince the police, and to make it public would be to tarnish unjustly the fame of a great, good man. On the other hand, if the police did accept the confession, it would mean Lionel's being let off comparatively lightly, Janet's being saved from hanging or life imprisonment (though the case of her conspiracy in Oswald's "suicide" would be pursued, no doubt), and therefore Robert's last wishes would have been respected.

How could I bring myself to disregard them? But then, how could I bear to dishonor his name? Who am I to conceal truth or to falsify justice? But which would serve truth and justice the better—to destroy his confession or to hand it over to the authorities?

I wish someone could tell me. . . .